A HANDBOOK

OF CHRISTIAN SOCIAL ETHICS

A Handbook
of Christian Social Ethics

EBERHARD WELTY OP

Volume One
MAN IN SOCIETY

HERDER

FREIBURG

NELSON

EDINBURGH-LONDON

This translation by Gregor Kirstein OP, revised and adapted by John Fitzsimons, is based on the second German edition of "Herders Sozialkatechismus, Band I, Grundfragen und Grundkräfte des sozialen Lebens", published by Herder, Freiburg, 1952

First edition published 1960 by Herder, Freiburg, West Germany
and Nelson, Edinburgh-London

Library of Congress Catalog Card Number: 59-14568

© 1960 by Herder KG

Made and printed by Herder Druck, Freiburg, West Germany

CONTENTS

Introductory Questions   1

1 What is ethics? (1) · 2 What is social ethics? (2) · 3 What do
we understand by social ethics? (7) · 4 Is the Church entitled to
speak at all on social questions? (9) · 5 To what extent do social
and moral questions come under the moral law? (14) · 6 From
what sources does Catholic social ethics draw its teaching? (20) ·
7 What is the basic line of thought in Catholic social ethics? (23) ·
8 Is Catholic social ethics necessary today? (24) · 9 What should
be our attitude towards non-Catholic social ethics? (27) ·
10 What is particularly incumbent upon Catholic social ethics
today? (31) · 11 What are the main divisions of this Handbook
of Christian Social Ethics? (35)

BASIC QUESTIONS AND FORCES OF
SOCIAL LIVING

Part One: Man in Society   39

Lesson One: On Man

12 What is man? (41) · 13 What are the prerogatives of man as
a person? (46) · 14 To whom do the prerogatives of the person
belong? (51) · 15 Are there certain general duties imposed on
every individual? (52) · 16 What is the significance of the dignity

Lesson Three: Fundamental Human Rights 261

Lesson Four: The Virtue of Justice 281

A. COMMUTATIVE JUSTICE 292

B. Distributive Justice 299

C. Universal or Legal Justice 309

D. Social Justice 317

Lesson Five: Charity in Social Life 324

PAPAL PRONOUNCEMENTS

THE following papal pronouncements are cited in the text with the abbreviations given below. Where other papal documents are cited in the text these are given their full title.

Leo XIII (1878–1903)

D. I.	*Diuturnum illud,* 29 June 1881, on the origin of the power of the State.
I. D.	*Immortale Dei,* 1 November 1885, on Christianity and the State.
L. P.	*Libertas praestantissimum,* 20 June 1888, against Liberalism.
S. C.	*Sapientiae Christianae,* 10 January 1890, on the duties of Christians as citizens. (Image Books, New York, 1954.)
R. N.	*Rerum Novarum,* 15 May 1891, on the condition of the working classes. (C. T. S., London.)

Pius XI (1922–39)

D. I. M.	*Divini illius Magistri,* 31 December 1929, on the Christian education.
C. C.	*Casti Connubii,* 31 December 1930, on the Christian marriage.
Q. A.	*Quadragesimo Anno,* 15 May 1931, on the social order.

M. S.   *Mit brennender Sorge,* 14 March 1937, against
            National Socialism.

D. R.   *Divini Redemptoris,* 19 March 1937, condemning
            the errors of Communism.

C. C. C.   *Caritate Christi Compulsi,* 3 May 1932, on the
            necessity of penance, and prayer to the Sacred
            Heart (C. T. S., London.)

Pius XII (1939–58)

S. P.   *Summi Pontificatus,* 20 October 1939, on the reli-
            gious decadence of mankind and the need of a
            religious education.

H. G.   *Humani Generis,* 12 August 1950, on preaching.
            (C. T. S., London.)

C. B.   *Christmas Broadcast*

P. B.   *Pentecost Broadcast*

ABBREVIATIONS

C. T. S.   Catholic Truth Society, London

C. M.   *Catholic Mind*

C. D.   Catholic Documents, Pontifical Court Club, London

C. M. W.   Image Books, New York, 1954

N. C.W. C.   National Catholic Welfare Conference

U. A.   The Unwearied Advocate, St. Cloud, 1956

PREFACE

A WORK such as this is something new among books dealing with social questions. The author, Fr. Eberhard Welty, O.P., a distinguished social scientist, has made use of an ingenious method for giving clear, concise, and yet comprehensive answers to the questions posed. Teachers, students, and others interested in social problems, who have used the work, are enthusiastic about the wealth of knowledge it contains and the clarity and directness with which it clears up controverted social problems, all too often clouded through lack of that light on social principles which permeates the social encyclicals of the Sovereign Pontiffs.

Pertinent passages from these papal pronouncements are placed at the beginning of the discussion of several questions or, if better suited to the exposition of particular points at issue, directly in connection with them. This arrangement facilitates the study of the various social problems.

Solid doctrine, well-balanced judgement, and apt arrangement of the contents characterize this Handbook. It is an achievement of masterly scholarship in the wide field of sociological literature. In addition to the exposition of the principles of social ethics, actual examples illustrate the principles involved. This practical feature adds immeasurably to the value of the work. The author has been at pains to set forth the matter in precise, simple, language. A glance at the well-arranged table of contents and at the comprehensive index will testify to the thoroughness of treatment as well as to the fact that all the facets of social ethics have been covered.

When I was asked by the author whether the work should be translated into English, knowing of its excellence and aware of the need of such a work of scholarship in English-speaking countries, I did not hesitate to give an affirmative answer. It is precisely in these countries that interest in social studies has not abated; on the contrary, new controversial social issues have made it imperative to direct attention more than ever to constructive social principles, if reliable answers are to be given to the questions that agitate the minds of men.

Young people, in particular, who strive to widen their knowledge, will welcome the work. From it they will obtain a fuller understanding of the social teaching of the Sovereign Pontiffs and its practical application. The question-and-answer method makes the book especially useful for discussion groups, which are being organized in increasing numbers.

It is a pleasure to send this up-to-date work, carrying a much needed message of social principles and social ideas, with a hearty God-speed on its way into schools, libraries, homes, and discussion groups.

Aloysius Cardinal Muench

INTRODUCTION

THIS work is, as its title indicates, a handbook of Christian social ethics. It deals simply and solely with the ethics of social living. Its primary task is to consider the fundamental questions of social ethics, in such a way as to include all that gives Christian social ethics its own special value and character.

I should like to make three suggestions concerning the use of this book.

1. Wherever it has seemed necessary, the point of doctrine being explained has been illustrated by examples which are not always placed at the beginning of the question but are worked into the text or added at the end of a section. If the work is being used as a textbook, that is, in study groups or in classes, I would recommend that the exposition begin with the examples.

2. The lay-out of a book of this nature makes it inevitable that the reader (and especially the teacher) will need, from time to time, to go more fully into some matters, and will need to refer to the literature. Frequently a question of ethics, and above all of social ethics, will give rise to a number of new questions which are not easily solved, even though one has at hand the answer to the relevant fundamental question. The application of ethical principles often depends on many and diverse circumstances, and the measure of freedom or obligation must be carefully defined in each case.

3. The quotations from papal documents are intended primarily as verifications of the actual answers given. It seemed to me not only right and desirable, but also expedient and necessary to support by the authority of the popes the correctness or at least the tenability of the answers given. They are intended furthermore to show the mind of Christian social ethics as a whole, how it meets the errors and tendencies of the times. As such they are integral parts of the text.

The use of the term "Handbook" does not imply that it is authoritative, but rather refers to the method of question and answer that has been used. It does not limit itself to the consideration of problems concerning which Catholic teaching has already been proclaimed by the Church, but deals also with matters concerning which the Church has as yet made no definite pronouncements or on which there is still no unanimous teaching. I have honestly endeavoured to consider thoroughly and weigh carefully answers and explanations. Due account has been taken of differing opinions in controversial matters, and in matters of particular importance I have expressly pointed out that the opinion which I myself hold to be the correct one is not shared by others.

Eberhard Welty, O. P.

Introductory Questions

1. *What is ethics?*

Ethics is the science of the morality of human conduct.

MAN is capable of acting morally, that is, freely and responsibly, and he is obliged so to act (Qs. 15–16). He *can* do right
or wrong, but he *may* only do right. In order to do right his
conduct must be in conformity with the ultimate and supreme
end of his life, with his final end, which is God. To put it another
way: he must fulfil the will of God, no matter in what form and
by virtue of what authority this is presented to him. Or again,
man's conduct must be in accordance with right reason (Q. 16).
Human reason is right when it judges and ordains in conformity with the intrinsic and extrinsic end of life. The intrinsic
end of life consists in perfection (holiness, becoming God-like,
Christ-like); the extrinsic refers to God and to union with him
in the next life.

Ethics examines and sets forth the general norms according
to which man must regulate his conduct so that it be morally
good, pleasing to God, in accordance with the ultimate end of
life. This as opposed to morally wrong, not pleasing to God,
contrary to life's ultimate end. Ethics is called the science of
norms because it sets forth imperative propositions which
do not merely instruct and inform man on some matter or
other, but rather impose on him, demand of him, or forbid

1

him something. These imperative propositions bind man to make decisions and to choose his motives in accordance with what they lay down for him. "Honour thy father and thy mother!" "Love thy neighbour as thyself!" "Be so minded as Christ was minded!" They bind him by virtue of a higher authority, they call upon him to take up a definite standpoint, to act or to forego. "I am the Lord thy God!" "Thou shalt . . . !" "You cannot serve God and Mammon!"

2. *What is social ethics?*

Social ethics is that part of ethics which gives us the moral standards for the social life and conduct of men.

MAN is a social being (Q. 20); God gave him a social nature and destined him to live as man among his fellow men. But he does not cease for that reason to be a man. His entire conduct, because it is human, must be in conformity with his final end; must be morally good. His entire conduct is, therefore, subject to the dictates and directives of the moral law.

1. Social ethics has a double function:

a. to tell the individual what rights and duties he has towards his fellow men, what he owes to them and what they owe to him – "Do to other men what you would have them do to you" (Matt. 7:12);

b. to tell the different human communities what aims (values) they may or must pursue, what order of things they have to observe or realize, to what extent they are entitled to exercise authority over men, what they should achieve and to what extent they are bound to help – "God has more right to be obeyed than men" (Acts 5:29. See also Qs. 25–7).

2

2. Social ethics, as the science of norms, differs essentially from sociology, which is merely descriptive. Sociology is a science of pure fact and experience, that is, it observes and establishes what the social behaviour, the ideas, tendencies and structures of society have been among different peoples and classes at different times in the course of history. It compares these results and produces a number of norms and so-called types which merely tell us how, in fact, men have thought and argued about their social obligations, how they behaved in various circumstances, and in what stages and forms development actually took place. This is all very important and indispensable, since we learn from it the conditions of society and the prospects of success allotted to the one or the other ideal, what conception of social order is binding on men, what the moral standards of social living are. It is not a proper basis for ethics, because a purely factual investigation and review does not lead to the inner nature of things, of men or of society. The genuine imperatives of moral conduct can only be derived either from revelation or from the nature of man and of human conduct. Not all principles of moral conduct, however, are so universally valid and binding that they can be applied everywhere and at all times in like manner and without restriction. Time and place, the character of the people, economic and social development — all play a considerable part. For this reason ethics must take into account the results of sociological research; and to that extent one may say that sociology presents the norm for the application of moral principles and directives.

One cannot, for example, define once and for all to what extent and in what manner property has to fulfil its social function, since this depends among other things on the degree of prosperity or poverty prevailing. The question of what virtues a people ought particularly to cultivate depends, not only on the general ideal of virtue, but also on the peculiar type, outlook, historical development and situation of the people in question. The principle that the authorities have to serve and satisfy the demands of the common good will work out very differently according to the internal and external situation in which the community finds itself. Thus districts with a predominantly rural population do not present the same moral and social problems, for example de-proletarianization, as urban populations. Ethics must, then, have recourse to sociology in order to know what it has to proclaim, and in what manner it has to stress its imperatives.

3. Social ethics, as part of the complete science of ethics, takes from general ethics those primary fundamental notions and norms which concern man's moral conduct in general. Under this heading belongs the following: Man may strive only after what is good and must avoid evil; in order that a man's conduct be right in every respect, it must be good in respect of its object, motive, and circumstances; a man's conscience is the immediate and inescapable norm of his conduct; spiritual goods are higher than material goods; no finite good can be the ultimate end of the life of man; God possesses the unrestricted power to rule over and command all created things and institutions; God can bind men of all ages and in all parts of the world to an order of life freely chosen and laid down by him. Social ethics is not limited, however, to applying these and other principles of general ethics to the questions and conditions of social living. Rather has it to examine social living in respect of the latter's own aims, laws, claims, and obligations.

4. The extensive fields comprising the subject matter of social ethics are often taken separately, each as a special ethic. Thus

4

we have ethics of the family, ethics of social economy, political ethics, professional ethics, ethics of property. We are dealing here with parts of one single ethic, but the division and separate treatment is justified, since each of the various fields includes its own extensive and difficult questions.

5. Social ethics is not to be confused with:

a. The Social Question. Not until the age of capitalism was there talk of a "Social Question", although former epochs also had their social problems and questions, often very difficult ones (the condition and freeing of slaves; the fate and the overcoming of serfdom; the frightful ravages of war and plagues). But the capitalistic age brought with it, as a pernicious evil, a progressive deterioration of the broad mass of the workers, and the term "Social Question" first came into common usage for the discussion of how and with what means the condition of wage earners (in industry and agriculture) might effectively be bettered. For a long time the terms "Social Question" and "Labour Question" were taken as more or less synonymous. This was understandable, since the labour question was really the most important and most difficult and because it was not conditioned by occasional reverses but by the system of private capitalism. Yet we must not overlook the fact that in the period in question other sections and classes underwent serious crises and it was constantly pointed out that their distressed condition was part of the Social Question. Today, as a result of the war, the difficulties and distress have become so acute, and changed to such a degree, that the existence of classes not belonging to the labouring class is endangered. (Refugees and deportees; the plight of the middle classes.)

As the economic and social system of private capitalism shows itself less and less capable of producing a right social order from within itself, the Social Question becomes a question of the radical renewal of society. Social ethics sets forth the moral norms and motives for the solution of the social question (the dignity of the human person, the right of all to a life in accordance with human dignity). It must see social distress in its whole tragic range, in order to urge social obligations as effectively as possible, and in order to know precisely where social duty arises and what is its extent.

b. Social Policy and Social Reform. These two notions are not everywhere understood and explained in the same sense, and sometimes they are even taken to mean more or less the same thing. The most correct and best interpretation is, surely, as follows.

By Social Policy is meant the tendencies, efforts, and measures of the State and public taken as a whole which serve to remove, as far as possible, the evils within an existing social order, thus to overcome present crises without questioning or wishing to change the general system obtaining.

By Social Reform is meant the tendencies, efforts, and measures of the State and public taken as a whole which aim at a new social order, since the existing one is judged to be no longer just and in accord with the times.

The distinction is made, then, in relation to the actual existing social order. Where this order is accepted in principle, where one is convinced that things are basically right and therefore can, or even must, remain essentially as they are, intentions and measures are limited to making good what is lacking, to rectifying the faulty, and to developing and improving the system. This is Social Policy. On the other hand, where the system itself is considered wrong or at least outmoded, where the conviction prevails that only a radical transformation of the whole situation can help and consequently is demanded, one cannot be satisfied with measures of Social Policy, but must pursue with determination and steady purpose a programme of Social Reform.

Both, Social Policy and Social Reform, need the direction of social ethics, so that they recognize the seriousness and full import of their obligations, as well as the moral rectitude of their ends and means. Any social movement or reform, if it is to be right, must be carried out according to moral principles. If it is to be effective, to be taken up and carried through with courage and a consciousness of responsibility, then it needs the highest and strongest incentives. Catholic social ethics in no way opposes genuine social reform (Q. 10). At the same time it teaches and defends unyielding norms which no reform may overlook or violate.

PIUS XI (Q. A., 128, 130, 147).

PIUS XII (Address of 2 June 1948; C. M., Aug. 1948).

"Only on the principles of Christianity and in accord with its spirit can social reforms, called for imperatively by the necessities and aspirations of our times, be carried out. They demand from some the spirit of renunciation and sacrifice, from others the sense of responsibility and endurance, from everybody hard and strenuous work."

3. What do we understand by Catholic social ethics?

By Catholic social ethics we understand social ethics as advocated by the Catholic Church, or recognized as being in harmony with her teaching.

THE Church has, in the course of time, spoken on most of the important questions of social ethics, laying down the basic principles and giving many decisions on particular questions (Q. 6).

She leaves it to science to present as a connected whole the entire range of questions in social ethics.

This social ethics is called Catholic, not in the sense that it contains only supernatural revealed truths of practical life, and certainly not in the sense that all its principles are recognized and accepted only within the Catholic Church, but rather quite simply in the sense that it puts forward what the Church, and science in the name of the Church, teaches on social living and social questions. Catholic social ethics presents a connected, systematic body of doctrine. It does not merely tackle isolated questions, but treats all questions of social ethics and gives the "Catholic" solution – the solution which either has been given directly by the Church, or is at least in conformity with, or may be inferred from, the Catholic deposit of truth.

The construction and development of such a social ethic is the hard and constant work of centuries. Special manuals and primers of Catholic social ethics, as we know them today, are recent innovations. But already in the early days of the Church the Fathers had begun to study the social teaching of the Gospel, applying it to the conditions of their time and developing it further. Succeeding ages continued this work, pursuing it more or less vigorously according to the needs of the time. Among the great teachers in the Church may be mentioned St. Augustine (354–430) and St. Thomas Aquinas (1225–75). Among the various social catechisms there is one which is particularly important, that compiled and published by the International Union of Social Studies, founded by Cardinal Mercier at Mechlin in 1920. A revised edition of this catechism was published in 1948.[1]

[1] English translation: *A Code of Social Principles* (Catholic Social Guild, Oxford).

4. Is the Church[2] entitled to speak at all on social questions?

When social questions have a bearing on the moral life of man, the Church is not only entitled but is actually in duty bound to speak.

LEO XIII (R. N., 13).

"We approach the subject with confidence, and in the exercise of the rights which manifestly appertain to Us, for no practical solution of this question will be found apart from the intervention of Religion and of the Church. It is We who are the chief guardian of Religion and the chief dispenser of what pertains to the Church: and by keeping silence we would seem to neglect the duty incumbent on us."

PIUS XI (Q. A., 41–43).

"But before proceeding to discuss these problems, We must lay down the principle, long since clearly established by Leo XIII, that it is Our right and Our duty to deal authoritatively with social and economic problems. It is not, of course, the office of the Church to lead men to transient and perishable happiness only, but to that which is eternal; indeed 'the Church believes that it would be wrong for her to interfere without just cause in such earthly concerns.' But she never can relinquish her God-given task of interposing her authority, not indeed in matters of technique, for which she has neither the equipment nor the mission, but in all those that fall under the moral law. With regard to these, the deposit of truth entrusted to Us by God, and Our weighty office of declaring, interpreting and urging, in season and out of season, the entire moral law, demand

---

[2] By "Church" we do not mean Catholic theologians but the Church as teacher. "To speak" is not to be taken as meaning "to express an opinion"; it means to judge and decide authoritatively and to lay down as binding. The Church claims it as her right and her duty to come forward as judge and to make her decisions binding in these matters.

that both the social order and economic life be brought within Our supreme jurisdiction. For though economic life and moral conduct are guided each by its own principles in its own sphere, it is false to maintain that the two orders are so dissociated and so alien to each other that the former in no way depends on the latter. While the so-called laws of economics, derived from the nature of things and of the body and mind of man, do indeed determine what it can attain and by what means; so reason itself also clearly deduces from the individual and social nature of man and things, what in the designs of God the Creator is the end and object of the whole economic order. The same moral law which commands us to seek in our general conduct our supreme and final end, also commands us in every particular kind of activity to aim at those ends which nature, or rather the Author of nature, has established for that order of action, and to subordinate particular aims to our last end. If this law be faithfully obeyed, the result will be that particular economic ends, whether of society as a body or of individuals, will fall into their proper place in the universal order of ends, and we shall rise by them as by steps to the final end of all, God, who is to Himself and to us the supreme and lasting good."

PIUS XI (D. R., 48).

"*In the social and economic field the Church has admittedly never propounded any definite technical system. This is not her function. But she has nevertheless laid down fundamental principles and general directions which while capable of adaptation according to differences of time, place, and people, do point out to civil society the safe path towards an era of improved culture and greater happiness.*"

PIUS XII (P. B., 8–10).

"*A profound conviction that it is not only right but also the duty of the Church to pronounce authoritatively upon social matters prompted*

10

Leo XIII to give his message to the world. Not that he intended to lay down any regulations for the purely practical or technical side of the social structure; he fully appreciated, as Our Predecessor Pius XI of holy memory declared in his commemorative Encyclical Quadragesimo Anno *ten years ago, that the Church disclaims any such mission.*

Within the general sphere of labour, in the sound and responsible development of all the physical and spiritual energies of individuals in their voluntary organisations, there is a vast field of manifold activity in which the public authority intervenes to complement and regulate; directly through local and professional corporations, and ultimately through the power of the State itself, whose higher and governing social authority has the important task of forestalling any disturbance of economic balance which may arise from the variety and conflict of competing interests, whether industrial or collective.

But it is unquestionably within the competence of the Church, where the social order touches the sphere of morals, to judge whether the foundations of a given social system are in harmony with the immutable order which God the Creator and Redeemer has manifested through the natural law and through revelation. To this twofold manifestation Leo XIII rightly appeals in his Encyclical; because the dictates of the natural law and the truths of revelation are like two streams, not contrary but concurrent, flowing by different courses from the one divine source; also because the Church, the custodian of the Christian supernatural order in which nature and grace converge, has the duty of instructing the consciences of men, including the consciences of those who are called upon to find solutions for the problems and duties arising out of social intercourse. The benefit or the detriment of souls will depend on the conformity or otherwise of the social structure with the laws of God; on this it will depend whether human beings, all destined to be quickened by the grace of Christ, are to lead their daily lives in the healthy and envigorating atmosphere of truth and moral virtue or in the poisoned and often

11

lethal air of error and depravity. In such circumstances how could the Church, the loving Mother who cares for the good of her children, legitimately witness their dangers with silent indifference, or pretend not to see and weigh with concern social conditions which, whether of set purpose or not, make difficult or practically impossible the practice of a Christian life in accordance with the commandments of the Supreme Lawgiver?"

PIUS XII (C. B., 1942; C. T. S., 2).

"The Church would be untrue to herself, she would have ceased to be a mother, if she were deaf to the cries of suffering children which reach her ears from every class of the human family. Between the various concrete forms by which individual peoples and States are endeavouring to solve the gigantic problems of internal order and international collaboration, she does not intend to discriminate, so long as such forms respect the law of God. Nevertheless, the Church, since she is "the pillar and ground of truth", since she has been appointed by the will of God and by the mandate of Christ to be the guardian of the natural and the supernatural order, cannot forgo her right to proclaim fundamental and immutable laws to her own children and to the whole world, protecting them against all perversion, obscurity, corruption, misinterpretation, and error. This function of the Church is the more necessary because upon the observance of these laws, and not merely upon the efforts of any upright and courageous will, depends the final stability of that new national and international order which is ardently desired by all peoples."

PIUS XII (Address of 16 July 1947; C. M., XLV, 117).

"Not that the Church has a mandate directly to regulate economic life. But the social and economic orders cannot be divorced from the moral, and it is her privilege and duty to affirm and proclaim the unchanging principles of morality. They rise above the storm-tossed

sea of social controversies as beacons whose piercing light should guide every attempt launched to bring a cure to social sores."

In these pronouncements the emphasis lies on the words "moral law". The Church clearly distinguishes between the technical and organizational side of economic and social living, on which she is neither willing nor competent to give an opinion (Q. 5), and the moral side, which comes under her authority to judge and direct. Here we have, then, the extent and motive of the Church's authority. The Church examines and decides her limits where moral matters are concerned, for she is commanded and empowered by Christ to lead men to eternal salvation. Man can find and work out his eternal salvation only by doing what is morally good, that is, by acting as God commands him to act. What is morally good and morally evil is not, then, left to the personal judgement of men to decide, rather it must be learned from objective norms. Objective means independent of human opinion, laid down for man, to be accepted and fulfilled by him. (At the same time it is not denied, of course, that human judgement has an important part to play, but subordinated to, and supplementing the objective norms.) In the final instance it is for the Church to declare and lay down as binding what, within the various spheres of life and human activity, is in accordance with the will of God. She must fulfil this duty if she is to teach and lead men along the "narrow" (Matt. 7:14) way of truth and salvation.

No single sphere of human choice and action is excepted. For always and everywhere it is the human person that acts, and his decisions, one and all, are subject to the moral law. They must be carried out and answered for as human acts. The individual must consider and know whether that which he intends doing, or which is demanded of him, will pass before

13

God, and it makes no difference whether it is a matter of earning money, tilling the fields, taking recreation, making political decisions, or anything else. This will be made clearer in the following Question.

5. *To what extent do economic and social questions come under the moral law?*

Economic and social questions come under the moral law in so far as they are, or may be, related to man's final end.

THERE is only one final and ultimate end: God. But there are innumerable and various proximate (single or partial) ends. Every sphere and every activity, every social structure has its own particular end, corresponding to the particular character of each. Thus, economics: supplying demand; science: the search for truth; family: begetting and bringing up children, mutual love and help; a sports club: the cultivation of sport. The doctor: health of the sick and injured; the architect: erection of suitable buldings, highways; the miner: producing coal; the woodman: felling trees.

The final end is all-embracing. All other ends are secondary and subordinate to it. Their significance is to lead to the final end, not away from it. Hence they must be so pursued that they do not divert and deter men from their final end. If that happens a man becomes so intensely and exclusively absorbed in them that he forgets and mistakes his true destiny.

As every sphere of life has its own proximate end, so it has also its own laws, its own ways and means, its own techniques and organization. Science works from hypotheses and with methods different from those of art; an operation carried out on a human organism proceeds differently from that on an atom; an economy which is distinctly industrial is created and developed in a different manner from a purely agricultural economy. One is justified, then, in speaking of the autonomy of the different spheres.

But this autonomy can only be relative and never absolute, that is, it remains conditioned and limited, conditioned by the necessities and circumstances of the sphere in question and limited in its value and importance for the life of man taken as a whole. Such laws may never be interpreted and followed in such a manner that they conflict with the moral law. On the contrary, they may be fulfilled only in accordance with the moral law.[3]

Neither the Church nor Catholic social ethics lays down particular laws for each sphere of culture, neither denies the right to abide by and develop according to such laws. That would indeed be foolish, since these laws are unavoidable as a practical necessity. On the other hand, the Church must fulfil the following tasks.

1. To see to it that the human temporal spheres of life do not assume undue autonomy and thereby become a danger to men spiritually and morally.

2. To state where, when, and in what manner the moral law applies.

3. To point out, and condemn, false notions, encroachments, and prejudices.

EXAMPLES:

Technical-organizational side:	Moral side:
Church not competent	*Church competent*
1. How the farmer should sow, harrow, thrash; how the tailor	1. Whether the purchaser is being defrauded (exorbitant prices, usurious interest); whether this or that

[3] See Vol. III of this Handbook of Christian Social Ethics: Economics in Society

15

should make a garment; how the artist should mix and apply colours; how the doctor should perform an operation.

business practice is to be considered honest or dishonest ("compensation", smuggling, illicit trading); whether a picture, no matter how valuable as art, offends against a sense of decency and propriety; whether, and where, a medical operation is permissible or not.

2. How large the capital investment and reserve must be in order to assure the continuance of a firm; what process is most suitable and productive; where and how mines might be sunk, blast furnaces and rolling-mills constructed and maintained in a state of efficiency; whether this or the other form of payment is most in keeping with the particular nature of the undertaking.

2. What wages, as a matter of principle, should be paid, or at least be aimed at, according to the demands of justice; what amount of work may be demanded of the individual; in what relation the profits of the concern should stand to the wages of the workers; whether it is justifiable to lay off workers, considering all the grievous consequences it entails; whether the production of certain types and quantities of goods is at all permissible (birth preventives, luxury goods).

3. What form of government a people chooses; with what neighbouring peoples it should maintain friendly relations; in what form family assistance is granted; what standard of instruction is to be attained in the different schools; whether protective tariffs are necessary and opportune.

3. What aims and tasks are, as a general principle, proper to the State; whether a constitution and government (totalitarian) leave sufficient scope for the safeguard of general human rights; what laws must be considered unjust in themselves; whether the rights of parents are sufficiently acknowledged and guaranteed; whether the family policy is in keeping with what is demanded by nature; whether State interference is admissible in the fields of business and culture.

It follows from what has been said that the Church is all the more entitled to put forward her point of view, the more immediately and gravely the moral life of men is affected or threatened by the aims and methods of secular power and influences. For that reason the Church has felt herself called upon more than once in our time to defend vigorously and unequivocally the fundamental rights of the individual and of smaller communities against the totalitarian states, as in the encyclicals of Pius XI against atheistic Communism (1937); *Mit brennender Sorge* against National Socialism (1937); the Christmas messages of Pius XII (1940-9), as also the decree against Communism (1949). On the other hand, the Church leaves men free to choose the form of society they like provided it allows them to develop their moral life. Pius XI has expressly approved (Q. A. § 71) the efforts to approximate the position of workers as wage-earners to that of partners, without laying down the law in this respect; and Pius XII in his 1943 Christmas message put forward and discussed in detail the democratic form of state as particularly suited to modern times. In this he did not contradict the traditional Catholic standpoint, that the choice of the form of state and constitution (whether monarchical, aristocratic or democratic) is a matter for the free decision of the people. He demanded only that in every state the principles of the natural law be fully honoured, and the Church guaranteed her God-given freedom. It is not at all the practice of the Church to pronounce on each and every matter which falls within her competence, rather does she observe the march of events and wait until she is convinced that her sacred mission obliges her to speak; and then she confines herself to saying what is necessary or opportune from the spiritual and moral standpoint.

The Church does not by her pronouncements interfere in an

unwarranted manner in purely secular affairs, as she is again and again reproached with doing ("political Catholicism"). If the Church were to enter into purely technical, organizational matters and lay down rules in their respect, then the reproach would be understandable and justified. But since she judges and stresses only the spiritual and moral obligations, she in no way exceeds her divine commission. The world should be grateful to her for every encouraging and enlightening word.

In all her social messages and instructions the Church's real concern is ultimately the Kingdom of God, that is, the honour of God, and the eternal salvation of men entrusted to her. It is certainly a matter of great importance to the Kingdom of God whether men are able to live their lives in a right order of things, whether they are correctly or falsely advised in their social decisions, whether temporal values are subordinated to, or given predominance over, eternal values, whether the goods of the earth are justly or unjustly distributed, whether power serves justice, or justice power, whether freedom of conscience is respected. The reproach, that the Church by constantly stressing the eternal discourages men from pursuing temporal tasks, is foolish and is blatantly refuted by the facts of history and of everyday life. On the contrary, it is precisely this concern for higher ends and higher goods which should inspire and oblige men to take temporal affairs more seriously and cooperate in creating worthy social conditions. The higher and more comprehensive the end, the more apt it is to awaken responsibility.

PIUS XI (D. R., 46).

"In proclaiming her clear teaching on this subject the Catholic Church has but one object: to realize on earth that glory to God and peace to all men of which the angels sang in their joyous message over the cave of Bethlehem; to establish true peace and true happiness so far as

these can be attained, at any rate by men of good will, even during this mortal life, in preparation for the perfect happiness of heaven."

The Church expects the renewal of human society not only from a reform of conditions, but also, more decisively, from a reform of morals. She does not at all deny, but rather emphatically demands, that proper, just, and worthy conditions be created, so that men may be in a position to lead morally good and peaceful lives. But she does not overlook the fact that betterment of conditions will remain pointless and fruitless if men's outlook continues to be wrong. Indeed she knows that such a reform of conditions can be effected only by men with a right outlook. From the many papal pronouncements on this point let it suffice to quote the following:

PIUS XI (Q. A., 97).

"However, all that We have taught about reconstructing and perfecting the social order will be of no avail without a reform of conduct; of this, history affords the clearest evidence. At one period there existed a social order which, though by no means perfect in every respect, corresponded nevertheless in a certain measure to right reason according to the needs and conditions of the times. That this order has long since perished is not due to the fact that it was incapable of development and adaptation to changing needs and circumstances, but it is due to the fact that men were hardened in excessive self-love, and refused to extend that order, as was their duty, to the increasing numbers of the population; or else, deceived by the attractions of false liberty and other errors, they grew impatient of every authority, and endeavoured to throw off all government."

19

6. From what sources does Catholic social ethics draw its teaching?

Catholic social ethics draws its principles and directives from whatever source presents it with the truths of moral living, but especially from the natural law, from revelation in the Old and New Testaments, and from the official pronouncements of the Church.

No truth, no matter what its source, or who first discoverd it, is alien to the Church, the guardian and proclaimer of the truth. She searches also for the truth concealed in error and is always ready to learn from friend and enemy alike. At the same time, the different sources of truth vary in importance for her according to how close they stand to her own origin and mission. In this also, Catholic social ethics follows the Church, whose social teaching it has to deal with scientifically.

1. Its highest and most authoritative source is the Word of God as contained in the writings of the Old und New Testaments, and in the tradition of the Church. The morality of men redeemed by Christ and reborn in the Holy Spirit is supernatural in its nature: as a state of existence and being (grace), and as a source of action and conduct (the infused virtues and gifts of the Holy Spirit), in its aims and motives, in its laws and model (Christ). The social commands of our Lord (Sermon on the Mount) take precedence of all other commands of society (Q. 18).

2. Natural law and natural rights form the primary basis for a considerable part of social questions, especially for those which concern the building up and ordering of life in society. Social life has its origins in nature and must develop according to the laws of nature; wherefore a genuine social ethics must pay the greatest attention to the natural law (or the order of creation), and seek to penetrate ever deeper into it (Qs. 61–77).

3. Further knowledge is provided by human experience and human sciences, above all by the different branches of sociology. Our knowledge begins with experience and must always remain closely linked to experience, to the reality of the world and of life. That holds particularly for ethics, the science of moral conduct. The findings and conclusions of the other sciences, for example psychology, history, ethnology, economics, juris- prudence, the various branches of theology, are carefully considered and utilized as far as they are necessary or helpful for the solution of the social question. Man-made laws (positive law), and especially the deliberations and records in connection with these, also give at times valuable pointers, and not always of a negative kind, since they can bring to light hidden coheren- ces, focus attention on particular questions, open up, or at least indicate new avenues. In many cases, however, the Church has been forced to protest vigorously against human laws, as, for instance, she did against the National Socialist law of 1934, which imposed sterilization on those afflicted with hereditary diseases, but such an attitude is altogether in the interest of truth.

4. The Church's teaching finds its truest and most authoritative expression in the pronouncements of her magisterial (teaching) office, among which the encyclicals and other messages of the popes take first place. But the numerous pastorals and exhortations of bishops – especially when the bishops of entire provinces, of countries and continents speak as a body – are also of great im- portance for both doctrine and Christian practice. It is generally acknowledged, by friend and enemy alike, that the social messages of the popes show, in a form and abundance nowhere else achieved, those very merits which should characterize documents dealing with both the doctrinal and factual side of social living: exact knowledge of the actual situation, of existing

21

conditions and current ideas; an open minded attitude to contemporary society; prudence and balance in judgement; courage in discussing and solving new questions, together with absolute loyalty to principle and respect for tradition, yet without rigidly clinging to it; the enlightened insight into, and appraisal of, the complete Christian order of nature and the supernatural (grace), reason and faith, creation and redemption, temporal and eternal values; apostolic charity, sincerity and fearlessness.[4]

[4] See the list of the most important pronouncements of the popes given on page x. To these should be added, as typical of episcopal pronouncements on these questions:

i. The Joint Pastoral Letter of the Hierarchy of England and Wales, June 1942, *On the Social Question* (C. T. S., 1942).

ii. The Statement of the American Episcopate, 7 February 1940, *The Church and Social Order* (N. C. W. C., 1940).

iii. The Annual Joint Pastoral Letters of the Australian Hierarchy.

iv. The Pastoral Letter of H. E. Cardinal Suhard, Archbishop of Paris, February 1947. English translation, *New Life* (London, 1947). American translation in *The Church Today: the Collected Writings of Cardinal Suhard* (Fides, Chicago, 1953).

The great number of the Church's pronouncements completely refutes the charge that the Church does not express her mind early, comprehensively, and forcibly enough on social questions. There is really no important matter on which the Church has not expressed its point of view, in unequivocal and moving language. Though the great social encyclical *Rerum Novarum* did not appear until 1891, it was preceded by innumerable statements and exhortations by popes and bishops, not to mention the incalculable amount of work done by the Church up to then in both the scientific and practical fields of pastoral ministry and social welfare. Before Rome speaks to the world on such difficult, and to a great extent new, questions, especially in the important form of a great papal encyclical, it observes developments for a sufficiently long time to weigh everything exactly. Confusion is caused all too easily by precipitate statements.

7. What is the basic line of thought in Catholic social ethics?

The basic line of thought in Catholic social ethics is :
1. **Realistic – true to reality.**
2. **Teleological – with a final end in view as determining all things.**
3. **Theistic – taking God as beginning and end of all things.**
4. **Christo-centric – taking Christ as the centre of all things.**

THE answer to this question derives from the fact that it is the task of Catholic social ethics to find and set forth the right norms within the order of life laid down by God and founded on Christ. Ultimately, then, everything must centre round the person and Gospel of our Lord: everything is related to him, measured by his standards, done in imitation of him and according to his mind. But for one who believes in Christ, the only-begotten Son of God become Man, there can be no vagueness or distortion in his conception of God, he *must* think theistically. He sees the world and man as the work of the one, personal, divine Creator, to whom everything that exists belongs inalienably, and to whom everything is subject in absolute obedience. Catholic social ethics is true to reality in its basic line of thought, because it affirms the reality of the world and of men, and recognizes and draws from experience as the source of natural knowledge. The oft-repeated reproach, that Catholic social ethics is unreal, "high-flown", since it stands for ideals not of this world, is false and unjust. Finally, Catholic social ethics is teleological, because it is convinced of, and sets out from the irrefutable principle that "all created things act always for an end, and in fact, for a final end" (St. Thomas, I–II, 1, 1; see Q. 47), and because it holds that whatever is good or valuable has the character of an end, for which we are obliged to strive. Teleological thinking must be taken together with what is called causal thinking, although actually causal thinking is subordinate to it. We call causal that mode of thinking which takes into account only the connections between cause and effect perceived by us (fire—smoke; a shot fired—impact). Undoubtedly men act with, and on, one another; but this mutual activity and reaction does not suffice to explain social living. Men are moved by ideas and purposes; they set themselves a goal; they make plans and aim at an order of things which is yet to come. They act teleologically, and everything depends on their striving for, and reaching the right ends.[5]

8. Is Catholic social ethics necessary today?

Catholic social ethics is necessary because the social questions of the present day simply cannot be solved without it, and certainly not in opposition to it.

PIUS XI (D. R., 47).

"It is a doctrine opposed equally to all erroneous extremes and to the violent methods and policies of those who embrace them."

PIUS XI (D. R., 75).

"But for the greater efficacy of this social action it is quite essential that Catholic sociology should be more closely studied, and that the principles of this science, under the auspices of the divinely constituted authority of the Church, should be given the widest possible publicity.

[5] By reason of this characteristic way of thinking and reasoning, Catholic social ethics is safeguarded against unfounded and capricious hypotheses, unreal and forced constructions, biased and subjective false notions, and against the dangers of both false materialism and false "intellectualism".

If the conduct of some Catholics in the social and economic sphere has left something to be desired, this has often happened because they had not duly considered the teaching of the Popes on the subject. Everyone, therefore, no matter to what class of society he belongs, ought to receive fuller instruction on social principles according to his degree of education, and the social teaching of the Church must be made widely known among the working classes.

Let Catholic principles enlighten men's minds with their sure radiance, and so move their wills that they will find therein the right rule of conduct to guide them in the strict and careful observance of their social duties. So will everyone help to banish from the lives of Christians that inconsistency which We have more than once deplored."

PIUS XII (C. B., 1942, C. T. S., 3–4).

"Never has it been so capitally important to understand clearly the true foundations of all social life as in these days when humanity, diseased by the poison of social errors and perversions, and tossed about by conflicting desires, doctrines, and aims, has become the unhappy prey of disorder, and is experiencing the disruptive effects of false social theories that neglect and contravene the laws of God. Just as darkness with all its oppressive horrors cannot be dispelled by a will o' the wisp but only by the light, so disorder can be banished only by order, and by an order that is not fictitious but real. Only in one way can we hope for salvation, renewal, and true progress, and that is through the return of numerous and influential sections of mankind to a true conception of society, a return which will require an extraordinary grace of God and firm and self-sacrificing resolution on the part of men of good will and far-sighted vision. If such men are brought to perceive and appreciate the fascinating beauty of just social principles, they will be able by their influence to spread among the masses a conviction of the truly divine and spiritual origin of social life; and they will thus prepare the way

25

for the re-awakening, the development, and the consolidation of those ethical conceptions without which the proudest achievement in the social sphere will be nothing but a Babel; its citizens may have walls in common, but they will speak different and conflicting tongues."

PIUS XII (Letter, 18 July 1947; C. M., November 1947).
"The present hour, from whatever standpoint it is viewed, summons the faithful to exert their every energy to render to the social teaching of the Church a maximum of efficiency and of practical results."

No intelligent and fair-minded person will deny that today human society is in need of a thorough renewal in every respect. This renewal will only succeed when men return to, and follow, what God himself has taught and shown us as the one and only right way. This means that in all spheres of social living the ends and norms of the Christian order of things in its entirety, embracing natural and supernatural, must again be recognized, accepted and put into practice. The world will not be put right without God and against his will. The social ethics of the Church acknowledges without reserve God and Christ, the forces of nature and grace, the divinely established order of men and values. It omits nothing of what God has given to, or imposed upon, the world, by way of potentialities and tasks, freedom and restriction. At the same time it does not overlook the fact and the power of evil. It is aware of man's need of redemption and of the inevitable failure of every imaginary or attempted self-redemption (Q. 19). In short, because Catholic social ethics both ventures to survey in all candidness the life of man in its entirety, and is able, directed by the irreproachable and reliable judgement of the Church, to put forward the ends and means of the one and only genuine and fruitful renewal, it can effectively and in every sphere help the present-day world.

9. What should be our attitude towards non-Catholic social ethics?

With all due recognition of what is true and good in non-Catholic social ethics, we are forced to conclude that they are not suitable, or not sufficiently so, for the renewal of society.

NON-CATHOLIC social doctrines, including those which taken as a whole must be definitely rejected, have unquestionably seen and brought home to men much that is right, sometimes earlier and more forcibly than Catholic social ethics. Even today they offer indications and conceptions of social order, which we often approve to a considerable extent, and sometimes can welcome as being stimulating and helpful. Taken all together, the many forms of non-Catholic social ethics, in spite of major differences and conflicting doctrines, have one thing in common: they attain neither the depth and wide scope, nor the accuracy and reliability of Catholic social ethics, of its vision, its principles and decisions. These various forms of social ethics do not draw from all the sources of truth accessible to us, or do not do so with complete logical consequence, freed from all prejudice. Either they start from premises too narrowly conceived, if not actually wrong, or they do not go the whole way.[6]

Non-Catholic social ethics may be divided into two main groups:

1. Those which rest on quite false hypotheses and consequently lead to completely distorted conceptions of man and human society; they are irreconcilably opposed to Catholic social

[6] Only the main tendencies are here outlined according to their most general characteristics. A more precise description and criticism is given in the relevant articles of the Handbook, where individual points of doctrine are discussed and judged.

27

ethics (although they also contain things that are right). To these belong:

a. Materialistic ethics, represented in scientific form, for instance, by Marxism (but in practice widely adopted by many people of all classes). Matter is the only, at any rate the all-determining, reality; the spiritual is denied, or interpreted as the mere reflection of the material, and so immortality, freedom and personal responsibility go by the board; spiritual values are not only very seriously threatened, but attacked at the core; life in society and its development are governed by force and utility; the community becomes a collective, to which the individual is subordinated without any means of asserting himself.

b. Liberal or individualistic ethics. Its slogan is *laissez faire* the complete liberty of the individual; the "struggle for existence" becomes the supreme law of life in society; real obligations binding men by virtue of a higher authority are not recognized. In all spheres of man's life this error has had dire consequences: inordinate pursuit of wealth; the substitution of might for right; "free love"; the destruction of morals in married and family life; the separation of art and morality; false nationalism.

c. Totalitarian ethics (the ethics of totalitarian states). The collective, collective actions, collective values, all of which can have only a conditional and limited importance, are turned into supreme values and sole norms (people, race, nation, State, economy, class). Raised to the absolute, the collective justifies every demand, and every measure put forward or taken in its name; the inevitable consequence is servitude and terror, a "never-ending horror". True, totalitarianisms operate in different ways; but all have this in common, that they regard the individual as a mere unit in the collective, and dispose of him accordingly (Q. 32, No. 5).

d. Naturalistic ethics. This embraces many types. Thus the three previously mentioned belong to it. It confines itself purposely to the purely natural sphere of human action and social living, because it rejects every supernatural order and obligation. It recognizes no transcendental, eternal goal, but only a temporal, this-worldly ideal of life and society. God's revelation and Christian belief are banished to the realm of fairy-tales and myths, or at best dismissed as something which has a certain historical importance, but is now out of date. Since God has redeemed and renewed the world in Christ, and since he has established his Kingdom in Christ, to which he has called all men, every naturalistic conception misses the decisive centre of the world and of men. For this reason, naturalism can be described as the great and diabolical error in the history of mankind.

2. Those non-Catholic ethics which start out from hypotheses, and follow lines, that are right in themselves but which either fail to see important things, or do not draw the obvious conclusions. More often than not these inadequacies go together. Almost invariably these social ethics, because of a lack of vision, succumb to the danger of whittling down or overstressing, the very truths at which they arrive. We mention here two groups:

a. Purely natural social ethics. It rests solely on reason and experience, and not on revelation and faith. However, since it abstracts from the supernatural divine economy of salvation, or at least does not deny or oppose it, it is not naturalistic in the strict and malicious sense, but rather in a broader and in itself harmless sense. For what is natural is, when correctly understood and developed, completely necessary and in place in the supernatural order. In so far as it observes, judges, and

29

infers correctly, it does not contradict Catholic social ethics, but rather forms their natural basis; hence it is carefully applied within Catholic social ethics.[7]

It may admittedly have very unhappy and menacing consequences, if for example it makes itself unduly independent and thereby seduces men away from their true final end, and forces them out of the true supernatural order of things. In that case it would drift into naturalistic ethics. The so-called "humanitarian" ethics of today, in its manifold forms and with its numerous following, has its place here, since it seeks to build up a complete and adequate moral code purely from man's natural understanding of himself (without revelation). Unfortunately, humanitarian ethics holds itself – for the most part consciously – aloof from every revealed ethics, and is at times openly or indirectly atheistic, denying God and our obligation towards him.

b. Non-Catholic Christian social ethics, as represented especially and in very different forms within the Protestant Churches. It has, unfortunately, all the faults peculiar to Protestant Christianity in general: complete or partial rejection of the natural law (Q. 62, No. 2); private interpretation of Scripture, which means foregoing the sure and comprehensive judgement of a teaching authority; dangerous oscillation and hesitation in coming to agreement on decisive principles and inferences (thus its compromising attitude on the questions of divorce, birth-control, abortion, sterilization).

The Protestant Church was not, and is not in a position to produce a conception of social order for human society comparable to that given in the papal encyclicals. At the same time we acknowledge the efforts being made in this

---

[7] Q. 6, paragraph 2. See the section on the natural law, Q. 61 et seq.

direction, as also its open-mindedness towards Catholic social teaching.[8]

Catholic social ethics, as a result of careful sifting and of necessary discussion, seeks and accepts whatever is true and good in order to compare it with its own teaching and, so far as it is in agreement with this, fits it into its own structure. Yet it is in no wise a heterogeneous "mixture", a composition of parts gathered from "outside" and worked more or less successfully into a single whole. Rather it is something completely apart, forming an intrinsic and consistent whole. It is important to make this point perfectly clear, since one hears in this connection peculiar and unfavourable opinions. The basic views, teachings and decisions of Catholic social ethics are intrinsically and necessarily bound up together, following one from the other, and are thus unique. Nowhere else in the world is the like to be found, and it can in no wise be explained as a mere synthesis of related or fitting parts. Each section of this *Handbook* proves and illustrates this in detail.

10. *What is particularly incumbent upon Catholic social ethics today?*

Two things are of particular importance at the present time :

1. To diagnose the causes and extent of the prevailing disorder.

2. To apply clear and indisputable principles correctly and as the times demand.

[8] E.g. the discussions and results of the Evanston and Amsterdam meetings of the World Council of Churches. See E. Duff, S.J., *The Social Thought of the World Council of Churches.*

1. BOTH the Church herself, and scholars guided by her teaching, must fulfil their mission to the world of today: "every time is God's time", and it should be possible for men of every age to see where their salvation lies.

In the present century we are in a crisis so great that it cannot be halted. Everywhere the former order has given way to disorder as frightful as it is distressing, so that we are forced to speak of an age of "total uprooting", of "nihilism" (where life has lost every genuine basis and security), an age of fear with the sense of being hopelessly lost. No single sphere of man's life has remained unaffected. But the most serious aspect is that the individual himself has reached a crisis where he can see no way out, no escape. Everywhere there is religious and moral confusion, indifference and depravity, lack of any solid convictions; a "philosophy of life" is substituted for religious belief; the demon of technology has come to dominate over man, its creator; men are divided into classes, nations, great powers, "East and West"; totalitarian ideas and powers have gained fatal influence; complete worldliness of outlook and culture has become deeply rooted. The deepest cause of this crisis lies in the alienation from Christ and God, which has grown steadily since the decline of the Middle Ages (influence of the natural sciences, the philosophy of the modern period: Renaissance, Enlightenment, Humanism). The saying has been proved true in the case of mankind, that "when the unifying principle is lost, the parts fall asunder". The falling away from God leads to dissension and disintegration. What has become uprooted must be planted anew, must be grafted onto the root from which mankind has sprung. To attempt anything else would mean inevitable failure, for man cannot be planted in any soil chosen at will.

It is the task of Catholic social ethics today to go back to the ultimate and deepest sources, to point out the renewing power of its basic principles in order to come to grips, convincingly and effectively, with the present disorder. Men must be made conscious of the original order of things, which is always valid and which no age can violate or destroy with impunity.

2. Every age has its own particular problems and difficulties. It is characteristic of our time that great and, as is generally agreed, inevitable transformations are taking place. These transformations are due not only to a change of outlook and mentality, but also to the fact that the conditions and order of things hitherto prevailing have for the most part broken down, and cannot be restored again in the same form. The false aims and the false ways of attaining them of the last centuries have made further development along the same lines impossible. This development has gone awry and come to a standstill. The world is really faced with new questions and decisions, which affect deeply both the life of society and of the individual. Catholic social ethics derives from reason and revelation basic and most general principles and postulates which never lose their validity and efficacy either wholly or in part, since they are outside place and time. From these follow other principles and postulates which are not so primary and universal and which, while they allow of no real exception, admit of a certain accommodation and elasticity (see the section on the natural law, Q. 61 et seq.). Human action, because it is always (in the concrete) singular and bound up with changing circumstances, is extremely diverse and, even when it produces similar effects, must be diversely evaluated (murder and killing in self-defence have the same effect, but morally and legally they must be judged differently). Social living should always be worthy and ordered, but how it is to be set up cannot be postulated once and

for all from any general conception of order, no matter how good. A monarchy is differently constituted from a democracy; the distribution of wealth which in a rich country would be considered well ordered might, in a poor country, be considered quite the opposite. An application of social norms in keeping with the actual situation must, then, be ever sought anew. Catholic social ethics is confronted with the very difficult task of combining the necessary broadmindedness and flexibility with the requisite firmness and circumspection. Men are to expect that demands, which may include considerable burdens and sacrifices, be made of them only to the extent that can be fully justified, that is avoiding all unnecessary restrictions. But this "accommodation" must not mislead us to surrender what reason and faith pronounce inviolable, nor to allow freedom such latitude that social living is thereby shattered. Social living is so multiform, and in the problems to be solved so difficult, that, naturally enough, opinions differ considerably even within our own camp. Hence it is not only good form but it is our duty to be tolerant towards one another.

The example of interpretation and application in keeping with the times and true to principle is given, as has already been said (Q. 6, paragraph 4), in the pronouncements of the recent popes. They do not hesitate to go to the root of social evils and to speak their mind clearly to the world. Free from any narrow, preconceived ideas, they show what is today the right and practicable way for healing and renewing society.

PIUS XII (C. B., 1941; C. T. S. 4–5).

"It is impossible to shut one's eyes to the unhappy spectacle of a gradual apostasy from Christianity in individuals and in society; a process which, beginning with moral laxity, has caused men to doubt and then openly to reject the truth, and to repudiate the forces

which enlighten the mind concerning good and evil and so strengthen private, family, civic and public life. . . .

Estranged from God and from the practice of the Christian religion the spirit of man was thus plunged into a moral abyss. It only remained then for every thought, plan, enterprise, estimate, action, and work of man to be directed and focused upon the material world, every effort and endeavour being made towards spatial expansion, towards an unprecedented acquisition of wealth and power, towards an unrivalled speed and efficiency in the production of all that material progress and advancement might seem to require. The result in politics was the prevalence of an unbridled impulse towards expansion and a political advantage that took no account of ethical standards; in the economic sphere, the domination of gigantic enterprises and trusts; in social life, the overcrowding of great cities and industrial and commercial centres with great masses of the population, followed by that general instability which is inevitable when multitudes of men are uprooted from house and home, district and trade, familiar friendships and interests."

11. *What are the main divisions of this Handbook of Christian Social Ethics?*

This Handbook is divided into four main parts:
1. Man in Society
2. Community and Society
3. Economics in Society   **1447856**
4. Church and Society

IT will always be a difficult matter to find the correct division of a handbook of social ethics. One can raise objections to every form proposed, since the questions are frequently interdependent and overlap. As has been said in the Introduction a handbook must be clear and easy to grasp. It is best, then, to have as few main divisions as possible. Since the Church's pronouncements have been continually referred to throughout, it seemed advisable to devote one main part to the Church's attitude to social living, although, naturally, the Church's attitude is discussed in each section relative to the matter treated there. In this main part it is intended – apart from the relation of Church and State – to examine in particular, in the light of the Church's teaching, the various conceptions of society current today, and so these conceptions of society will be given there in full.

BASIC QUESTIONS AND FORCES
OF SOCIAL LIVING

There are certain socio-ethical questions and answers of a
general nature which one must grasp in order to get a true perspective, and to be able to judge properly in the sphere of
individual questions. There are certain moral attitudes and
obligations which must be upheld in every society, since men
cannot otherwise live together in a dignified and orderly
manner.

The first volume of the *Handbook* deals with the most important aspects of these basic questions and forces. It is divided
into three parts:

1. **Man in Society (Qs. 12–42)**

2. **Basic Laws of Social Order (Qs. 43–52)**

3. **Justice and Charity (Qs. 53–124).**

Part One

Man in Society

PIUS XI (C. C., 13).

"Even his rational nature alone sets man above all other visible creatures. Add to this that God's purpose in willing human beings to be born is not merely that they may exist and occupy the earth, but far more, that they may worship him, and that they may know and love him and finally enjoy him for ever in heaven."

PIUS XII (C. B., 1942; C. T. S., 5, 7, 13).

"The original and essential purpose of social life is to preserve, develop, and perfect the human person. . . .
Whatever happens, whatever change or transformation may take place, the purpose of all social life remains the same, ever sacred, ever obligatory: the development of the personal values of man, who is made in the image of God. . . .
He who would have the star of peace to shine permanently over society must do all in his power to restore to the human person the dignity which God conferred upon him from the beginning."

PIUS XII (C. B., 1944; N. W. C., 84).

"The Church has the mission to announce to the world, which is looking for better and more perfect forms of democracy, the highest and most needed message that there can be: the dignity of man, the call to be sons of God."

39

ALL right thinking begins with experience. Now two incontestable facts of experience are that (a) there are many men, of whom each is an individual and (b) these men live together in community, indeed, in a great variety of communities. Experience shows that one cannot separate the individual from the community, nor the community from the individuals. So the first important question of social ethics is: What is the position of the individual in relation to the community? Which takes precedence, the individual of the community or the community of the individual? This question will be resolved one way or the other according to one's conception of man. And according to how one resolves this question, one will draw further conclusions, which will be a blessing or curse to man and to the community. One must not approach these questions too hastily and with a biased mind, but rather warily, appreciating fully both facts of experience. The one who holds from the start that man is indebted to the community for the sum total of his reality, even though he afterwards protests vigorously that he admits the individual and unique value of man, nevertheless contradicts himself, for on the basis of his supposition man is forfeited for better or worse to the community. On the other hand, the one who declares from the start that the individual alone is a reality and has right to existence, champions egotism and selfishness as the supreme law of life, and destroys therewith every social order and every social obligation.

Lesson One

ON MAN

12. What is man?

Man is a rational animal. He is constituted of a body and a spiritual soul, and possesses alone among visible creatures the independence and the dignity of a person.

PIUS XI (D. R., 38).

"Man has a spiritual and immortal soul, and being a person and endowed by the Creator with quite marvellous gifts of mind and body, he is rightly called a 'microcosm' (to use the expression of the ancients) because in perfection he far transcends the whole measureless world of inanimate nature. His final end, not only in this life but also in the everlasting life to come, is God alone; and because he has been raised up by sanctifying grace to the dignity of a son of God, he is united to the kingdom of God in the Mystical Body of Jesus Christ."

IN the answer given we are considering man according to the innermost constitutions of his being, thus saying what kind of being man really is, what it is that ultimately and essentially makes him a man, distinct from all other things.

There are other definitions of man which are also correct and merit our attention, particularly today. But they do not disclose that innermost heritage of this being, "man". Rather they stress the one or the other characteristic or characteristic activity, as when it is said that man is the only being with a "history", or that man alone "works". Only man lives in history. God stands above history. Things lower than man, it is true, come to be, develop and pass away, but they lack mind, that force which forms history in the real sense. To enable a being to work

41

(not just to perform certain actions), it must possess a twofold ability: the mental talent of discovery and invention, as also the skill of craftsmanship. Man alone possesses both. God can, of course, bring about everything that human labour can produce or attain; but God does not "work", he creates, that is, he and he alone calls things into being out of nothing by virtue of his all-powerful will. The essential definition of man which we have given is anything but new. It goes back to Aristotle and St. Thomas Aquinas. It contains the following truths which for social ethics are very important:

1. To the essential nature of man belong body and soul, which are joined together by God's creative power in a unity of being and acting. The two different basic elements which constitute man, unite and fit together in such a manner as to form the one human nature, the one man. From them arises the one subject of being and acting: man. Man, the whole man, comes to be, lives, acts, suffers; he needs, in order to act, definite abilities (predispositions, faculties, powers), but it is *he* who acts and experiences, who thinks and wills, moves his hands, feels pain, and is subject to influences. It is not that the soul merely lives in the body and moves it, rather it penetrates it through and through, penetrates and forms it, builds it up and fashions it. This interaction and coexistence of matter and form (body and soul) is called essential unity, unity of essence, in contrast to every other type of unity which is not essential since it presupposes the essence of the thing, for instance, the unity of the soul with its powers; the unity of parents and children; the unity of a people or a business concern. Now the real greatness of man does not lie in his possessing a body so formed and endowed (although this body is one of the most beautiful works of art of the Creator, and for that reason should

be treated with reverence) but in his possessing a spiritual soul, invisible, sublime and exalted above matter (Qs. 13–19).

2. There are innumerable independent things (every stone, every plant, every animal), as distinct from qualities, which are not independent but inherent or adherent (size, colour, form). But to man belongs a special, namely a spiritual independence which is founded in the fact that the spiritual soul in itself is independent of matter and its laws. The independent being in the world of spirit-nature is called a "person". So "person" designates primarily, not a moral attitude, but a state of being; more correctly, a "person is an individual being which is spiritual in its nature, or, which is the same thing, endowed with mind.

3. Man, in common with all finite things, takes his origin from God, is created by God. But here also man has something distinctive; for each individual human soul is brought into being by a particular creative act of God, and implanted in the body prepared by the parents. For this reason the person towers above all other, impersonal things. Person is a title of dignity, nobility, honour, inner greatness. The person is "the most perfect thing in the whole of nature" (St. Thomas); but the imperfect is always there for the sake of the perfect, not vice versa.[1]

4. A man is not only a person, but also an "individual", a unique being. That does not mean merely that each man is precisely one, and thus the one is not the other, but it means that each man possesses a particular stamp and essential character of his own. Notwithstanding all specific conformity in essence (nature),

[1] The false conceptions of man nearly all agree in this, that they either overlook, deny, or do not view in the proper light and misinterpret, the spiritual element in man; some of them, such as modern theosophy and anthroposophy, ascribe to man what amounts to divine attributes, make of him a kind of component part of God.

each man has, as experience shows, his own particular way of seeing and experiencing things, his own particular merits and faults, his own "disposition". Life's fortunes are as manifold as men themselves: what comes easily to one, another can scarcely cope with, and what suits one man and attracts him is often positively rejected by another. How difficult it is for one man, even with the best will in the world, really to understand another, to put himself really in the other's position. Descent and heredity, family and race, education and milieu, and many other factors and influences combine in an ever-changing variety of ways to fashion men not only outwardly, but inwardly as a unique individual. So men must develop, each in his own way. Thus the individuating note in and about a man is something given by Nature. And yet this individuating note must not be so intensely sought after and so strongly stressed that the general laws and obligations suffer thereby (Q. 15), or that the just claims of the community are passed over (Qs. 31–2). A man is limited by his "individuality" so that he cannot do all he would like to, but only what is in keeping with, and can be achieved by *his* ability and *his* individual character. But apart from the case where someone is born with particularly unfavourable predispositions (affliction with hereditary disease), a man is enriched by his individuality. Only by it does he become really effective. Since he possesses particular gifts, abilities, and inclinations, he is particularly fitted for certain things (science, art, teaching), and can approach his speciality with good prospects of success. It is one of the most unhealthy and most regrettable facts of the present age that many are unable to follow their natural bent in the choice of occupation, and are simply forced by material circumstances to take whatever employment happens to come their way. Thus one and the same man is both individual (single being with his own particular character), and person (spiritual independent being). It is not here a question of two component parts, but of two aspects, decisive characteristics of one and the same man. Man can and must be regarded:

a. as one single living and acting being, with his particular character and temperament – an individual;
b. as a being endowed with mind (spirit), independent and sovereign in being and acting – a person.

5. The following might be noted here. Because, and in so far as, a man is a spiritual being, he remains, despite all social obligations, in a very definite sense always by himself. He may never "spend himself" to the extent that he loses sight of himself and neglects his own perfection (Q. 15). There is a false form of self-renunciation. To put it another way: each person is essentially and inevitably turned inwards, self-regarding. He may never leave himself out of account. His primary and inseparable legacy lies in his being able to find, and rest in himself; his highest and most personal form of action, contemplation and the love that flows from it, is not originally and certainly not exclusively focused outwards or of a practical nature, but first and foremost an expression and growth of the interior life, or-dained to the end that the person should develop and perfect his spiritual self. And all this is indirectly important for social living, because the *whole* man is social by nature (Q. 31). But one would thoroughly misunderstand the social nature of man, if one were to imagine that there was nothing in and about man that did not derive its primary and sole significance from the social aspect (Q. 20, No. 5). This way of being turned inwards, towards himself, is shown most clearly in man's encounter with God, the source of all truth and the essence of all goodness. Knowing and loving God, who is most intimately present to

man and actually "resides" in the soul of any one in the state of grace, are first and foremost in themselves personal activities, not only performed by a person, but related to the person and his perfection. And, indeed, man can and should gain much by way of incentive, strength, wisdom, and counsel for vigorous and self-sacrificing social action precisely from this very encounter with God. In an age dominated by the machine and completely given over to external things, it is truly necessary to stress with all possible emphasis the importance of this return of the person to itself, and to do everything to guard it from insolent, presumptuous or just thoughtless interference. The whole modern situation, its progress, complications and necessities divert man's attention from the "intimate sphere" of his own person. False philosophies presume to "co-ordinate" man down to the very depths of his being, begrudging or preventing him from enjoying the happiness of the retreat and quiet of his own soul. Only that which can be seen is of value, and man's worth is defined (if not "rated") according to the measure of his external activity and success.

13. *What are the prerogatives of man as a person?*

As a person man is:
1. **The image and likeness of God in the Blessed Trinity.**
2. **Immortal, having an immortal soul.**
3. **Of inalienable and inviolable individual worth.**

THESE prerogatives are already implied in the answer to the previous question.

1. All creatures bear witness to God, since they have their origin in him. Irrational creatures, however, merely, provide a

46

"clue" to his existence. They proclaim by their very existence their richness and their order, that an infinitely wise, powerful, and good Creator exists, who has brought them into existence and guides them. But a clue does not imply a likeness, it merely proclaims that another must have been its cause. It shows that the clue must have been left by someone, but gives no idea what that being looks like. One can only infer the form and appearance of this being if one knows beforehand whence the clue originated. Image, on the other hand, implies likeness; it represents someone, reproduces the features of the being whose image it is. An image is something valued and dear, worthy of being revered; it is cherished as a jewel or a keepsake.

That man is made in God's image is clearly shown by the account of the Creation and elsewhere in Holy Scripture, and is accepted faith in by the Church and her teaching. "Let us make man in our own image and likeness!" (Gen. 1:26); "For man was made to the image of God" (Gen. 9:6); "... and made him after his own image" (Ecclus. 17:1); "For God created man incorruptible, and to the image of his own likeness he made him" (Wis. 2:23); "You must be clothed in the new self ... so that the image of the God who created it is its pattern" (Col. 3:10); "... to be moulded into the image of his Son" (Rom. 8:29).

PIUS XII (S. P., 16).

"The very first page of Holy Scripture records, with that nobility of phrase which is native to it, that God crowned the work of creation which he had begun by making 'man in his own image'. The Bible further teaches, that man was enriched with supernatural gifts and properties, destined for a mysterious and eternal happiness."

This consciousness of being created in God's image and likeness and of being called and commissioned to extend that image, must surely remind man most forcibly of his own greatness and the nobility of his life. God does not make an image of himself for it to be disfigured or passed over unnoticed, but rather that it be further worked on and formed, that it may gain increasingly in clarity and beauty and ever better reflect the original.

2. Because it is spiritual, the human soul is intrinsically imperishable (immortal). God could, of course, allow it to fall back into nothingness, but he will not do this, as revelation quite clearly testifies (Matt. 10:28; 25:46; John 8:51; 10:28; 2 Cor. 5:1-2). The human soul is simple. This means that it has in it no component parts tending to repel one another and bring about dissolution. It cannot disintegrate, but must continue in being. The immortality of the soul shows again how serious an affair is the life of man.

3. Because his soul is spiritual and imperishable, man possesses an individual worth, as opposed to a mere utility value to others. Irrational things are instruments; tools in the service, and for the benefit of man.[2] Man is more than that. He forms the noblest part of all God's visible creation, enjoys special guidance by God's providence and must not be degraded to a mere thing. This individual worth is inalienable; man himself may not forego it. It is inviolable; the community must recognize it.[3]

---

[2] Irrational creatures also must be looked upon and valued first of all as testifying to God's glory and creative power; they also are destined primarily to praise the Creator. But since they are by their very nature perishable, they are created by God himself to be the basis of existence and for the use and benefit of man. They are God's gift to man, to be used by him in working out his perfection.

[3] St. Thomas, III c. G., 111-13.

All other attempts to establish man's dignity and worth, when they are correctly argued and developed, resolve themselves into the reasons given here. They are based ultimately on the personal immortality and consequent intrinsic individual worth of man. Where such arguments are one-sided and restricted they have not the force to establish man's genuine individual worth, nor are they proof against all arbitrariness. To this group belong arguments that would base man's worth on race hereditary qualities, class, military or labour value or general utility.

4. The conditions and influences of a man's immediate surroundings are without question decisive factors in his formation. Men of different nations, ages, classes, and professions differ considerably in mentality and physique. In their way of thinking, feeling, expressing themselves, "reacting", they are far from being alike. Qualities which we find in a pronounced and remarkable form in one man may be completely lacking or scarcely noticeable in another, as for instance, courage or cowardice, diligence or indolence, candour or cunning, genuine passion or apathy and melancholy.

Numerous forces and influences act as causes or motives upon the unborn child and the living individual to make of him a man of his particular age, people, class, sphere of culture (climate and country, heredity and education, habit and custom, rich or poor circumstances, type of work and manner of employment, even – not to be overlooked today – propaganda and terror!). These factors form the environment out of which a man grows and which he can escape only with great difficulty. Nor can it be denied that technical economic changes and progress are very definite co-determinants in the development of men, in so far as they demand of mankind in general or of individual groups certain measures and

49

decisions. The industrial age changed living conditions and with them men and their problems changed too. The arrival of the atomic age confronts us with new problems and new decisions. Nevertheless, the basic thesis of Marxism, that man is the product of his environment, the result of economic social conditions, is false and must be most emphatically rejected,[4] for this theory makes man subject to development which he suffers but cannot control. If we grant that economic social conditions have such power over man that it is not he who fashions them, but they him (and that in his entire development, in all that he is and does) this means that man is ruled by the laws of necessity and compulsion. It means that man is denied all that raises him above the world of matter. He is robbed of his true origin, for he has not been created by God, but brought forth by material conditions, of his individual worth, since as a mere product of environment he has only utility value for the world that surrounds him, of his true destiny, which is to reach God, not to serve the collectivity. It must be admitted that under certain circumstances it is only by putting forth all his energy that a man can free himself from the demands of the world surrounding him, and that he may be living in constant danger of being overwhelmed by the world and submitting to prevailing conditions, but it is still *he* who loses himself and submits, for he has the power to resist, actively or passively. Motivated either by fear or pride, or even by a genuine desire for progress, men may indeed continue along the way technical economic deve-

---

[4] This conception of man is known as the "theory of environment". Marxism is not its only follower and defender, but the most important and most widespread one today. On this theory is based the Marxist materialistic conception of history, according to which history is a continuous stream of compulsion, which man directs, it is true, but only in so far as he succumbs to it and is forced to his decisions by it. Man lives history in the sense that history passes over and through him.

lopment is pointing. They have it in their power to call a halt or at least to direct that development into reasonable, and for society acceptable, channels. The world, if it really wanted to be sensible and peace-loving, simply could not be powerless in the face of atomic energy, mass poverty, nationalism! Conditions can effect much, but man can effect more.

14. To whom do the prerogatives of the person belong?

The prerogatives of the person belong to every man, and that from the first moment of his existence.

THE independence and dignity of the person belong to a man by virtue of his nature, simply for the reason that he is man. They are independent of birth and profession, talent and wealth, race and heredity, health and sickness, independent of whether a man be already born or only as yet conceived in his mother's womb. It suffices that man lives. There are cases in which the individual may, by reason of personal and very serious guilt, forfeit his dignity to the extent that he loses his right to live, and yet he has not thereby become devoid of all rights, in every respect (Q. 60), for he never ceases to be man; even in the most wicked criminal there still flickers the dignity of man.

There is no other way than the one shown here of safeguarding the individual effectively against interference from the community (Q. 17). Only when a man's worth is deducible not from external circumstances or practical considerations, but from himself is it possible to resist the claims of the state with firmness; for it is only from this standpoint that it can be stated irrefutably where the limits of all earthly power are fixed. All other conceptions leave room for evasions, for

51

extending those limits, since they lack the safe criterion for the nature and extent of authority. The community would always hold the trump card with which to "prove" its precedence regarding the individuals subjected to it.

Totalitarian states, no matter what their particular form, or what their immediate aim, have offended and continue to offend atrociously against the general principle of man's dignity and the respect due to him. Their basic error has already been mentioned: they evaluate man falsely and one-sidedly according to his usefulness, according to racial-biological, political, military or economic points of view.

15. Are there certain general duties imposed on every individual?

It is the duty of every man:
1. **To pursue his last end so effectively as to achieve it.**
2. **To perfect himself by doing good (practising virtue).**
3. **To play his part in the ordering of temporal affairs according to the measure of his capabilities and existing necessities.**

PIUS XI (Q. A., 118).

"For according to Christian doctrine man, endowed with a social nature, is placed here on earth in order that, spending his life in society, and under an authority ordained by God, he may cultivate and evolve to the full all his faculties to the praise and glory of his Creator; and that, by fulfilling faithfully the functions of his trade or other calling he may attain both to temporal and eternal happiness."

THIS question is decisive for a man's conception of and attitude to life. The answer is universally binding, regardless of

52

when or where the individual lives, regardless of sex or age, profession or position, race or nationality. The answer applies also to the community, which is *not* competent to stipulate or abolish legally those obligations which flow from man's own nature (Qs. 26–7).

1. Being a person is not only a natural disposition, but also a calling. A man is strictly bound to develop himself by suitable activities. Nature and revelation teach him how he is to behave.

The ultimate end of life can only be God, not any finite good, neither external not internal, not the "honour of the Nation", the well-being and progress of mankind, the classless society of the future the preservation and "purification" of the race. Man strives after God by knowing and loving him and by doing his will, and only in Christ can he do this in the right way (Q. 18). And so, considered under the aspect of his highest destiny, man is that being unique in all visible creation who is capable of knowing and loving God, and to this he is called.

2. To love God means to do his will, or to do good and thereby become good (perfect). For God is the supreme Lord and at the same time the supreme good. Only the good man becomes like unto him. Thus a man conforms with the primary and most essential meaning of his life, not by attaining certain external proficiencies as, for instance, by becoming an efficient craftsman, or a skilled orator or anything else of that nature, but by remaining steadfast in virtue, in every virtue on which the right ordering of life depends.

A virtuous life (the morally good life) is the primary duty of every man, from which no one, neither himself nor others, can free him. For a man must strive after perfection if he is to comply with the command of his nature and of his Creator.

Christ calls upon us with the most impressive words to fulfil this duty, and he means the fulfilment which is attained only by his grace and by imitating him.

The morally good and morally mature person we call a "personality", and mean by that, one who has overcome the vacillations of an uncertain, unstable character, one who is advanced and steadfast in virtue. According to the particular qualities of an individual we speak, for example, of a strong or balanced personality. In many expressions, however, it is not so much (or not at all) the moral nobility, but rather the high position of the individual which is meant when we say of him that he is a highly placed, respected or influential personality.

3. God has appointed man to be lord of his creation, to bring it to completion. Man should subject the world more and more to himself, make it serve him, elevate and enoble it, open up its latent sources of power. Thus he bears, indeed, world responsibility. The responsibility for the external achievement of this task is that of mankind as a whole, or of the communities in charge of the different parts of the world. At the same time, each individual lives in the community of his fellow men, must use things in common with others, and must work to ensure that the community is able to live in a worthy manner. Thus he, too, must co-operate to the best of his ability in fulfilling God's commission to rule over and cultivate the earth. In certain circumstances, in a general emergency, for example, this co-operation can become a duty, and may be imposed by the community as binding on the individual.

PIUS XII (C. B., 1948; C. D., I, 25).

"A convinced Christian cannot shut himself up in a comfortable and selfish 'isolationism' when there are rampant the needs and the

wretchedness of his brothers, when there reach him appeals for help from those of scanty resources, when he knows the aspirations of the working classes towards more normal and just living conditions, when he is conscious of the abuses of an economic ideal which sets gain above social duties, when he is not ignorant of the errors of an intransigent nationalism that denies or tramples on the solidarity of peoples – a solidarity that imposes on each of them manifold duties to the great family of nations."

What our worldly-minded age quite overlooks and refuses to recognize is that there exist in the world hidden, seemingly fruitless and unimportant activities, which are of great value for it, such as, for instance, intellectual work and what is achieved through example, prayer, and sacrifice. No one may shrink from world responsibility, but there are numerous ways of sharing in it. External withdrawal and seclusion do not mean that an individual is indifferent to the world, that he is leaving it to its fate or to the efforts of those who are directly engaged in the "battle of life". The researcher and the scholar, quietly and perhaps without any visible success, endeavouring to serve truth, the hermit and the contemplative who do not "produce" anything tangible, carry and fulfil their share in the general world responsibility. The Christian knows that a life of prayer and sacrifice not only demands a more than ordinary amount of energy and perseverance, but also that it is actually of decisive influence for the world and its development. The important thing is not so much that progress should be achieved in the many fields of culture, but that such progress should bring a blessing to the world and to man and, for that, grace from above won by prayer and sacrifice is necessary.

16. What is the significance of the dignity of the person in man's conduct?

As a person, the individual is both qualified and obliged:
1. To act independently according to his reason and on the free decision of his will.
2. To answer for his actions before God, his conscience, and human society.

1. THE previous question concerned more the matter, the present question more the form or manner, of human action. A man must so act as befits his nature and consequently his capacity. As a spiritual being he possesses two mental faculties which determine his manner of acting: intellect, with which to know the truth; will, with which to strive after good. Accordingly he must act intelligently and freely, in other words, independently, from personal conviction, and on his own free decision.

a. His intellect (reason) enables a man to acquire the necessary knowledge about the meaning of life and the ways that lead to, or away from, the true end of life. The intellect, the faculty of mental insight and judgement, is able to recognize and determine whether an action is good or evil, just or unjust, whether it can be upheld or not. God has so made man that the highest principles of moral living are self-evident to him and he can, by right reasoning, deduce further principles. In so far as the human reason "spontaneously" knows these highest principles, that is, without long reflection and danger of erring, it (the reason) is called the "original conscience", because this original insight precedes, and, indeed, must precede, all individual decisions of conscience. In thus fashioning the human mind, God's providence has bestowed on man one of the greatest benefits. True, man is not spared the trouble of frequent and, often enough, very fatiguing reflection; true, original conscience does not safeguard him against even considerable errors in recognizing further obligations, whereby these errors are certainly occasioned in the first place by perversity and stubbornness of the will (Q. 19). But a sure foundation is laid, and the individual possesses solid and handy criteria for examining and revising subsequent decisions.

b. His will enables a man to do or refrain from doing, to strive after, or reject, the good put before it by the intellect. God implanted in the human will an insatiable appetite for the good, which is so strong and so extensive that the will, whenever it acts, must needs act from desire for the good, even when it desires what is only apparently good or in fact even is the opposite of good. The good moves and attracts the will, because by his very nature man seeks to become good and happy (Q. 69). At the same time the will is not intrinsically necessitated towards any individual good (even the highest and most worthy of being striven for). Because the will is sovereign, it has the power to choose, to decide to act or refrain from acting, among two or more goods to choose one rather than another. But this freedom does not imply absolute lack of restraint, since the will is bound to the good and may never strive after or do what is not good.

2. Man's responsibility is founded on the freedom of his will and on his reason, which guides the will, and is therefore called the "root" of freedom. To be responsible for one's conduct means to answer personally for one's conduct, to be able, and to be obliged to account oneself for what one does. A man is immediately responsible to his own conscience, which provides the nearest norm for his conduct, and to the clear dictates of which he must bow (Q. 42); then to the community in so

far as it may lie in the competence of the latter to command and requite (Q. 37); ultimately and always to God, to whose authority all man's conduct, both exterior and interior, is subject.

Those who oppose the freedom of the will and genuine responsibility are uncommonly numerous. At the present time, for instance, there are those who believe in the materialist interpretation of history. A certain type of liberalism (or individualism) has a false, because exaggerated, notion of human freedom. It declares man to be absolutely unrestricted in his freedom, at any rate not subject to any interior restriction binding in conscience (Q. 20).

17. How is the independence of man to be understood?

It is not sufficient for a man to be independent as to the manner of carrying out the tasks set him; he must be in a position to take responsibility for them in their substance, regardless of whoever imposes them.

PIUS XII (C. B., 1942; C. T. S., 13).

". . . he must favour, all by legitimate means and in every sphere of life, social forms which render possible and guarantee full personal responsibility in regard to things both temporal and spiritual."

THIS answer, following logically as it does, has far reaching implications, since belief in the independence of the person can be, and in a great number of instances has been, decisive for man's fate. In itself, the obligation to act independently, with personal responsibility, knows no limit; whenever a man's conscience clearly and unhesitatingly judges that something ought not to happen, he must refrain from doing it, even though it means opposing the community's power of compulsion (Q. 42). A man cannot be said to act in accordance with this individuality by being independent merely in the execution of tasks imposed upon him, and not concerning himself about whether such tasks are in their substance right and permissible (technical independence). No one can reassure himself with the thought that he is doing something merely because it is ordered or desired or expected of him, without considering what is at stake and whether it conflicts with the moral law ("Orders are orders!"). Rather the individual must be able to accept in conscience the task itself, the substance of the order, the matter demanded of him. He must at least be convinced that the order does not conflict with the sure and clear judgement of his conscience (genuine independence).

Wherefore, in respect of social living, the independence of the individual has a twofold validity, in that,

a. the individual remains inwardly free in the discharge of his social obligations;

b. the individual refuses whenever he cannot in conscience take responsibility for what is demanded of him.

Thus it is an error fraught with grave consequences to limit the personal responsibility of the individual to the major decisions of his life, and to hold that where the individual is under command, it is his duty merely to carry out "according to orders" whatever he is commanded to do. Such a conception degrades man to a mere tool, a machine operating mechanically. It demands of him to deny his individuality as a person, to trample on his nobility as a human being; it splits a man, as it were, into two halves, of which the one, given over to the community, sinks to the level of the subhuman.

Every attempt to justify totalitarian power is brought to nought by human freedom rightly understood, which is quite certain to be disregarded and crushed by such systems. At the same time, their intrinsic falseness and injustice are exposed by the shameless denial and destruction of the dignity of the human person, by blotting out the dividing line between good and evil (moral nihilism), by idolizing authority (demon of power), by the base attitude of pure convenience, and policies with slavery, robbery and extermination as their obligations.

From the conflict between false (technical) and genuine independence there arise for the individual at times the most frightful mental strain and conflict of conscience, which have ended not infrequently in despair and suicide.

18. *What does faith teach concerning man?*

Faith teaches that in the supernatural order the human person:
1. Is recognized in his natural dignity and autonomy.
2. Is raised to a new and greater dignity by grace.
3. Is placed under allegiance to Christ.
4. Is bound to pursue supernatural ends, to cultivate and comply with supernatural institutions, and to adopt supernatural standards.

LEO XIII (I. D., C. M. W., 38).
"This honourable liberty, alone worthy of human beings, the Church approves most highly and has never slackened her endeavour to preserve it, strong and unchanged, among nations."

LEO XIII (L. P., C. M. W., 4).
"As the Catholic Church declares in the strongest terms the simplicity, spirituality, and immortality of the soul, so with unequalled constancy and publicity she ever also asserts its freedom. These

truths she has always taught, and has sustained them as a dogma of faith, and whensoever heretics or innovators have attacked the liberty of man, the Church has defended it and protected this noble possession from destruction."

PIUS XI (D. I. M., 123).

"Far from renouncing the activities of this life, far from suppressing his natural powers, the true Christian nurtures and perfects these, uniting them with his supernatural life in such a way that the life of nature is enhanced and provided with more effectual aids, not only for the attainment of spiritual and eternal goods but also for needs of the natural order."

PIUS XII (Address to the Cardinals, 1946; U. A. vol. I, p. 190).

"The Church living in the heart of man and man living in the bosom of the Church – here, Venerable Brethren, is the most deeply rooted and efficacious union that can be conceived. Through this union the Church elevates man to the perfection of his being and of his vitality. In order to give to human society men formed thus, men established in their inviolable integrity as images of God, men proud of their personal dignity and of their sound freedom, men justly jealous of their equality with their fellows in all that touches the most essential basis of men's dignity, men firmly attached to their land and traditions – men in a word, characterized by this four-fold element; this is what gives to human society its solid foundation and obtains for it security, equilibrium, equality, normal development in space and time."

A well known principle of St. Thomas is that "grace does not destroy nature, but presupposes and perfects it". In the Christian order of life all natural values are fully recognized (science, art, economics; family, home, fatherland; work and profession; cheerfulness and good fellowship; rank, Nation, State). The supernatural order attaches the greatest importance to the cultivation of the natural virtues and naturally good motives (love of parents, relatives, and friends; industriousness, happiness in one's profession, thrift and generosity, politeness, and gratitude).

1. Man's natural dispositions, merits, and tasks are not, as is so often quite falsely maintained, overlooked and viewed with suspicion, but respected and appreciated. The Christian is a man in the full and true sense of the word, and precisely when he makes earnest of being a Christian exclusively. Every human or naturalistic conception is contrary to the Christian idea of man (Q. 9, No. 1, d), because it neglects the "new man" made holy in Christ and called to the vision of God in the next life. Naturalism has also penetrated into Christian circles. Liberal theology may refer to God while rejecting any genuine allegiance to the God of revelation. Modernism has a predilection for what is "new", undermines the God-given truths and facts of faith, substituting personal feeling for these.

2. Man, justified and raised to the supernatural order in Christ, has not lost his worth but has gained immeasurably. Grace, that is, the adoption of the children of God, membership in Christ, makes him richer and increases his worth more than any natural abilities and achievements could possibly do, it endows him with a new divine presence ("we will come to him, and make our abode with him"; John 14:23). Man raised to the supernatural order is, therefore, obliged all the more to respect and be true to himself, and the community is bound to further him and his development.

3. The charge is unjustified that Christian, and above all Catholic, morality destroys the independence of the individual. The Church is alone in having defended effectively human

62

freedom against all attacks. She demands of everyone absolute fidelity to his conscience, but she is not so foolish as to let pass every kind of extravagance as genuine fidelity to conscience, or as something accountable for before God. Christ confronts man with the decision for or against his own person, his Kingdom, his grace, his command that every man must answer for his conduct personally to him. He wants followers strong in faith, ever ready to be his witness, straightforward and courageous, not the unreliable type, the weakling who, by sheltering behind the responsibility of others, seeks to escape his own.

4. Corresponding to the "new man" raised to the supernatural order in Christ, there is a new and higher ideal proclaimed by Christ which consists in imitating him, and can be attained only by the supernatural power of grace. Forming the centre of this new life are what we call the theological virtues of faith, hope, and charity (love of God and our neighbour), to which are added the infused (that is, not naturally acquired) moral virtues (Q. 89, No. 1). The gifts of the Holy Ghost, too, are bestowed on man in the supernatural state as spiritual powers, the effectiveness and dominating influence of which increase with the growth in holiness of the individual. But the individual himself always continues to act and to be responsible for his actions. Even where the Holy Spirit of God enlightens and moves him beyond the normal, his own action and responsibility are in no way superseded, but on the contrary raised to their highest potentiality.

In this connection it might be appropriate to refer to the "superman". The superman, as Nietzsche (1844–1900) and his followers saw him is really God's opponent, indeed his usurper, who arrogates to himself the right to change all values and looks on it as in the natural order of things that all other men should be subject to his will and do his bidding. Apart from Christ, the God-Man, who infinitely excels all other men in knowledge and holiness, the Church speaks of superhuman action where an individual, under the impulse of the Holy Spirit, attains to a manner of knowing and willing of which neither his own ability nor even the supernatural virtues of themselves render him capable. The superhuman here implies neither opposition to God, nor the elimination of the fundamental disparity between the creature and God; it implies rather the highest form of union with God and obedience to him; wherefore it presupposes, and at the same time implies man's living to the full that friendship with God in which supernatural charity consists.

5. The supernatural order of life and the economy of salvation is built upon the natural order, and in such wise that it is the supernatural which sets forth and imposes the authoritative aims and norms. There is only one single comprehensive order having absolute validity, namely, the natural-supernatural. Hence it is man's duty to pursue and promote natural values so that they do not endanger the supernatural, eternal element in man. The proper Christian virtues and duties must not be deposed from their predominant position. The constitution and activity of natural communities, as well as service in these communities, must be such as to preserve for communities of the supernatural order (especially for the Church) the possiblity of free development.

6. Within the supernatural order also, man lives as a social being. This is made quite clear in Scripture where the Church is spoken of as "the Kingdom of God", "God's people", "the community of the redeemed", "the mystical body of Christ". We refer to the Lord's vicarious suffering for *all* men, to the

sacraments which he instituted to unite in fellowship all those who partake of them. We speak of the "communion of saints" and pray with and, for one another, to our Father, just as our Lord and his disciples prayed together in common, "where two or more are gathered together in my name there am I in the midst of them", that is, drawing them together, unifying them. We are commanded to show charity towards our neighbour and to practise the other social virtues of justice, kindness, gentleness, and so on. How highly the individual is rated for his own personal worth in the Kingdom of God is brought out very strikingly in the parable of the Good Shepherd and in the parable of the Talents. Everyone redeemed is a child of God and heir to heaven.

19. What are the effects of Original Sin on man and his conduct?

Original Sin did not destroy man's nature but weakened his natural powers. Man is therefore unable without the help of grace to attain to a natural and right order of life and society.

THE significance of this very Christian doctrine, which all those reject who are opposed to the idea of revelation, is frequently lost sight of. Man continued to be man even after the fall. He did not, with the loss of sanctifying grace, and all other supernatural prerogatives, forfeit the ability to think and to will. He did not fall so far into disorder as to have the power to know truth by natural means completely barred to him, or to be unable to strive after and do what is naturally good.[5]

Nevertheless man has been weakened; his powers have been

---

[5] Cf. the encyclical of Pius XII, *Humani generis* of 12 August 1950.

blunted and fettered. This applies especially in his moral life, since his vision of the good has been darkened and his resolve to do good rendered extremely difficult by his weakened will and the violence of his passions. As a result of his falling away from God, the only supernatural end of life, the will is no longer directed towards its ultimate end. "Nature has fallen back upon itself" says Saint Thomas. Until he is again linked to his true and final end, by God's grace, man tends to see himself as the ultimate end of life. In this way the true order of things is reversed and can only be restored by grace. Grace also has the task and the effect of healing fallen and corrupt nature and restoring man to the state in which he can bring to realization what is naturally good. Grace gives man power to overcome inordinate desires and to restore the supremacy of the spirit within him.

Only the doctrine of Original Sin can explain why man so often goes astray — not least in the social field, where, because of the many factors involved, the possibility of error is very great — and why all purely human endeavours to reach a true and just social order are doomed. The heavy burden of selfishness and egotism resulting from Original Sin has acute effects on society. For it is in this field, above all, that selfishness must be overcome, and where it matters to realize and to seek what is due to our neighbour and to the community.

The world, then, must become Christian if it is ever to be in a position, and to have the will, really to renew itself socially (Q. 8). Hence from the outset all Christian social reform must aim at the conversion of the world, leading men back to a belief in Christ and to a Christian life. History supplies the proof of experience. Where men have turned away from Christ, his teaching, and his grace, society has fallen into disorder, and selfishness, in economic, national, political forms, has triumphed. Recent popes have never tired in their efforts to persuade mankind that it must again recognize Christ and his law if it really wants order and peace.

LEO XIII (R. N., 22).

"And if Society is to be healed now, in no other way can it be healed save by a return to Christian life and Christian institutions. When society disintegrates, the wholesome advice to give to those who would restore it, is to recall it to the principles from which it sprang; for the purpose and perfection of an association is to aim at and to attain that for which it is formed; and its efforts should be put in motion and inspired by the end and object which originally gave it being. Hence to fall away from its primal constitution implies disease; to go back to it, recovery."

PIUS XI (Q. A., 127).

"However, if we examine matters more diligently and more thoroughly we shall perceive clearly that this longed-for social reconstruction must be preceded by a renewal of the Christian spirit from which so many people engaged in industry have at times lamentably departed. Otherwise, all our endeavours will be futile, and our house will be built, not upon a rock, but upon shifting sand."

PIUS XII (Address of 20 November 1946; U. A. vol. I, p. 186–7).
"She (the Church) seeks out, above all, man as such. Her study is to form man, to model and perfect in him the Divine Image. Her work is done in the depth of each man's heart, but has its effects, extending throughout his life, in all his activities. Through men thus formed the Church prepares for human society a basis on which it can rest securely. Modern imperialism, on the contrary, goes in just the opposite direction."

PIUS XII (C. B., 1949; C. D., II, 32).

"To those who give support to one or other of those social systems, both of them foreign and opposed to the divine plan, may this Our

persuasive invitation to return to natural and Christian principles find a favourable answer. For on these principles is based effective justice, together with respect for true freedom. May the recognition of the fact that all men are equal in the inviolability of personal rights, put an end to the futile struggle which makes brother hate brother!"

Lesson Two

ORIGIN AND NATURE OF HUMAN SOCIETY

20. *Must men live in society?*

By their nature men are destined, fitted, and obliged to live in society.

LEO XIII (L. P., 21).

"God it is who has made man for society, and has placed him in the company of others like himself, so that what was wanting to his nature, and beyond his attainment if left to his own resources, he might obtain by association with others."

LEO XIII (D. I., 3).

"It is not difficult to determine what would be the form and character of the State were it governed according to the principles of Christian philosophy. Man's natural instinct moves him to live in civil society, for he cannot, if dwelling apart, provide himself with the necessary requirements of life, nor procure the means of developing his mental faculties. Hence, it is divinely ordained that he should lead his life – be it family, or civil – with his fellow men, amongst whom alone his several wants can be adequately supplied."

68

PIUS XI (Q. A., 118).

"For according to Christian doctrine man, endowed with a social nature, is placed here on earth in order that, spending his life in society, and under an authority ordained by God, he may cultivate and evolve to the full all his faculties to the praise and glory of his Creator; and that, by fulfilling faithfully the functions of his trade or other calling, he may attain both to temporal and eternal happiness."

MAN is "a social animal by nature"; by reason of the natural constitution of his being he tends towards, and is obliged to live in society. But natural man is not an enemy of his fellow men as Hobbes and Rousseau thought, nor a "predatory animal" as Oswald Spengler held. He is neither absolute master of himself (autonomous–sufficient unto himself, a law unto himself), nor a recluse, but is sent into society, standing right in it (Q. 9, No. 1, b; Q. 16). The theory of social contract, according to which men, solely by mutual agreement, forego part of their innate sovereignty and liberty in exchange for the necessary security otherwise not assured them, is against human nature and, therefore, against truth. It is significant that in Soviet Russia and in the satellite countries, where the workers are supposed to enjoy freedom and equality, a new ruling class has risen which dominates and oppresses the people. That should be a warning to those who regard Bolshevism as fundamentally nothing more than taking man seriously as a social being! An unprejudiced consideration of man suggests that he is socially inclined and that he has a social nature. This is not a subsidiary quality, an incidental duty in respect of the community, but an indication that living in society is proper to man in virtue of his very nature, that because, and in so far as he is man, only in society can he fulfil his vocation to live as a man. The following facts support this view:

69

1. In every individual the one and the (specifically) same human nature is realized. Each is one of the many who all conform in that they are men and share in a common human nature. On the basis of this common nature men belong together. They form the great family of mankind, of the human race.

2. Man's dependence on the community during the whole course of his life is materially very evident. He is born into it and materially dependent on it as well as intellectually and morally. Contrast the inventive and constructive power of reason with nature's provision for creatures that lack reason. Only in his fellow men does he encounter that intimate personal response which understands him, which can receive and return his love (marriage, friendship). This dependence necessarily arises from the fact that man is a being composed of body and soul. As such he needs society as his proper sphere of life. Any real human activity (knowing, willing, acting) presupposes the social environment (education and training as social phenomena). Culture and technology are socially conditioned.

3. Man is only able to perfect himself in the manner proper to him, when he accepts society and lives socially. There are the so-called social virtues which can be practised only within society, but which are indispensable for moral life: truthfulness, obedience, fidelity, justice, charity. Without society man cannot adequately fulfil his highest duty, which is to know and love God. Only society, at least in view of the actual human situation, will help him towards a sufficiently clear and sound knowledge of God.

4. God has so endowed human nature that man is fitted for social living: the desire for the company of his fellow men; the spirit of sacrifice; language as the means of mutual understand-

ing, of exchanging ideas and sentiments; the differences and mutual attraction of the sexes. Hence man is obliged to live as a social animal. To be unsocial or asocial is not a harmless thing, but is detrimental to man. Everyday life gives expression in countless ways to the fact that men regard themselves as originally and obviously socially inclined. The individual who is always ready to help is respected spontaneously; the hardhearted, on the other hand, is despised. Those who are sorely tried will be comforted and relieved by kind words and deeds from others in sympathy with them. Cain's question, "Am I my brother's keeper?" is regarded as singularly callous by all of us.

The account of Creation in the Sacred Scriptures shows very clearly that God made men for one another: "And the Lord God said: It is not good for man to be alone; let us make him a help like unto himself" (Gen. 2:18).

5. Man is a single essence (Q. 12); that is, body and spiritual soul are so united as to form one human nature, the one and complete man. Hence it is false to limit social living to the realm of the body and the senses, and to exclude the spiritual. Spiritual beings, or persons, it is true, are first and foremost selfregarding (Q. 12, No. 5), and man is no exception to this order. But we must not forget that the spiritual soul of man is what is called his "essential form". It was designed to be united to the body, to form and fashion the corporeal, material element so that from spiritual soul and body is constituted man (and not something else, a plant or an animal). Human nature results neither from the body alone nor from the spiritual soul alone, but rather from the union of both in a single essence, and this complete nature is, for the reasons given, a social nature, a nature which is, as such, in its entirety, at the same time both individual and social. Also,

and, indeed, precisely the spiritual side of man inclines him towards his fellows, towards society, and that by nature, of necessity, in his capacity and relative character as a spirit (cf.Q.71). To attribute to the human spirit an immanence above and beyond society is to tear man as he really is asunder. It is to advocate a very dangerous form of spiritual pride under the pretext and semblance of preserving man's spirit from getting entangled in the world and its affairs; it is to debase social living to something that is in reality beneath man.

21. What do we mean, generally speaking, by community (society)?

Community (Society) is the unity of order of human persons who are united in (origin and/or) purpose and act in common.[6]

PIUS XI (Q. A., 84).

"Order, as St. Thomas so well defines it, is unity arising from the proper arrangement of a number of objects; hence, true and genuine social order demands that the various members of society be joined together by some firm bond."

PIUS XII (C. B., 1942; C. T. S., 3).

"All social life deserving of the name has its origin in the desire for peace and aims at attaining it; it aims at that orderly and tranquil common life in which St. Thomas, echoing the well-known definition of St. Augustine, sees the essence of peace. Two essential elements, therefore, are necessary for social life: an orderly *common life, and a common life which is* tranquil."

[6] "Community" is to be understood for the moment in its broadest sense, without any distinction between community and society (Q. 28). It is not easy to define community, since social being, on account of its diversity and ever-changing, "fluid" character, is extremely difficult to comprehend.

1. COMMUNITY (SOCIETY) is not a mere product of the imagination, something outside and beyond reality, as some social scientists would have it. According to this view men do not really belong together, or depend on one another, but do so only by supposition. That such a view is false, is shown if we were to ask a father if his family exists solely in his imagination, if he only thinks that he is living in a family. He may give you a surprised look and probably a very drastic answer. He is perfectly convinced that his family actually exists, and exists as a community. Community belongs, then, to the order of real being. There is such a thing as community. Real relations exist between men. Community is more than a total, more than a mere conceptual unity of men.[7]

2. Men who form a community have undoubtedly some mutual interest. They have to do with one another. Either they are related by common origin (closer or more distant ties of blood: family, kin, clan, race), or they are striving by their united efforts for the attainment of a common goal, thus being united in purpose. This purpose can be very varied. It is always super-

---

[7] It is not the task of a handbook to engage in learned controversies and theories. Nevertheless it must be pointed out that the community has, in the language of metaphysics, not substantial but only accidental being. It does not exist after the manner of a thing, as a complete being, but as a dependent relation which unites two or more persons with one another. Social being belongs, then, to the category of real relations which in turn is classed as dependent (accidental) being. We cannot subscribe to the view that social being is *sui generis,* i.e., neither substantial nor accidental being, but something lying in between. At the same time we must remember that metaphysics when it defines community as a unity of relation or order intends merely to place it metaphysically and in no wise to explain the manner and profundity of functions of community in every direction. Finally, community must be seen and grasped in the concrete, in its members, as men related to and bound up with one another, it must be seen not so much as order and unity, but rather as men living and acting in order and unity.

personal in the sense that it does not affect and concern the one or the other as such, but rather the many as such (Q. 24). The simplest example is that of any working group formed by a number of people deciding to solve a single problem by common effort. Such a group lives in the carrying out of its concerted activity, that is when all are co-operating in the spirit and in the interest of the common task (instruction, discussion, management, sessions etc.). Whoever wishes to join it must subscribe to its aims and co-operate in realizing them.

3. When our answer speaks of "origin" and "purpose", this must not be taken to mean that where men live together in community by reason of origin there is no common purpose present. Every community has its proper purpose which it must pursue and realize (Qs. 24 and 28). But communities founded immediately on a relationship of origin are much less numerous than those which do not presuppose, or which preclude such a relationship (marriage, friendship, most study groups and cultural societies, sports and social clubs, not to mention the political society with all its ramifications). In fact, apart from the family taken in its narrower sense (parents and children), quite often only very loose connections are maintained between relatives, and such natural ties do not lead to a genuine community. We might add that very often indeed external circumstances and mere chance lead to the forming of communities or social relations. The necessities, tasks, and eventualities of life, conditioned for example by technical and economic developments, by misfortune, sickness, and danger, by opportunities of work and education, force or urge men to live close together in a neighbourhood, parish, village or town; to change their residence and place of work (moving house, moving to another district or province, flight

74

and banishment). They are forced to seek other surroundings for reasons of health, education, training (hospitals, schools, universities). In this way men are constantly meeting different people (and conditions), or they meet those already known in a new way. All this results in the growth of new communities and in the consolidation or disintegration of existing communities.

4. Thus, whenever men form a community they stand in relation to, and enter into relation with, one another. They form a unity of relationship, of order. Parents and children, brother and sister, master and apprentice are in relation to one another. The "form" of the community is that which makes a social unity out of a mere plurality of persons. Form in the philosophic sense designates that which gives a thing its proper nature. It is the intrinsic reason of the thing's very definition, not an extrinsic cause. The form of a man, for instance, is his spiritual soul, and it is through it that man becomes man.

5. "Unity of order" may be contrasted on the one hand to mere plurality and to mere conceptual unity, and on the other to the unity of the person. Unity of the person is something quite different from unity among persons. This is an important distinction which will have to be further explained.

22. How does the order of community differ from any other order?

The order of community is the work of man and is of a moral nature ; it does not exclude the independent being and acting of the person, but rather includes it.

PIUS XII (C. B., 1942; C. T. S., 3).
"Order, the basis of social life among men – among intelligent and responsible beings, that is, who pursue an end appropriate to their nature – is not a mere extrinsic connection between parts numerically

75

distinct; it tends rather towards an ever more perfect achievement of internal unity, a unity, however, which does not exclude differences grounded in reality and sanctioned by the will of the Creator and by supernatural laws."

1. EVERY human community presupposes common being, that is, its members have human nature in common. Now there are communities, such as the family, which rest immediately on "dependence in being". But these communities also owe their origin to human action (the generation of new life by the parents); they can be preserved only by human action and aim at human action. It is clearer still in the case of other communities that they only come into existence where men are drawn together by common action. Every community is rooted, exists, and is completed in human action. The reason is obvious. All human development and perfection consists in action and is based on action. St. Thomas says that everything exists for its own perfection and consequently for its own proper action. Men are drawn together to overcome their insufficiency, or because they want to be together.

The definition of community as unity of action does not deny or weaken in any way the relation of being between men; but it suggests that the relation of being between men has its source in human action and is ordered to it. Nor does unity of action prove that it is a question of mere conceptual unity. It merely stresses that the origin and meaning of community are not to be understood immediately (although of course mediately) in terms of being, but of action. Community is often described, therefore, as "dynamic", or functional unity. Aristotle and Thomas Aquinas, as well as many others up to the present day, describe man's practical reason as the immediate creator of the community. The practical reason is the reason in so far as it is related to action, to the thing done or made, and in so far as it is moved by the will to act or produce. On the other hand the task and purpose of the pure (speculative) reason is knowing as such, not applying what it knows to doing something.

2. Man creates many kinds of unity and order. He puts in order his thoughts, his house, his finances. The craftsman fits together and orders a variety of things, mostly prepared materials, to form one thing, a cupboard, a garment, a vehicle. The result is always a man-produced unity of order, but of a mechanical and artificial nature. In the case of the community, however, it is a question of order among men of whom each person is endowed with free will and subject to the moral law. Men cannot be fitted together like bits of timber or metal. The ordering of them must be in accordance with the dignity of their nature. Ordered unity among men is, therefore, of a moral nature; to be aimed at, achieved and worked out only in accordance with the laws of morality, and through personal responsibility. Two features characterize this moral unity of order:

a. Persons united in community do not lose, but preserve in their unity the independence proper to their nature. In this lies the peculiar character of this unity of order, that each one in it remains, and continues to live, his own spiritual (personal) self.

b. The activities (functions) of the individual remain always distinct while they are actually being carried out, and often in their relation to one and the same end, which specifies a plurality of functions without, however, allowing the individual ones to be absorbed in one all-embracing function. Hence there is no such thing as a social body, and no such thing as social soul in the sense of compact entities.

EXAMPLE. In a workshop the master craftsman, the journeyman, and the apprentices form a single community of labour, but each does his own work. The master gives his instructions to the journeymen and apprentices. He lends them a hand in order that they may learn, and until such time as they are able to work independently. But no one of them can actually do the work of the other. True, the one can take over the work of the other, but then it becomes his work and is no longer the work of the other. Even where several work in immediate co-operation (in building a wall, making a suit of clothes), each has his own function to fulfil. In the case of very simple jobs such as carrying a load or pulling a car out of the mud the functions are similar (each one carries, pulls or pushes); something like a homogeneous cause is produced. And yet each is just as active as the other. Even here there is, strictly speaking, no collective action (see the following Question).

23. Is there such a thing as collective action?

The community as such is incapable of acting. However, we speak of the action of the community in so far as its members act in the name, or in the interest, of the community.

PIUS XI (D. R., 40).

"For it is only individual human beings, not any association of them, that are endowed with reason and moral freedom."

EXAMPLE. At the command: "Company – halt!", all halt. Each individual, and, therefore, the company as a whole, halts. When a team is playing, each individual plays, but according to a certain order, each in his place, all in contact with one another, and all with the same purpose in mind. The community has various forms of operating. In a parliamentary or congressional election all the voters co-operate (positively or negatively). Parliament or Congress debates and passes laws which bind the whole people. Soldiers go off to war, having been called up and sent to the front by the military commanders. Teacher and pupils read and do sums together. There is not a collective action in the sense that the action

78

of the individual is absorbed into one single, total action, but rather in the sense that the individuals stimulate or direct one another, plan and vote together, direct their actions with a single purpose towards some particular goal. They act in common with, and for one another. In this individual action, directed towards the common goal and towards one another, consists the action of the community, and not in a superpersonal action posited by the body of the community as such.

It follows that we have to be extremely cautious in speaking of collective responsibility and collective guilt. Collective responsibility in the sense that mere membership of a community makes one co-responsible for everything that happens, would presuppose that the collective as such can know and will, which is an impossible supposition. All deeds and misdeeds of the community are the responsibility of the individual only in so far as he has had a personal part in them, be it by positive co-operation, by neglecting to oppose them as far as he personally might have been able to do so, or by approval and agreement, which is also a kind of co-operation. In order to fix the measure of responsibility and guilt, other valid principles concerning the degree and extent of freedom must also be taken into account (vincible and invincible ignorance; fear due to threat and intimidation; the evil consequences bound to follow, such as the increase of terror; the attitude of others, especially of more mature and conscientious men). But the question of collective guilt is not to be confounded with the duty of the members of the community to acknowledge the wrong that has come from out of the community, and has been perpetrated by members of the community and in its name. It is not to be confounded with the burden of restitution which must be borne by all; with the honest will and energetic tackling of a necessary re-education; with getting rid of all influences endangering order and peace.

24. What do we understand by the common good?

By the common good we understand both the end and the order of the community.

PIUS XI (D. I. M., 49).

"This end, the temporal welfare of the community, consists in the peace and security which families and individual citizens need for the exercise of their rights, and it consists also in the maximum of prosperity, spiritual and material, which can be attained in this life through the combined and co-ordinated efforts of all."

1. EVERY community has its end, an intrinsic or extrinsic purpose proper to it. It is designed for something which it intends or should intend to attain. Likewise every community has its own order; it is constituted, arranged, built up in a particular manner.

EXAMPLE. The purpose of a working team is to accomplish a certain task; its order is the proper assignment of functions. The purpose of the State is to seek the total human good, that is, the totality of natural values for the whole community; its order lies in its specific political form, its social structure, the proper distribution of offices.

2. The end is not for the sake of the order, but the order for the sake of the end. The principle that the end is the first of the causes holds good also for the community. The end specifies the type, extent, necessity and employment of the means. The community must be ordered in accordance with its end; it must distribute and exercise office reasonably, and choose a particular form of living and working together.

There are certain communities (such as the family, the Church), the order of which nature or God himself has prescribed. These communities are not competent, therefore, to determine their order for themselves. They are obliged to order themselves as God and nature have ordained.

25. What ought the end of a community to be?

The end of every community ought to be :
1. Morally justifiable.
2. A common good.
3. Properly related to all other values.

THE answer applies to each community taken singly, and to all communities taken collectively, that is, as they are related to one another.

1. It is unfortunately true that men come together and even form associations for unworthy purposes. Such associations do not merit the name of community, for they do not fulfil the first condition demanded of every community, namely that its purpose ought not to dishonour men, but ought to be consistent with man's dignity. Men may not, either individually or in common with others, strive after or indulge in what is morally wrong (criminal association, concubinage, secret societies aimed against Church or State, associations directed against God).

2. Only a good which concerns the members as a whole and not merely this or that individual can be the proper end of a community. Not some private interest, but the common good establishes a community. Hence, there is no genuine community where one or a number of individuals employ the labour of others solely in their own interests. Such structures have the character of mere interest groups, for example, industrial concerns which employ and possibly exploit workers exclusively from profit motives; or modern forced labour camps (Q. 28). It is essential that the common goal is seen and pursued as common. As soon as individuals or groups neglect this, and under the pretext of the common good pursue their own interests (power, gain,

81

indulgence), they harm or even destroy the community (tyranny's crime is misuse of the common good for selfish ends; terrorizing the community; placing the party above the community as a whole).

3. The community, too, is bound by the objective order of values. It must, therefore, avoid false emphasis and one-sidedness in the pursuit of its ends. It must take particular care that no values pertaining to the complete perfection of man are obscured, overlooked or even deliberately suppressed. Particular circumstances (when, for example, the common weal is endangered) may necessitate certain tasks or requirements. But this does not mean that other values can be ignored or that the restrictions and measures which may have been justified at a particular moment can be perpetuated.

26. *How are we to determine what are the natural ends of the community?*

The natural aims of the community are determined by what is called the "total good of human nature".[8]

PIUS XI (M. S., 34).

"To overlook this truth is to lose sight of the fact that the true common good is ultimately defined and discovered from the nature of man with its harmonious co-ordination of personal rights and social obligations, as well as from the purpose of society which is determined by the same human nature."

[8] The supernatural ends of the community are prescribed or indicated by God's redemptive purpose. They are not discussed here. That these ends are good and rightly demand priority over the natural ends of the community, follows from the fact that God has expressly laid down these ends, and has assigned them their proper place in the order of values.

If the conditions set out in Question 25 are observed, then there is no limit either in extent or degree to the development and effectiveness of the community as such. All values which present appropriate objectives for common endeavour or action may constitute proper ends of the community. Men may seek to acquire material goods, promote the sciences, cultivate social life. Purely contemplative activities alone are not immediately suitable for community ends (Q. 37).

1. All these values are summed up in what Thomas Aquinas defines as the "total good of human nature". By that he understands both the final and the immediate ends which are given to, or are attainable by, man by reason of his nature, destiny and potentialities. This total good of human nature is so profound and so immense that neither the individual, who is necessarily limited, nor the whole of mankind could ever exhaust it.

2. St. Thomas again sums up this human total good as "the virtuous life". "The life of virtue is the end of the human community" (De reg. princ. I, 14). By virtue he means first and foremost being confirmed in moral goodness by habitual practice, that is, unwavering fidelity to the dictates of the moral law (truthfulness and justice, temperance, reverence, devotion) and besides, all that is worthy of being striven for by men (all genuine cultural values). It is evident that St. Thomas views the community as intimately and absolutely bound up with man as an individual (Qs. 29–31). The spiritual and moral perfection of man dominates everything, the personal as well as the social aspects and activities of men. It is not for the community to set up, apart from what concerns men personally, another different order which more or less has nothing to do with a man's personal decision and development. That brings us to the next question:

83

27. Can man himself decide the ends of the community?

There are two kinds of social ends : those which are given to man by nature (by God) and those which men can freely choose for themselves; the former have priority over the latter.

MAN is not free to pursue or reject the total good of nature. If he were he could do what he liked, and any perfection in accordance with nature would lose its meaning. Therefore, man must as it were consult his nature in order to find out to what social activities it obliges him, and how and where it would have these activities carried out. That brings us to what are called the natural communities, those which as such are absolutely demanded by nature. They have their origin, then, in nature. Nature has determined the purpose and functions of these communities. Men forming, or belonging to, such communities are not competent to fix or alter their purpose and function. Rather they are obliged to acknowledge their natural ends and norms as valid and binding.

There are not many natural communities in the proper sense: the family and the political community; then, more remotely, the different degrees of relationships, neighbourhood, kin, tribe, people; finally, mankind as a whole, about whose aptitude for a real, that is, unified and integrated community, opinions are very much divided. That does not mean that it is simply left to men to establish all other communities just as they please. It does mean that men ought themselves to judge upon the necessity or suitability of other communities according to the particular circumstances, and then decide which communities answer their needs or legitimate wishes, and how they might best and most suitably be established.

Historical development ought also to be taken into account

in the general development of the community. It is not only the character of certain groups of people which fate has linked together that has found expression in the traditional forms of community; practical necessity has been a more basic factor still in leading to such forms of social life. Thus tradition also plays an important part. We cannot, for example, without further ado pronounce the political structure of one nation or country as ideal and even obligatory, for others, since natural conditions and traditional customs and outlook differ widely among individual nations and countries.

1. Apart from natural communities, there are social structures to be set up which, according to the stage of development reached, are necessary for the attainment of life's purposes to which men are obliged. Thus there must be economic and educational communities to cover material needs and ensure moral education. There is, for example, also a need for the preservation of health and the protection against the ravages of nature.

2. Communities concerned with the promotion of learning and art deserve special consideration and encouragement. They are not, or do not appear so at first sight, as necessary as those previously mentioned. But we must remember that man is to develop the powers within him as much as possible, for he has received the most comprehensive cultural mission. Different fields of knowledge, for example, are required in no small measure if men are to be able at all to live in material security and with moral dignity. Mankind is not to remain at the spiritual, moral, or material level of primitives. Progressive development requires an ever increasing store of knowledge, mechanical and technical skill, discoveries, and inventions. Thus the formation of such communities is an ever increasing

duty. It is for man himself, however, to work out the particular shape and extent of these communities, according to the particular subject and stage of development.

3. Men have a natural right to associate together, be it for social purposes, or for representing and protecting their common interests (freedom of association). And they must not be impeded from doing so as long as they exercise or protect their right with morally permissible means, and do not infringe on the legitimate claims of other, and particularly higher, communities (see Qs. 50–52).

4. Communities freely chosen by men are not entitled to oust the natural communities from their tasks and privileged positions. Rather they must acknowledge them and endeavour to supplement and support their aims, and to make possible their existence and unimpeded development.

5. The number and diversity of such freely chosen communities is vast, since they embrace all spheres of life, and in every sphere there are innumerable possibilities. In most cases the number of people in these communities is limited, since otherwise the community would become unmanageable and incapable of functioning, or because the particular character of the community admits of only a small number of members. Accordingly, bigger communities are sometimes divided up into branch communities. (Trade unions set up regions and branches; a conference may set up committees and commissions; a sports club has several teams; political communities are divided into states, counties, cantons, provinces, etc.). This arrangement follows either natural conditions (difference of professions, position in one's profession, age and sex), or practical necessities (limitation of area or subject in order to ensure greater efficiency).

6. Among voluntary communities, those devoted to sports have become enormously widespread and important. They represent an unconscious defensive reaction of men against the constraint to which their profession and work today subjects them. Not by any means all men find the activity which might have become their vocation in a real sense. To a great extent their work is empty, monotonous, rushed, causing excessive nervous tension. Consequently they seek forms of activity which will compensate for the bitterly felt lack of nobility and of pleasure in their work. Apart from making for physical fitness sport allows relaxation and diversion and can also become the basis and opportunity for genuine social contacts. Thus it can call forth and develop values which are so much neglected today, and which, in spite of our efforts for a work and vocational system in conformity with nature, can as yet be expected only in very small measure.

Pope Pius XII in an address on 20 May 1945 to 10,000 young Italian sportsmen on the purpose and value of physical training and sport, said:

"Sport is an affective antidote against an effeminate and soft life; it awakens a sense of order, promotes self-control and self-mastery. Sport trains us to despise danger without boasting of it, yet also without faintheartedness. You will realize that it goes far beyond ordinary physical resistance, aiming as it does at moral strength and greatness. . . . Sport is a school of decency and courage, of perseverance, resolve and general brotherliness. These are, indeed, natural virtues which provide secure bases for the super-natural virtues; they prepare us to carry the burden of heavy responsibility without weakening . . . . If, thanks to your physical training, you manage to discipline your bodies, in order all the better to submit them to your spirit and moral obligations, if your example contributes towards giving forms to the

87

life of sport which are in greater accordance with human dignity and the divine laws, then your physical training will attain supernatural value."

Voluntary communities (taking "community" in its widest sense) embrace not only social structures with purely material ends, but also and particularly, associations which have an immediately personal character. Thus, for instance, friendship, which after all, implies the closest personal union, is a free community, since a man is free to decide whether he will choose friends and whom he will choose. It is a fact that much modern social effort is aimed at reaching a human, personal relationship – even where material interests are the primary and essential motive for working together – and in this way to procure for man the respect and treatment due to him (fellowship and co-operation between employer and employees, workers councils, etc.).

28. What is the difference between "community" and "association"?

A social structure is termed "community" or "association" according to whether of its nature it affects and binds men in a personal and intimate manner, or for material and practical aims.

ETYMOLOGICALLY and in their original usage there was no difference between these two words either in idea or in meaning. ("Community" derives from the Latin *communis – cum-munis:* serving together; "association" from the Latin *socius:* a companion.) But gradually a difference of sense and meaning has emerged so that nowadays we use these terms to denote two different kinds of social structure.

Community sounds warmer, more personal, more intimate. It implies or indicates neighbourliness. In a community each member is personally concerned with the others. On the other hand an association is rather materialistic, impersonal and distant. Its members have only a temporary and external relationship, or else their association is for some common aim or interest while they themselves as persons keep their distance from one another. We call a family, a village or a people a community, but commercial groups, limited companies, and the like we call associations.

One of the first to stress the distinction between "community" and "association" was the German sociologist Ferdinand Tönnies in his book *Gemeinschaft und Gesellschaft,* first published in 1887. (English translation: *Community and Association* [New York, 1954; London, 1955].)

Tönnies wrote this book to uphold the correct organic idea of community and community order against the prevailing mechanist view of society and social order. According to Tönnies, community is based on "natural will", and association on "rational will". This latter is the individual will seeking material and practical ends. When not bound by natural ties or considerations, the individual will follow his own interests either alone or with others, depending on the position in which he finds himself. Thus associations into which he may enter with others, after weighing up the advantages on a contractual basis, have the character of purely administrative unions. The "natural will" is the exact opposite of the "rational will". It is connected with "natural" inclinations, impulses, and qualities none of which are intended for practical purposes, but which of their very nature, that is, without the intervention of the practical reason, tend towards development and fulfilment. They presume community and lead effectively to it. Notable scholars (and not only Catholic ones), while not denying the stimulation and enlightenment of his ideas, have raised serious objections to Tönnies' system and indeed have flatly rejected the basis of and argument for his

89

distinction between community and society; the most important objection being that he restricted the activity of the human person and of human reason to the rational will.[9]

But these objections do not disturb the fundamental necessity, correctness, and importance of the distinction between community and society. About this the following can be asserted:

As a matter of fact it can be shown that these two radically different social structures have different origins. There are

---

[9] Human personality is not just an expression that is used to describe the ambit of the practical reason. It is rather the very foundation of being which, although it may be distinguished mentally from nature and innate qualities, cannot be separated from them. "The whole man is the person", and as such he possesses his own dignity and importance. Nevertheless, independence of being and action does not imply that man should outgrow his natural origin and ties to the point that they are no longer part of him nor affect his life, development and actions. The nobility and distinctive character of the human person are completely misinterpreted and indeed dissipated if one sees an antithesis in man between personality and nature, for this means cutting human personality off from its roots and hence destroying the whole man. It is equally false to assume that whenever human reason is active or engaged thought and will are confined to the sphere of the practical reason; that would mean denying the innate creative power of our intellectual capacities. It is as an intellectual being, with reason and free will, that man must deal with all his natural ties and conditioning, and with all the bonds that arise from his natural inclinations and desires. This does no harm to the originality, depth, and genuineness of his sensibility and experience; unless it be maintained that any guidance and control by reason and will over natural instincts, inclinations, and emotions implies a violation or a falsification of what is truly human. And this we cannot agree to, since it would mean withdrawing the whole sphere of natural impulses from ethical judgement and surrendering it completely to irrational compulsion. Moreover, it should be pointed out that "to seek an end" is not the same as "to be intended for practical purposes".

If Tönnies conceives the State as a work of the practical reason and so confines it to the rational will, then he is undoubtedly to a great extent correct – if he is speaking of the modern State with its *raison d'État* and its organization. But we must emphatically contradict this as applying to what in previous ages was called "the political community", for this community is a natural thing, natural in origin, purpose, direction, and authority.

90

some social structures which spring from the original inclinations and "ways" of human nature or from personal and intimate contact between individuals. We call these structures *communities*. They direct or cause men to have a true interior fellowship with one another. Then there are those social structures which are directly and properly speaking ordered to material and practical ends. We call these structures *associations*. They bind men together only in so far as they are concerned or interested in their common aims.

It is wrong to condemn social structures simply because they have the character of an association. These structures are necessary and are to be evaluated according to other criteria, according to the nature of their purpose and the means they employ, according to their extent and influence. Though undoubtedly community comes before society both in origin and in order of precedence.

It is wrong to think that reason and will (deliberation and freedom) are involved in the origin and development of association but not in that of community. All social structures of the natural order originate, develop, and endure through human reason and will. But what originally motivates reason and will, the manner in which they are involved and to what degree, differs fundamentally for community and society. A great deal of deliberation and decisiveness are called for before one forms a friendship or embarks on marriage (still more so if it is to endure); but the considerations involved are of a quite different order when it is a question of joining a joint stock company, a building society, or a savings group.

It is also wrong to think that while association exists for an end, community does not. "End" in the true sense of the word means a desirable and obligatory good, that is worth attaining for its own sake. This fits exactly the idea of community, but for association it is better to speak of its aim (practical purpose, interest, concern).

There are scarcely any associations or communities to be found in existence in their pure form – there are only greater and lesser approximations to one or the other. In every community there are values, considerations, activities, about which all the members must be concerned, about which they must come to an agreement and which must be adapted to one another. And no association can flourish if mutual relations remain absolutely impersonal (without shared inclinations, and a minimum amount of trust). It is often difficult to say whether given social structure belongs to a community or to an association.

Lesson Three

MUTUAL RELATIONSHIP
OF INDIVIDUAL AND COMMUNITY

On the basis of the two preceding lessons the question of priority must now be put and answered. Does the person take precedence of the community or the community of the person? Is the community there for the sake of the person or the person for the sake of the community? Few problems in social ethics are attended with similar consequences.

Here the saying of Aristotle and Thomas Aquinas is verified, that the least error in a principle must have dire consequences in the conclusions drawn from it.

LEO XIII (S. C., 2)
"Nature did not form society in order that man should seek in it his last end, but in order that in it and through it he should find suitable aids whereby to attain to his own perfection."

92

PIUS XI (D. R., 40).

"In the Creator's plan society is the natural means which every citizen can and must use for the attainment of his appointed end; and, therefore, society exists for the sake of man, not man for the sake of society. But this principle is not to be understood in the individualistic sense of those, who subordinate the community to the selfish interest of each single citizen. What it means is that their organic union in society enables all citizens, through their mutual collaboration, to attain true earthly prosperity. The grouping of human beings in society also develops and fosters in man those individual and social qualities with which he is naturally endowed, and which, transcending as they do the immediate and selfish interest of the individual, exhibit in human society an aspect of the divine perfection which man living in solitude could never display. In this respect, too, society is a benefit to man, enabling him to recognize this reflection of the divine goodness and to render thanks for it to the Creator by praise and worship."

PIUS XII (C. B., 1942; C. T. S., 5).

"The original and essential purpose of social life is to preserve, develop, and perfect the human persons, by facilitating the due fulfilment and realization of the religious and cultural laws and values which the Creator has assigned to every man and to the human race, both as a whole and in its natural groupings."

29. How is the common good related to private good?

Common good and private good condition and supplement each other, so that the one cannot exist without the other, and much less if the one be directed against the other.

By common good we mean the end or purpose of the community which concerns the individual precisely as a member of the community. On the other hand, private good means the end or good of the individual as such. Private good includes not only those material things which an individual has in his possession and for his use, but also and even more essentially higher goods which are proper to the individual as such; his human existence and his personal abilities, the obligation binding every man to live virtuously; all that which the individual has attained in the way of interior and exterior values.

The hypothetical case of there being only one individual in existence, when there would be private good but no common good is completely irrelevant, since men, one and all, do live in community and are dependent on it.

I

Concerning the relation of common good and private good St. Thomas says briefly and clearly: "The community has necessarily the same goal as the individual"; "The end of the community is to be judged in the same manner as that of the individual"; "The good of the individual is not a final end but is subordinated to the common good"; "Individual well-being cannot exist without the welfare of the community . . . therefore it is in judging correctly in the light of the common good that man must recognize what is good for him."[10]

EXAMPLE. In a football match the whole team as well as each individual player are intent on victory. The community and all its members have the same end in view. Victory can be achieved only when all (each individual player and so the whole team) work together in their proper places. Common good (victory in the match) and private good (active participation in the game) condition each other. When the team plays, each individual plays. (Mere training or just kicking a ball is not playing). In

[10] Taken in order, the texts quoted are from: De reg. princ. I, 14; I–II 90, 3 ad 3; II–II 47, 10 ad 2.

the common good the private good of individuals is made possible and at the same time defined and co-ordinated. The common good gives order and unity to private good.

For greater clarity let us consider the following points:

1. No community exists, and none can be formed, where there is no common goal, where a single good is not striven for by all and for all. A private good, taken in the strict sense and achieved as such, does not bind together, but differentiates and divides. For private good is that which is proper to some particular individual as distinct from all others, his personal outlook and attitude, the development of his talents, the possession of his property. If the individual keeps to his private good and seeks only this, then either he cuts himself off from his fellows or he employs them in his own private interest. In any case he does not help to form a genuine community, nor does he live a genuine social life; possibly he disrupts or misuses it.

2. Natural ends, that is, those determined immediately by nature, apply to all and hence to each individual, since each individual has a human nature. They are consequent on human nature and, therefore, are as general as it. Thus in order to attain his ends (his individual good, for this consists in the attainment of his ends), as these are shown to him by nature, the individual must strive for those ends which are common both to himself and to his fellow men. Only through those values man as such becomes good. And so he can attain his individual good only by acting in accordance with the common good of (human) nature.

We ought to remember also that every end is first willed (desired, intended) and then attained (realized, possessed). The attainment is always concrete and singular. Thus the common good in being attained passes into the private good of the members.

3. This unity of goal (among all and for each one) does not at all mean that individuality and the particular rights of the individual are destroyed. It does not in any way give rise to the dangers of the collective man. Each one must himself act with the common end in view; he must pursue the common goal for himself and in accordance with his individual character; he must take personal responsibility for himself (and so also for others). Each one must become that which nature demands of all: just, temperate, kind, industrious, etc.

4. Now since the common goal concerns one as much as another, the common good is rightly called the "virtual unity" of private good. Virtual unity means, to be one in power and in root. When a number of individuals pursue one goal, then this common goal is the root from which their unity grows and by which this unity is assured. By all being set on the one goal and by achieving it together, they necessarily intend and pursue at the same time their private good, because the common good establishes and ensures the right order of private good.

The common good unites the members of a community in many ways:

a. As a common goal which is binding on all and which is accepted by all as binding, the common good establishes unity among the community members.

b. As a goal achieved by each one, the common good forms and perfects individual personalities without dissolving the unity among them.

c. As a common goal, the common good demands the active co-operation of all who belong to the community; (it requires also mutual respect and help). Therefore we can state that a man can maintain a proper proportion in the pursuit of his private good only when he pursues it in due relation to the common good. In promoting the common good he enhances his private good, works for himself, for his own perfection as a person.

To serve the common good, to make it one's concern, to protect it against dangers are, therefore, actions which are morally good in themselves, since their object is the total good of human nature. True, no actual community could exhaust this total good. But it suffices when men take an active part in the attainment of this good within an actual community.

II

What is true of the goal of the community is true also of its order. Order is never an end in itself (Q. 24, No. 2; Q. 45), but is always for the sake of the end. The order within a community is obviously of a different kind from the order in a man, but the following principles apply also to the latter:

1. The order in a man depends to a great extent on the order in the community, both in the good and in the bad sense. The favourable or unfavourable development of youth depends largely on the conditions prevailing in the family (good or bad housing conditions, adequate or inadequate income), in the school (religious spirit, discipline), in the State (laws, public morality). A working team may give the individual valuable encouragement and help. Well regulated conditions of ownership may guarantee and protect the property of the individual.

Even under unfavourable external social conditions a man can preserve order within himself, since the will (supported by the grace of God) cannot be forced to betray human ideals (the heroism of voluntary or unavoidable poverty; the exemplary bearing of many inmates of labour and prisoner-of-war camps).

But surely the natural order of things is that the individual should develop into a good man, not in spite of social disorder, but supported by social order. One particular, and at times very obstructive, type of disorder is exaggerated, extravagant order (bureaucracy, the endless referring of a matter from one department to another).

2. The order of a community depends to a great extent on whether, and how far, those living in the community are well ordered in their own lives. A capricious individual who is hard to please and lacking in self-control will upset the order in the family; avarice and miserliness lead to social hardship and injustice; weariness and indifference in political life may give rise to grave dangers.

3. Although the order of the community immediately and properly affects the community as a whole, still it concerns – in its totality – the members of the community. True, each member can co-operate only for his own part and in his own position in making the order a reality. But these partial functions should make up the order of the whole, and the individual member as such must have a concern for the order of the whole, because the whole is his; it is the whole of which he is a member.

EXAMPLES. The smooth running of a business is to the advantage of all its members because trouble in any part reduces its total productive capacity. Disorder in a working team (unpunctual work, distraction) retards the progress of the whole. It is particularly true today that conflicts arising in any part disturb the rest of the world, since they endanger world order.

30. Has the community an intrinsic value?

The community has an intrinsic value, but different, of course, from that of the person. Its purpose is not

confined to creating favourable conditions for the development of the individual.

PIUS XI (Q. A., 118).

"*For according to Christian doctrine man, endowed with a social nature, is placed here on earth in order that, spending his life in society, and under an authority ordained by God, he may cultivate and evolve to the full all his faculties to the praise and glory of his Creator; and that, by fulfilling faithfully the functions of his trade or other calling, he may attain both to temporal and eternal happiness. Socialism, on the contrary, entirely ignorant of and unconcerned about this sublime end both of individuals and of society, affirms that human society was instituted merely for the sake of material wellbeing.*"

PIUS XII (C. B., 1942; C. T. S., 4).

"*Social life is a reflection, however imperfect, of the triune God who by the mystery of the Incarnation redeemed and elevated human nature; and therefore, viewed in the light of reason and revelation, the ideal and purpose of society possess an absolute character transcending all the vicissitudes of time.*"

"INTRINSIC value" is in contrast to mere service or utility value, that is value merely as a means and as a tool. That may be said to possess intrinsic value which has a significance beyond that of providing the prerequisites, conditions, and aids that help others to attain their goal, which is of value for its own sake, in itself and of its own nature. At the same time, even inevitably, it may by reason of its nature fulfil the functions of serving others, and of making a worthy existence possible for them. But it has also an importance and a value in itself. It is no mere utility. Being and value condition each other. The height and degree of intrinsic value differ according to the diverse nature of being.

The ordinary man and ordinary speech clearly indicate our answer. We speak of the "good family" as a positive value, meaning that the family as a community is good and worth striving for in itself. It is very significant that people say: "That bunch is no good" though "they may be all right as individuals".

We ought to recognize clearly that "a unity of persons" is something other and something more than a plurality of individuals which is merely thought of as a unity (Q. 21). Community is not something outside and apart from the persons forming it; rather the actual persons living and acting in unity and order are the community. Thus the community, about whose peculiar character we are enquiring, contains the persons in itself, and necessarily so, since one cannot conceive of an order without the ordered persons (the family is the parents plus children in so far as they belong together and form a unity among themselves). Yet this does not mean that the intrinsic value of the community is identical with the added intrinsic value of persons. On the other hand the intrinsic value of the community cannot be separated from that of the persons, as otherwise the community would just dissolve into nothing. The community possesses the distinctive value of a complete order which comprises as its members independent persons with individual value. And so the community is a new, super-individual but relative reality, and consequently forms a new, super-individual category of value. The value of the community is based on, and consists in, the fact that it brings to light and unfolds human values in a unique manner; that the community as such bears witness to the greatness and the creative power of man as God's image and likeness, and so reflects the divine attributes to a degree which men can only attain by willing and acting in common. It is no exaggeration to say that the community is a particular revelation of God's glory.

100

Certainly it is an essential function of the community to serve the perfection of the individual person. But this function gives no justification for depriving the community of any intrinsic value, and for holding that the common good serves as a mere condition for the private good.

31. In what sense is a man a member (part) of the community?

The whole man is part of the whole community, and, therefore, he is incorporated in, and subordinated to it. However, the community is not the sole, the ultimate and highest end of the individual in the sense that he would fulfil the purpose of his existence by serving in the community.

PIUS XI (M. S., 10).

"Whoever transposes Race or People, the State or Constitution, the executive or other fundamental elements of human society (which in the natural order have an essential and honourable place), from the scale of earthly values and makes them the ultimate norm of all things, even of religious values, and deifies them with an idolatrous cult, perverts and falsifies the divinely created and appointed order of things. Such a man is far from true belief in God and from a conception of life in conformity to it."

PIUS XII (P. B., 1941; C. T. S., 10).

". . . it would be succumbing to the erroneous doctrine that society is an end in itself and that man has no other life awaiting him save that which ends here below, to hold that society is the proper place of man on earth."

THE answer is given almost literally by St. Thomas: "Each individual person is related to the whole community as the part to the whole" (II–II 64, 2); "The whole man is related as to an end to the whole community of which he is a part" (II–II 65, 1); "Since the individual is part of the community, so each individual in what he is, and in what he possesses, belongs to the community, just as each part in what it is belongs to the whole" (I–II 65, 1).

1. A whole does not consist just of parts, but of its own parts, that is, of the parts corresponding to it. The planning of a whole does not proceed in such wise that the whole is first planned without reference to the parts proper to it, and then when the plan has been completed things are put in which are to be its parts, because it is made up of these parts. The peculiar character of the parts and of the whole presuppose and require each other. It can happen, of course, that things not originally intended and fashioned as parts of a whole are seen later to be suitable as parts of an artificial whole. But this is an exception which, moreover, proves the rule. For they are accepted as parts precisely because they suit this particular whole.

2. As the community is an ordered unity, so it is an ordered whole. It is the nature of such an ordered whole that things independent in themselves are related to one another in such wise that they form a whole within this relationship. Yet such parts are not so completely absorbed in the whole that they are incapable of existing or acting apart from the whole.

EXAMPLE. The individual grows away from his family and matures into an independent man. He can neither deny nor shake off his origin. Yet even if all the members of his family should be dead, if his family no longer exists, he can still live on for years. And even within the family he is always capable of going his own way, of thinking and acting independently.

3. With these principles in mind we may say that the whole man is a member of the whole community, because he is always related to, and incorporated in the community. But since the community is a whole made up of persons, it includes its members precisely as persons, that is, independent, spiritual and moral beings, and not as mere parts whose entire purpose and right of existence consists in their being the parts from which the community is formed. In short, man is a member of the community while retaining at the same time his own intrinsic worth and his own personal responsibility. No community is an end unto itself, none is the highest end of its members, but both community and men have their end in God. "The end of human life and of the community is God" (St. Thomas, I–II 100, 6).

PIUS XI (Q. A., 136).

"This is the perfect order . . . which places God as the first and supreme end of all created activity, and regards all created goods as mere instruments under God, to be used only in so far as they help towards the attainment of our supreme end."

It follows from this that:

a. When community states the advancement of its own honour, expansion, material and cultural development to be the ultimate and highest duty of its members, it violates their personal dignity in the worst possible way, and by so doing it harms itself, as it is dependent on its members (Q. 27).

b. Man is absolutely subject to God alone, the origin and goal of his life. Man is immediately united with God in knowledge and love (not by means of the community, as if there were no such thing as personal contact between man and God). Any subordination to the community must be in accordance with the dignity and freedom of the human person.

4. Every form of collectivism as well as all types of totalitarianism are completely opposed to this view. In both systems the members are totally, that is in every respect, subordinated to the community as a whole. The individual is nothing more than a part of the community and is completely absorbed by it. Hence the community has unrestricted rights in respect of its members. It alone has full, unrestricted powers to determine the individual's rights, to what extent he may pursue his personal perfection, what he is in duty bound to do, or not to do. We know from the mock trials of totalitarian regimes that this sovereign authority of the collective can be brought to the pitch where persons accused of sabotage and other crimes freely confess themselves guilty against their better knowledge and conscience for the sake of the collective.

A different explanation of the relationship between person and community was given by the Austrian theorist Othmar Spann (1878–1950). According to Spann the development of social life proceeds from above, descending downwards through the continuous and progressive formation of lower units from the higher, down to the individual man. This theory contradicts both the sound principles of philosophy and the experience of human life, although as an opponent of individualism Spann made a valuable contribution to sociology.

The exaggerated organic theory is also untenable. It conceives of the community as a real organism which comes into existence, lives, grows, and works like any living organism in nature (plant or animal). The structure, laws, and movements of the organism which have been established by science are blindly taken over and applied to the community, which is expected to exhibit cells, tissue, nerves, and a blood circulation like any living thing. This theory overlooks altogether the essential differences between the physical and moral orders.

But there is also a correct organic theory of community opposed to the mechanical and atomic social theory of 19th century Liberalism, which is held by many Christian moralists. It defines community as an organism, however in an analogous not in a figurative sense. The principle that the whole lives in its parts, that the parts operate in and through their unity with the whole, holds good also in the case of the community, but only in so far as is consistent with the peculiar nature of community, that is, to such degree and in such form as is appropriate to the unity of purpose and action of persons. In this way the loose application of biological laws to social living is avoided. Thus understood, an organic theory of community gives expression in an intelligible form to the vital and formative force of the community, without giving rise to the danger that the whole might devour its parts.

32. Which, then, should have precedence of the other: the individual or the community?

The relationship between individual and community is one of reciprocity; however, precedence is due to the person in so far as all social questions arise, and must be resolved, in relation to him.

LEO XIII (S. C., 2).

"Nature did not form society in order that man should seek in it his last end, but in order that in it and through it he should find suitable aids whereby to attain to his own perfection."

PIUS XI (D. R., 40).

"But God has also destined man for the civil society which his nature requires. In the Creator's plan society is the natural means which every citizen can and must use for the attainment of his appointed

end; and, therefore, society exists for the sake of man, not man for the sake of society. But this principle is not to be understood in the individualistic sense of the liberals, who subordinate the community to the selfish interests of each single citizen. What it means is that their organic union in society enables all citizens, through their mutual collaboration, to attain true earthly prosperity. The grouping of human beings in society also develops and fosters in man those individual and social qualities with which he is naturally endowed, and which, transcending as they do the immediate and selfish interests of the individual, exhibit in human society an aspect of the divine perfection which man living in solitude could never display. In this respect, too, society is a benefit to man, enabling him to recognize this reflection of the divine goodness and to render thanks for it to the Creator by praise and worship."

PIUS XI (M. S., 34).

"Society is willed by the Creator as a means to the full development of the faculties of the individual, and a man has to make use of society now giving and again taking for his own good and for the good of others. Nay more, those higher and more universal values which cannot be realized by individuals but only by society are intended by the Creator ultimately for the sake of the ultimate end of man, for his natural and supernatural development and perfection. Whoever transgresses this order shakes the pillars of society and imperils its tranquillity, security, and even its existence."

WITH this question we are drawing the conclusion from what has already been said.

1. Social ends can only be determined in relation to the human person. Definitions of the aims of community that have no reference to the human person are immoral and absurd. Totalitarian states which assert that they pursue their own honour and glory for the sake of their members are evading the issue.

2. As the person is "the most perfect thing in nature" (Qs. 12 – 13), and as, therefore, nature pursues the development of the person to his full nobility as its first and most important aim, it follows that the task of the community must lie in developing and perfecting the person, who, for his part, serves the glory of God in the most exalted way. The good of the community has been created or achieved for man.

3. Unfortunately a very important point is often overlooked. When emphasizing that the end of the community is the development and perfection of the person, we ought to think of the person not only as an individual; we ought to think of him equally as a member of the community, and so think of the community; the social ties and obligations of the person are inseparable from his full development. We must remember that the neglect of social duties makes impossible the real perfection of the person, that perfection which is true to nature and appropriate to man, that is, extended to the whole man and excluding no essential aspects of him. Social duties embrace not only what is right and proper in human intercourse; they also include such services as the community is entitled to expect, or can demand in virtue of lawful authority.

4. Once again it is evident (Q. 30) that the community is not merely a means to the development of the individual person. The end of the community, the common good, is more than the sum total of those institutions and arrangements which assist the individual in the attainment of his goals. It is the total goal of the unity of order we call community in which the persons are the community's responsibility and are contained in it as partial and yet individual goals possessing an intrinsic value of their own. In pointing out that each person represents an end of inviolable, intrinsic value, which is at one and the

same time a partial goal and yet complete in itself, we have said what matters. Such an end is not absorbed in the more comprehensive total end, but retains within the latter its own proper character, significance, and independence. The total goal is not a higher "something" floating in mid-air, but the unity and order of individual goals which themselves possess an intrinsic value. The common good cannot therefore justify any ordinance or measure contrary to the divinely appointed ends, norms, and values of the person; for that would mean violating intrinsic values and degrading persons to the level of utilities. Examples are abortion for eugenic reasons; the encouragement of illegitimate births; arbitrary arrest and detention; the use of force to make a person abandon his religious beliefs. (See Part 3, Lesson 3, p. 261.)

5. It is clear from what has been said concerning the relationship between person and community that the person restricted by social obligations is something totally different from the collective man, from "mass man".

a. In explanation we distinguish three meanings of the word "mass":

i. It can mean a large crowd, or the large majority of a people, class, community, group, or organization (the mass of the American or British peoples, of the faithful, of the educated, of the workers, of the army). This is to use it in the sense of numbers without implying anything about the attitude of the individual.

ii. Mass can mean a large number of people united by a common experience which, however, springs from a genuine, personal conviction in the case of each individual, and which has a definitely positive character: for example a religious demonstration where all take part voluntarily and in a spirit of faith and devotion. In this sense, "mass" and "mass experience" can be positive influences for good.

iii. Mass can mean a large number of people with no judgement and no mind of their own, carried away by some, ususally excited and hostile, general mood which may have been the result of a chance situation or may have been stirred up by some individual. Given this meaning, the mass is credulous, impatient, easily incited, courageous only as a mass and without any sense of proportion in its demands. Its mood changes quickly. (The best example is the trial of Jesus.) In the hands of clever or unscrupulous leaders it can become a frightful instrument of enslavement, terror, economic disasters, and political emergencies such as strikes, demonstrations or riots.

b. "Mass man" is not the individual who allows himself to be swept along on some rare occasion by the current of the mass, but one whose mentality is that of the unthinking, conformist in the mass. He possesses neither the strength nor the courage of personal responsibility, especially when it comes to standing up for something that is opposed to the accepted view, to the ideas of his class or profession, to a system and its rulers. Always afraid of attracting attention, he will choose the line of least resistance. He will do what "they" expect and want him to do, "they" being, for example, a political party, fellow-workers, a social class. There is no doubt that modern man is exposed to the danger of becoming "mass man". There are internal and external reasons for this, such as his being totally uprooted, his turning from God and hence from the source of strength and the basis of any genuine responsibility, his lack of firm principles, and his secularism. There is the trend of world economic and social development, urbanization, regimentation of modern industrial labour requirements, State direction and bureaucracy, military service, conflicts in the labour market between trade-unions and employers' organizations; ideological movements, powers, and influences; Fascism and Marxism; film, press, radio, and television.

It would be contrary to fact to believe that only members of a certain class, for example the wage-earners, were exposed to the danger of becoming "mass men", and that they alone succumbed to it. There are among the labouring class very solid and independent personalities, who will stand up against the demands of the collective. Among all classes are to be found some, even many and highly respected individuals, who will generally take no part in mass meetings and actions, but who, from a want of personal judgement or by surrendering it, by complacency and lip-service, by their malleability in adapting themselves to every situation, show that they lack the moral fibre and steadfest character of a true personality. In fact they do their best to submerge themselves in the mass.

c. We do not become "mass men" through extending our social obligation too far, or taking it too seriously, but rather through surrendering ourselves completely to the collective and its rulers and their demands, to the "party line", to the "movement", or simply to what we may regard as the spirit of the times. For instance, the demands made by the collective, or in its name, may be very unsocial, in fact basically so, although, and indeed because they appeal to social equality and equal rights. Worst of all, the collective arrogates to itself the right to determine the order and range of values, and the independence of the person is neither recognized nor safeguarded. The collective pretends to be superior to the individual and to have absolute authority over him, thus reducing the person, socially restricted in the true sense, to the level of the herd. What is social in and about man does not extinguish the dignity and individual responsibility of the person; on the contrary, it is made possible and intelligible only on the basis of the latter. Man's moral nobility cannot be undermined by what is truly "social". It is a distortion of his social function to induce him to renounce personal decisions for the sake of ideologies, party programmes, "Five Year plans", or political or economic blueprints. It is indeed better for him to have too much personal independence and responsibility, than too little.

33. How are we to understand the priority accorded to the public weal?

In the sense that the common good comes before private interest.

THE expression "public weal" suggests an exclusively utilitarian standpoint. Considerations of utility are necessary, no doubt, and are certainly not bad in themselves. However, as soon as they become predominant, especially when, as in totalitarian States, the ruling authorities decide what constitutes a public benefit, then the situation becomes intolerable, since arbitrary standards coupled with force and terror are substituted for objective standards.

This exclusively utilitarian standpoint is ruled out when we speak of the common good, for then the good as distinct from mere utility is emphasized as the purpose of the community (Qs. 25–26). It is clear that the whole is greater than the part, that the good of the whole (common good) comes before the good of the part (private interest), since it embraces all partial and private goods and unites them in a higher order. The first duty of the community is to itself as the whole which embraces the parts. It must therefore set its norms in such wise that the whole is served. For this reason also it must take measures that are suitable for the whole, and lead to, and guarantee, the right order of the parts within the whole. For example a family will appoint a time for meals to suit all its members and not just one or the other; the individual should conform and show consideration.

In the light of what has been said so far, the principle that the common good comes before private interest is valid and binding provided the following conditions are fulfilled:

1. The community may never demand of any individual something which is wrong in itself. Man is obliged, in virtue of his nature, to do what is good; nature nowhere releases a man from this obligation, neither the individual in the community, nor the community as an order of persons. Now there are things which are wrong in themselves and which no human explanations or evasions can make it right to do (Q. 47), for example, lying, cheating, killing innocent life, adultery, violation of conscience, disobedience to God's commandment; the community is absolutely bound to recognize them, and no appeal to the common good, no decision of a human authority can alter this.

2. The order of values must be respected and upheld. Since the common good includes several domains of the good which vary in value and importance (Qs. 25-7), since the parts constitute and carry the whole, since, consequently, the existence and favourable development of the whole depends on how far the parts realize in themselves the values of the natural order, the restrictions and sacrifices imposed on the members must be carefully weighed according to the order of values. The community ought to take care to foster values in accordance with

their respective status and importance (the law of subsidiary function, Q. 52). It must allow room for genuine progress and therefore allow liberty to members and member communities. The higher the values, the greater the liberty required. For example, it is more important to promote morality than to promote art, and more important for the Church than for economic interest groups to have freedom of development.

The degree of necessity will be a further limiting factor, thus:

3. The measure of what is expedient at a particular time should not be exceeded. In certain circumstances admittedly the general good can be maintained only by setting the higher values aside for the time being and concentrating on the attainment of lower values. The community will then have the right to take what measures are necessary. Such measures exceed the restrictions and sacrifices which are necessitated by the nature of community life, but they should be confined to the duration of the particular emergency.

EXAMPLES are: the need to keep certain public services going during strikes and in times of catastrophe; the obligation of farmers and manufacturers to deliver up agricultural or industrial products for the purpose of providing enough for all; the closing of schools during an epidemic.

In conclusion we wish to emphasize again that the purpose and task of the community is not to oppress but to uplift the individual and to develop his rights and opportunities. The members should find fulfilment in the whole, not be absorbed by it. This can be achieved only by their proper adjustment to the whole, otherwise they themselves will inevitably fail and the whole too will be a failure.

Lesson Four

AUTHORITY AND OBEDIENCE

The Power to Command and the Duty to Obey

EXPERIENCE shows that every society and every activity undertaken in common has need of direction, and of an arrangement whereby someone is at the head to whom the others are subject; it has need of authority (for example parents in the family; executive power in the State; a managing committee in a club; a chairman at a meeting). Authority (from the Latin *auctor:* author, originator) implies a relationship of origin. Now there is the order of being and the order of doing (action). Whatever takes its being from another is subordinate to him and owes him obedience: authority in virtue of origin (thus all creatures in relation to God, children in relation to their parents). Dependence in action is twofold: either it is personal, that is, dependence which is personally sought, as when someone seeks the advice of another and puts himself voluntarily under his direction, or it is social, being based on membership of a community. This is social authority.

Authority, as we know, plays a large part in the life of man. It can bring innumerable blessings, but it can also wreak havoc and be fatal for the individual and for the community.

Since the purpose of a social handbook is to set forth the moral norms of social behaviour, it treats the question of authority in relation to action (willing), and not in relation to knowing (knowledge, faith: authority of doctrine).

34. Why is authority necessary in society?

Authority is required by the ends and nature of community.

LEO XIII (D. I., 11).

"*But now, a society can neither exist nor be conceived in which there is no one to govern the wills of individuals, in such a way as to make, as it were, one will out of many, and to impel them rightly and orderly to the common good; therefore, God has willed that in a civil society there should be some to rule the multitude.*"

LEO XIII (I. D., 3).

"*But as no society can hold together unless some one be over all, directing all to strive earnestly for the common good, every body politic must have a ruling authority, and this authority, no less than society itself, has its source in nature, and has, consequently, God for its author.*"

1. WE are concerned with the source of authority. That there is and ought to be authority in society is not due to a voluntary agreement between men, but to the very nature of community as a unity of order and purpose of persons. A common end can be duly and effectively striven for and attained only when the various forces and activities are directed in relation to it. The individual has his own ends, ideas, characteristics, and abilities; if each one remains on his own and seeks his own interests exclusively, then individual not common ends are pursued. On the other hand the common end demands that private interests should be co-ordinated and in certain circumstances even set aside. It is not the lack of good will and false self-interest which necessitates a directing and co-ordinating authority; the reason lies in the fact that men differ naturally from each other and are

by nature self-centred – meaning love of self in the true sense – whereas the community as a new, overall unit has its special ends and necessities.

Catholic ethics has therefore consistently refused to seek an explanation of authority in original sin and the inclination to self-interest (selfishness) which results from it. It teaches rather that even in the state of original justice in Paradise powers of direction and the obligation of obedience would have been necessary, simply because men would then have lived in community, and life in community is not possible without authority. Catholic ethics of course appreciates and stresses the fact that the need for authority has increased considerably as a result of original sin and its evil consequences which make it necessary also to employ compulsion and punishment as a means of upholding authority. This would not have been necessary in the state of original justice (Q. 38).

2. Consequently there must be some organ in the community to which the care of the common good, of the community as a whole, is entrusted and which will set forth and impose on the members what has to be done for the sake of the common good. Hence authority is called the guarantor of the common good, and rightly so. Although authority is not the definitive form, not the soul of the community (the form of the community is its order, Q. 21), yet it must be considered an essential consequence, an essential characteristic which results immediately from the nature of community. Thus authority is not extrinsic, but intrinsic to community; not accidental, but necessary.

3. This shows that:

a. Wherever a community comes into existence, or already exists, it possesses and develops authority. Natural communities there must be because no ordered human existence is possible without them. The authority proper to them is therefore absolutely, that is inevitably and inescapably necessary. Voluntary communities need not be, or need be under certain conditions only; consequently the authority proper to them is only relatively necessary. The question, therefore, whether a particular authority (for example that of parents, of the State, of a firm) is indispensable, that is, whether it belongs to the social order of life as such, is to be judged according to the necessity of the community under consideration.

b. Communities based on an intimate, personal friendship, as well as those in which men live and work together in a perfectly informal way, seem to get along without authority. And that is true in so far as authority means the power to direct and command. It is also true that in such communities authority is scarcely apparent and should not make itself felt. Yet these communities are always ruled by a relationship of give and take, perhaps in a marked and harmonious reciprocity, in which case, however, one will be more decisive and give more abundantly than the other by reason of natural superiority, of greater riches of mind or heart, or because of other circumstances. For example, in a marriage based on a mutual love which is completely generous the husband will not dominate and order his wife about, yet the wife will, nevertheless, be the one who is sheltered, led, and protected; she will consent and desire to leave to the husband many decisions according to the natural circumstances.

4. Other explanations have been advanced of the source of authority, especially in relation to particular communities. Some see it in the power of the one who gets to the top (the struggle for survival; might and consequently right of the stronger). In this case authority is seen to derive not from objec-

117

tive necessity but from subjective arbitrariness; the holder of authority claims it as his "natural" right that he precisely and no other is at the head of affairs. As a rule this proves fatal for the community, since nearly always coercion, threats, and oppression are the result. The necessity for authority is also denied by anarchism (the unlimited freedom of the individual, rejection of all government), which seeks to overthrow all authority and has as its ideal a society devoid of all authority; a society which would be both contrary to nature and absurd.

5. By deriving authority from the nature and end of the community Catholic ethics has shown it to originate from God, the Creator and Lord of social life. Human authority points beyond its immediate source; it is of divine origin, and is a participation in the absolute authority of God.[11] Wherever men govern lawfully and justly they do so in the name and in the power of God (even where they are unaware of this fact, or even where it is not to their liking). All authority cannot, of course, claim to be derived to the same extent from God; within the natural order of life this must be judged according to how close in origin the community is to nature, or according to the legitimacy of the mission which the community fulfils (for example, the school to which parents entrust their children). The more voluntary the community, the less rooted in God is its authority (the head of a firm cannot claim to issue his orders "by the grace of God"). In these communities men can by leaving them evade authority.

LEO XIII (R. N., 28).

"As the power to rule comes from God, and is, as it were, a participation in His, the highest of all sovereignties, it should be exercised

---

[11] Eccles. 10:4; Prov. 8:16; Luke 20:20; John 19:10; Rom. 13:2.

as the power of God is exercised – with a fatherly solicitude which not only guides the whole, but reaches also to details."

LEO XIII (D. I., 11).

"But no man has in himself or of himself the power of constraining the free will of others by fetters of authority of this kind. This power resides solely in God, the Creator and Legislator of all things; and it is necessary that those who exercise it should do it as having received it from God. "There is one lawgiver and judge who is able to destroy and deliver" (James 4:12). And this is clearly seen in every kind of power. That that power which resides in priests comes from God is so well-known that among all nations they are recognized as, and called, the ministers of God. In like manner, the authority of fathers of families preserves a certain impressed image and form of the authority which is in God, "from whom all fatherhood in heaven and earth takes its title" (Eph. 3:15). But in this way different kinds of authority have between them wonderful resemblances, since, whatever there is of government and authority, its origin is derived from one and the same Creator and Lord of the world, who is God."

LEO XIII (S. C., 8).

"Law is of its very essence a mandate of right reason, proclaimed by a properly constituted authority, for the common good. But true and legitimate authority is void of sanction, unless it proceed from God, the supreme ruler and lord of all. The Almighty alone can commit power to a man over his fellow men, nor may that be accounted as right reason which is in disaccord with truth and with divine reason; nor that held to be true good which is repugnant to the supreme and unchangeable good, or that wrests aside and draws away the wills of men from the charity of God."

119

35. What is authority?

Authority is the precedence which one man has over others, coupled with his right to rule the community.

"AUTHORITY" is one of those current notions which are obscure and difficult to define.

1. Two facts or characteristics appertain without doubt to what we call authority:

a. Authority (that is to say the one holding authority; Q. 39) takes precedence in the community; it has a superior, exalted position and function.

b. This precedence carries with it the right to rule the community, and therein precisely lies the significance of authority, namely, that it empowers and entitles one to rule the community effectively. It is no mere precedence of honour or prestige, but one of power. We call this function authoritative, directing, commanding, regulating power. To the authority, that is to say to the one holding authority, is granted the right and the power to do what is necessary and what he judges to be necessary for the good of the community (Q. 38). This power is of a legal and moral nature. It is no mere actual superiority (physical or intellectual power).

2. Catholic ethics holds that all power of authority is based ultimately on the good. But there are two main schools of thought.

a. One school – and it has by far the greater number of followers – holds the definition given above, namely, "Authority is the power to command and to enforce".

b. The other school holds that, absolutely speaking, authority consists in the effectiveness and the binding power of the good. The good possesses a power to move and to bind in the true and proper sense, since it presents itself to man as something which he must strive after and do. A man may not have an indifferent or evasive attitude towards the good. He must decide in favour of the good. Now there are two species of good. One presents itself to the human will (to the person) as binding of itself without having to be imposed expressly as an obligation. The other type of good, on the contrary, if it is in fact to be binding, must be expressly imposed upon the will as a task. And for that there is need of another person who is empowered to impose the good as an obligation. He must recognize and desire the good himself first before he can impose it on others. We see, then, that those who uphold this second theory give a twofold meaning to authority. In the first place they hold that authority is the effectiveness and binding force of the good, and in the second sense (which is derived from the first) that it is in the power of one person to regulate and command others.

There is a wide measure of agreement in practical questions and conclusions between the two theories. The second view is criticized – perhaps unjustly – for allowing man a dangerously large measure of freedom, since he could appeal all too easily to "the good" as to the higher authority against the command of the legitimate authority and in this way make ineffective every inconvenient command.

36. Are the powers of authority restricted?

The powers of authority are restricted : in general to the good, in particular to a specific common good.

LEO XIII (R. N., 28).

"As the power to rule comes from God, and is, as it were, a participation in His, the highest of all sovereignties, it should be exercised as the power of God is exercised – with a fatherly solicitude which not only guides the whole, but reaches also to details."

LEO XIII ("In the midst of Solicitudes", 16 February 1892).

"[Civil Power] by its nature is constituted to seek after the common good, the supreme goal which is the source of human society . . . This good is, after God, the first and last law of society."

1. IT is self-evident to the man who believes in God that every human authority is bound by what the higher authority of God commands or forbids; for man has been granted no supreme power which is not subject to the sovereignty of God. But God's will is manifest not only in the divine and the natural law, but also in all that the Church in the name and in the power of her divine founder lays down for men to do. No authority can ever be empowered to command things to be done which are wrong, or contrary to the will of God. Where this is done, nevertheless, authority is misused and its claims are irresponsible and unjust.

EXAMPLES are: the legalization of euthanasia or abortion; the extortion of false testimony as in the trials of totalitarian regimes, but also matters which occur in a small circle and perhaps in secret; secret societies which bind their members to blind allegiance; parents who order their children to steal.

2. Acknowledgement of the moral law implies that human authority should recognize objective moral values and should allow man freedom where this is granted him by nature and revelation. Human authority must guide the community and rule its subjects in accordance with the dignity and needs of man (of Christians). It is not immaterial how man reaches the values which are held up before, or are attainable by, him, since he can only perfect himself properly and harmoniously when he observes the objective order of values, that is, an order independent of his own opinion or liking, and makes it the basis of his

122

conduct. Nor is it immaterial whether the individual realizes the rights and freedoms guaranteed him in virtue of a higher authority, and where and in what manner he shows this freedom for he cannot become a good man if he renounces these rights and freedoms in favour of the community (Q. 82).

3. To express it positively and concretely, the task and limits of human authority lie in the common good. Authority may and must encourage and carry out whatever is necessary in respect of the common good. Moreover, it is necessary in the first place:

a. to know how it can best direct and regulate matters from the point of view of the common good and in harmony with the ends and values of the total human good.

b. to assess as nearly as possible the measure of co-operation and sacrifice which the members (and member communities) owe to the common good.

c. to take timely and effective measures to prevent might coming before right.

Thus we are not surprised when St. Thomas, for example, (I–II 92, 1 ad 3) reminds the holder of authority that he must be a virtuous man, since otherwise he would lack the qualification necessary for ruling a community.

37. What actions are subject to human authority?

Only those external actions are subject to human authority which are in accordance with the task of the community and which are of importance for the good of the community.

HERE is a matter of the greatest importance. Totalitarian regimes expect the people to think just what they prescribe for them and to accept and blindly to consent to the aims which they have fixed. Accordingly they threaten, ostracize and persecute the individual when they suspect that his way of thinking is not in line with theirs. And if they cannot produce evidence, they will treat him as suspect and attribute to him things which they know to be false. In this way they have a useful device for condemning awkward opponents, no matter how legitimate they are, and for "liquidating" them.

1. Human intercourse and co-operation neither begins nor ends in external action, but is carried out in it. This is true even of the "I – thou" relationship (for instance in friendship) which comes into existence only when two people not only know of one another and of their mutual regard, but when they communicate this regard to each other and recognizably reciprocate it. It is even more true of those communities which demand unity of aim and unity of purposeful functions. Men must associate together and bring order into their associations in relation to a goal; but that is possible only when the relations with one another are conducted in an externally recognizable form.

2. It is a sound principle that men can regulate by norms and laws, only what they are in a position to judge. We may be able to suspect and surmise, perhaps after long enough experience even tell with a fair amount of certainty what another is thinking, from what motives he acts, why he does one thing rather than another, but it will be quite certain only when the person himself has told us. At most we can establish whether in the light of all the circumstances someone is fully responsible for his action, and even this is very difficult to decide at times. From the fact that every form of community is concerned with human relations it follows that these at any rate are within the scope of the community. Thus it has the right to prescribe or

forbid, to reward or punish external acts only. However, we may not conclude from this that the spiritual life of men is no concern of the community, and that the community can remain wholly indifferent to it. We must distinguish between the competence and the purpose of the community. External order is its proper domain, but it is certainly meant to contribute towards mens' inward perfection. This is the reason for the community as a unity of order of men, and it is easy to see how much external acts depend on internal acts, and external on internal order. Experience supplies any number of examples: members of a family who are wanting in inner affection and respect for each other become estranged; a people that submits reluctantly to its rulers may for a time be whipped up to great achievements, but it will lack morale in order to persevere; a business which is merely outwardly efficient as it were for "show" will be weakened in its productive power.

Therefore, the community, in keeping with its own proper development and in the service of men, is entitled to use all morally justifiable means in order to influence men for their inward good. It may and should instruct and encourage, and propagate its ideals effectively but truthfully. Naturally when men's consciences are subjected to force, blackmail, and oppression we cannot speak of morally justifiable means.

38. What in particular are the obligations of authority?

The obligations of authority are :
1. **To lay down exactly the aim and the order of the community.**
2. **To provide for the training and proper disposition of its forces.**
3. **To enact the necessary just laws.**

4. **To watch over and to enforce the observance of the law.**

5. **Justly to reward or punish the observance or the transgression of the law.**

THESE particular obligations are not to be taken as mere enumeration; they also indicate the proper order of the functions.

Experience confirms both the necessity and the order of these functions. For example, a working team begins by finding out exactly what work is to be done; or if there is already agreement about this, it immediately begins to consider and to define the precise order in which the work is to be carried out. Then the conditions are laid down and a committee is set up and invested with the necessary powers to direct and to supervise the work, to admonish and possibly to expel those who lag behind, and in general to see to everything that the activity of the team demands. In order to make sure that the work will continue suitable new members are recruited or trained.

1. It is not unimportant that the factor of force is listed last among the functions; because it is wrong to single out the power of coercion and punishment as the primary (possibly even the only or at any rate the most important) function and right of authority. Only when people disregard the law, or act contrary to it, can and must the community make use of the power of coercion and punishment which is one of its powers. Thus authority is not simply "the right of coercion", as Kant held. Coercion affects man from outside. It is contrary to the nature of man, who, because he is endowed with free will, can and ought to comply inwardly with the commands of authority.

2. The aims and the norms of the natural community are determined in their general content and character by nature (Qs.14–16). Nevertheless, the actual community must first of all find forms that

are suitable to it in distinction from the other communities of the same kind. This function of giving the community its particular inner structure is the right of the whole community (for the exception see Q. 39). Whether a people wishes to live under a monarchical or a republican system is a matter for the people to decide. Within this function the first question is to determine the organ of authority and to pass the constitution which is then binding on both the community and the authority. How far the community reserves to itself the passing of further laws depends on various circumstances. The greater and more important the community, the greater and more radical will be the powers which either must be conceded to authority in virtue of the natural law or may be granted to it by the community. At any rate authority must have the powers necessary for the vitality and effectiveness of the community. The community has the right and the duty to protect itself by sufficient safeguards against the misuse of authority.

We emphasize once again that every human authority, like the community, is bound by the God-given aims, institutions, and basic rights of man. History shows all too clearly how easily this can be forgotten. Voluntary communities ought to be conducted in such a way that they do not interfere with or make in any way impossible the activity of natural communities.

39. Who appoints the holder of authority?

The holder of authority is appointed either by nature or by the community itself.

THE holder of authority is appointed by nature itself only in the case of the family (the parents – pre-eminence of the father). In the case of all other communities men are free to decide to

127

whom they wish to confide authority, by whom they wish to be ruled. They can confer the power of authority on a single individual or on a group; he who is to hold authority may be elected, appointed or chosen by lot. But here also freedom does not mean licence. The community must ensure that the holder of authority is fitted for his task, that the aim and the order of the community are not disrupted. In the case of a public service an officer or manager (or whatever title he may have) must be appointed who is able to keep the service going. That is required by the good of the service and of those belonging to it and by the function which the service has to fulfil within the national economy.

Often the assumption and exercise of authority require a special qualification on account of the purpose and character of the particular community, and this is something additional to the general qualifications for leading functions in general. For example, authority in an educational community will have to be exercised by the person who imparts the education; otherwise the work will not be fruitful. Those taking others into their services, employing them and paying them for their labour, are authority for them.

40. How are the holders of authority to rule the community?

Holders of authority ought to rule the community with prudence and justice.

1. HE is a prudent man who knows how to rule with fairness and in conformity with the dictates of the moral law. The prudent man reflects and weighs up, judges and sees what ought to be done here and now. He will not be swayed by considerations of expediency, but is led in everything by

the point of view of the good. He will remember that he is set over men with free will and personal responsibility and that all human action, including service of the community, must be good in order to be justified. Prudence, therefore, differs from shrewdness or cunning. It is practical wisdom acquired or at least deepened and clarified by experience. It presupposes that man is inwardly disposed to decide in favour of, and in accordance with, the norms of virtue. The virtuous man "senses" the good and the demands of virtue, and his determined will safeguards him against perversion of his judgements and against any influences that might deter and distract him from the good.

2. Social prudence takes its standard and its limits from the common good. Its task is to point out and to lay down what must be done in order that the community may prosper and be successful from the point of view of its specific purpose and rank. Especially in questions and decisions of importance it must proceed carefully and respectfully, since in the last resort it is not dealing with things but with men. Therefore, the one who has charge of a community must obey the dictates of prudence. According to St. Thomas he should be a man of wide and expert experience, always keeping moral principles in mind, ever ready to learn, always careful to take everything into account before giving a decision, logical in reasoning, provident in relating means to end, circumspect, that is, taking into account specific circumstances, careful that nothing wrong or *apparently* good is mixed up with what is completely good (II–II, Q. 49).

3. He is a just man who gives to everyone his due. Distributive justice gives to everyone within the community what is his due of the common good, of work and earnings, of sacrifice and (in

129

the case of culpable transgressions) punishment. It judges not by calculation but by a standard of proportion, having to consider any existing inequalities. For example £ 5,000 distributed according to simple division among ten families gives each family £ 500. On the other hand, if it be distributed according to size and need among ten families which differ in the number of their children and in their needs, the result will show considerable differences (Q. 100). True, justice is no respecter of persons (Q. 102), but at the same time it must be based on recognition of man as a person, in fact on a strong and genuine love for man. Whoever holds and exercises authority ought to be mindful of dealing with those whom he commands in a dignified manner. The power of authority need not and ought not to lead to loss of self-control, resentment, and bitterness, not even where severity is called for.

41. What is due to those who hold authority?

Respect and obedience is due to those who hold authority.

LEO XIII (L. P., 13).

"Moreover, the highest duty is to respect authority, and obediently to submit to just law; and by this the members of a community are effectually protected from the wrong-doing of evil men. Lawful power is from God, 'and whosoever resisteth authority resisteth the ordinance of God' (Rom. 13:2), wherefore, obedience is greatly enobled when subjected to an authority which is the most just and supreme of all. But where the power to command is wanting, or where a law is enacted contrary to reason, or to the eternal law, or to some ordinance of God, obedience is unlawful, lest, while obeying man, we become disobedient to God."

130

1. RESPECT is due to every man, at least as long as he fulfils his obligations as a man. Special respect is due to authority on account of its position and power which are to a large extent independent of personal qualities and attitude; because respect is paid to authority for the sake of the common good and the community whose care is entrusted to it.

2. We owe obedience to no man but him who is placed over us in authority and who is entitled to rule over us. Power of authority without the corresponding obligation of obedience is senseless because it is ineffective. He who rules over the community must especially have the right to enforce his decisions; otherwise disunity and disorder will prevail.

3. Since no human authority has unlimited powers it forfeits its right to be obeyed as soon as it exceeds the limits of its competence. In four cases in particular human authority exceeds its powers:

a. When it makes demands which are contrary to the natural law or to any other divine law. To obey in such cases is sinful, consequently one must refuse to obey.

b. When its orders have nothing to do with the purpose of the community, thus encroaching on another's domain (for example, when a sports club lays down for its members when and in what manner they are to carry out their professional duties, or attempts to dispense its members from the obligation of Sunday Mass).

c. When it favours some and discriminates against others in an obviously unjust manner (for example, an employer who, while paying to all the same wages, demands more work from some than from others).

d. When it issues orders which are reserved to a higher authority.

42. What is to be done when authority conflicts with private conscience?

The individual must follow the clear and certain dictates of his own conscience, even against the injunction of a human authority; it is his duty, however, to examine objectively and carefully whether his conscience is in fact correctly informed.

LEO XIII (D. I., 15).

"The one only reason which men have for not obeying is when anything is demanded of them which is openly repugnant to the natural or the divine law, for it is equally unlawful to command and to do anything in which the law of nature or the will of God is violated. If, therefore, it should happen to any one to be compelled to prefer one or the other, viz., to disregard either the commands of God or those of rulers, he must obey Jesus Christ, who commands us to 'give to Caesar the things that are Caesar's, and to God the things that are God's' (Matt. 22:21), and must reply courageously after the example of the Apostles: 'We ought to obey God rather than men' (Acts 5:29). And yet there is no reason why those who so behave themselves should be accused of refusing obedience; for, if the will of rulers is opposed to the will and the laws of God, they themselves exceed the bounds of their own power and pervert justice; nor can their authority then be valid, which, when there is no justice, is null."

LEO XIII (L. P., 13). See under Q. 41.

THE answer is deliberately confined to human authority; the authority of God and of the Church is not included here. It is purposely kept general; individual and at times very intricate questions will be treated in the relevant sections (for example, the right to rebel against the authority of the State, conscientious objection, tax laws).

1. His own personal conscience is the proximate, uniform, and inescapable norm of a man's behaviour. A man must always act in accordance with his conscience, and he may never act against it, not even when his conscience is inculpably and invincibly erroneous.

2. It is a man's duty to see to it that his conscience is true or right, that his conscience judges and decides according to the truth and the actual situation, and not according to how he himself views the matter in question. In cases of doubt he must take the proper and available means to obtain clarity and certainty (personal consideration of the matter, prayer, the reading of relevant literature, the advice of competent men).

3. When a man's conscience tells him unmistakably and beyond all doubt either that he is obliged to do something which goes against the injunction of a human authority, or that he cannot take responsibility for, and may not do, something which a human authority demands of him or suggests to him, then his conscience and not the will or the wish of authority is the decisive voice. The individual must know what exactly is at stake, what he intends to do or what is demanded of him, and he must be firmly convinced either that his conduct is permissible or necessary, or that what is asked is unlawful.

4. However, the subject should realize that authority has the right and the duty to command and to forbid, and that consequently he is normally bound to obey. He should also realize that he himself could be mistaken. Often enough it is very difficult even for the expert or the conscientious man to decide whether a command is wrong in itself, or whether a prohibition infringes inalienable rights or prevents a person from fulfilling clear obligations. Indeed, the very fact that something is

demanded or forbidden is in many cases a guarantee of the lawfulness of the command or the prohibition. The person in authority, too, has a conscience. Especially in the case of important decisions we should not assume at once that the command or prohibition has been made lightly and without giving the matter sufficient thought.

When, however, it is actually established that authority demands something that is wrong in itself, or that forbids something to which the subject is undoubtedly obliged in virtue of a higher authority, then the subject cannot and may not obey (Q. 36, No. 1; Q. 47, No. 2). Parents cannot submit to the authority of the state when it prevents them from bringing up their children as Christians.

When the command or prohibition is not in itself wrong or the experts are not unanimously agreed about it, and the subject himself is firmly convinced that he must act otherwise than authority demands, then the greatest caution is necessary. Not every command which seems to be unreasonable or unlawful is really so. At times authority has to take into account factors which are not known to the subject and which, therefore, he cannot judge. Various motives, views and feelings might frequently prejudice us against those in authority. Obedience has an intrinsic moral value, while disobedience to lawful commands is morally wrong. (Regarding the case where an order has to be carried out before it is possible to consult authority, see Q. 77 on equity.)

5. If an individual does not succeed in resolving doubts concerning the lawfulness of a command, he must take into account the basic and general attitude of those in authority. If the one in authority is known to be conscientious and mindful of his responsibility, then the individual who is unable to resolve his

134

doubt may follow the injunctions of authority, since its attitude speaks in favour of the lawfulness of the command. On the other hand if we know from experience that the one in authority has no scruples about overstepping the limits of what is morally right, then (in case the doubt remains) we must seek to evade the command in every legitimate way, since the attitude of the one in authority speaks against the lawfulness of the command.

If evasion is impossible the magnitude and certainty of the evil which will attend the refusal to obey must decide. If merciless and harsh measures of reprisal and punishment are threatened, we may well be justified in carrying out the command (for example the serious and well founded doubt about the guilt of someone condemned to be shot – if the person or persons detailed to do the shooting refuse they may themselves be shot or, as happened in Nazi Germany, bitter revenge might be taken on their families).

6. The Catholic Church, therefore, neither undervalues nor overestimates the conscience of the individual. She demands only that the conscience should be carefully and systematically trained so that right decisions may be made and a genuine conscientiousness developed by the individual. Totalitarian states, on the contrary, show their inner vile nature precisely by violating the consciences of their people and praise as the highest expression of virtue an unquestioning obedience to even the most dastardly commands.

Part Two

Basic Laws of Social Order

Social Principles

TRUE social order ought to be based on certain fundamental laws which we call social principles. Men cannot and should not just drift along through life without concern for present or future. They need secure points of departure, solid principles and standards of action and development. Otherwise social life will disintegrate.[1]

Many errors or inaccuracies in social science are due to ignorance of these principles or to their false interpretation. Moreover, it is frequently overlooked that the sphere of social living has its own peculiar character which is quite different from that of

---

[1] Some of these principles have been discussed already in Part One (for example, the relationship of the whole and the part, of the common good and private good); but there are other principles which are no less important, and this book is surely the fitting place to give an exposition of social principles as a connected whole. In order to afford a complete survey we shall, therefore, include in this Part the more important principles of Part One, though this will mean a certain amount of repetition. We shall endeavour to explain the principles in logical sequence limiting ourselves to the fundamental principles which support and regulate social life as a whole. Those principles which pertain to particular spheres of social living (for example economics and ownership, culture, politics) will be treated in conjunction with them.

the physical and the organic spheres. When the laws of nature, established by science and natural philosophy, are blindly taken over and applied to social life this must inevitably lead to illogical reasoning and false conclusions. Let us take one example: The family is undoubtedly the primary cell of the human community, but this does not mean that all other communities develop from the family in the same way as the life of an organism develops from the cell. The point of comparison and agreement should not make us forget the essential differences.

43. How and where are the fundamental principles of social order to be discovered?

God's works, working, and nature reveal to us the fundamental principles of social order.

SOCIAL living is one sphere of the order of being and action established by God and embracing all creation. Man and community have their origin, their goal, and the model for all their activity in God. God's work in nature shows forth the manner in which he operates and the mysterious richness of his activity (and of his nature). But the deepest and at the same time the truest and clearest insight is given us by revelation, since through it God himself unfolds his own nature, his intentions, and his activity before the eyes of faith. And so we must inquire of nature and listen to the God of revelation if we would explain the fundamental principles of the order in creation, that is, if we would learn how created order is conceived and constructed; for all created order is constructed according to the "exemplary ideas" which God carries within him and which are nothing other than the nature of God himself in so far as this can be imitated and represented externally.

138

1. In all his external activity God has one dominant, inexorable purpose, namely, to show forth and to communicate his divine glory. He creates, conserves, and governs all things in order that they may proclaim his greatness and participate in his goodness and riches. God is infinite. No creature, even the most perfect, can reflect to any degree of adequacy the fullness of his divine attributes and his creative power. And so God created many and various things in order that they might make up as far as possible by their great number and variety for what they lack as individual creatures in the power of representation.

2. Faith teaches us that God is one in nature and three in persons. The three divine persons are not subordinate but related to one another, and that by reason of their origin from one another (the Son proceeds from the Father, and the Holy Spirit proceeds from the Father and the Son). Thus this most exalted community of all is "unity in order". Everything that God does externally is common to the three persons. It is to reveal not only God's power but also his wisdom, and it belongs to the order of wisdom. Hence God created a universe, not just a multitude of things but an ordered whole which has the one origin – God, one goal – God, and which has been constructed according to the law of the whole and its parts. In God's plan of order things are visualized as one whole in which they are related to one another in a unity of order. (Each thing is one in itself and intrinsically ordered; all things of the same category are related to one another and together they actualize the full value of this category; the lower categories are designed for the higher; irrational creatures are subject to the higher category and are meant for its use and benefit; all are subject to the Creator.)

3. God's plan of redemption and salvation also shows the unity and order of divine action: one Redeemer, the God-Man Jesus

Christ, in whom divine and human nature are hypostatically united in the one divine person; the wonderful order in his human nature itself; one Church hierarchically ordered; the order of the sacraments unified according to meaning, power, and goal (Christ in the Eucharist); the Communion of Saints.

4. All things have been created not only in order to bear witness to God by their existence and nature but also in order to become more and more like unto God, their model, by actualizing their potentialities. And where they act not according to blind instinct or inner compulsion but from knowledge and free will, they will be able to know and to imitate God's action, that is, they should make a careful study of nature, especially their own, in order to discover how God acts and how he bids them to act, and then they should set to work. If they do this the following will become clear to them:

a. All being and all (meaningful) action consists in unity and order and is perfected therein.

b. In social life too, men are in duty bound to act true to nature and for a right end.

c. Community life develops organically from smaller to bigger structures; these structures are not only linked up with one another but they support and supplement each other.

5. Accordingly we can enumerate nine fundamental principles which will be explained and further established in the following questions. These are 1. unity, 2. order, 3. acting true to nature, 4. acting for a right end, 5. the common good, 6. authority, 7. organic growth (of the whole), 8. solidarity, 9. subsidiary function.

44. What is meant by the principle of unity in social life?

Social life is not based on struggle and discord, nor on mere multiplicity (mass), but on agreement and concord.

WHATEVER exists and is meant to have permanency must in some fashion hold together intrinsically, it must not fall to pieces, since it would then cease to exist altogether or at least lose its own peculiar character (integrity). He who splits a tree or breaks off the leg of a chair (thus dissolving the cohesion of the parts) destroys or damages these things. Nature tends to preserve its unity and thus to preserve its parts. Atoms must be split by force, otherwise they will not surrender their unity.

Men can live socially only when they are united among themselves. Otherwise they live asocially, either in conflict with one another or merely alongside of one another. In both cases social life is suffocated or not even developed. Men are able to "live" in unity, that is, to attain or at least to strive for unity only because they are already united by a common nature to this end. There is accord in their nature, their capacities, their ends, in mutual dependence, in their desire for each other. But men are endowed with free will, and liable to error and deception as well as subject to various propensities such as the acquisitive desire, the desire for power and position. Hence social unity in the sense of a lived, actualized unity is not present from the beginning but must be created, achieved by men themselves. And this is only possible through the various forms of mutual understanding and consent; unanimity is required from which concord springs.[2]

---

[2] St. Thomas Aquinas wrote an instructive passage under the heading "Is peace the same thing as concord?" (II–II 29, 1). He points out that there is concord when several people are united in will and agree in desiring some one

Experience and insight show:

a. As long as men go along unconcerned beside one another, forming nothing more than a plurality, a crowd of people, we cannot speak of a community; the important thing is missing, namely, the sense of belonging together and of being there for one another and transcending the mere crowd.

thing; peace requires first of all order in the inner life of the individual being at one with himself, his will moving and directing his other faculties in accordance with the destiny of man, that is, in accordance with the voice and the will of God. Concord can exist among men in whom this inner order is missing, who as individuals do not lead lives which are inwardly well ordered. On the other hand, true social peace comes and is maintained only where men whose individual interior lives are well ordered live and work together, where men who are individually good or who are at least earnestly striving for the good meet and live together. Interior peace is the primary basis and the support of social peace. Taking man in his supernatural status and destiny, St. Thomas holds unity in the individual and true unity among men to be the fruit and proper effect of supernatural (Christian) charity. Charity unites man and relates him to God. He who lives in charity integrates his powers and aspirations according to God's will so as to please him. Charity also makes a man see his neighbour in his fellow man and love him "as himself"; he will therefore desire well for his neighbour as he desires well for himself. He will not selfishly think only of himself and try to get his own way, but will unselfishly think of the other and be ever ready to do what the other wishes. Thus arises true and fruitful concord in human intentions and actions. At the same time it is not necessary, as St. Thomas expressly remarks, that there should be no differences of opinion or no tensions of any kind among men. That would be impossible; and it suffices that men should be of one mind and united in their efforts *in principalibus bonis,* concerning the things that matter, while continuing to differ *in parvis et minimis,* on the unimportant and insignificant things. This remark was intended for smaller social groups, but it is surely permissible to give it a broader application and to say that in weightier questions, in questions which perhaps decide the fate of whole nations and epochs, even considerable differences of opinion and heated discussions need not endanger genuine concord where men show good will and where the *principalia bona* are kept in mind and honestly striven for by all (See Q. 123 where the article of St. Thomas is further explained).

b. It is even possible, as in the case of the mass, to have a large crowd of people with the feeling of being one, who are united in some common cause (in protesting, or making demands), yet mere factual agreement cannot establish or imply a genuine community since there is too little individual, personal responsibility. The mass follows the slogans and headlines; it is carried away by the influence of the demagogue; it is easily infected, it "reacts", creating a typical collectivity consciousness. Yet social living presupposes and demands unity; for even such a heterogeneous multitude which has been brought together by agitators is strong only so long as it holds together and is filled or moved and borne along by a single will.

c. Struggle and resistance are inevitable in social life. And where there is good reason for them and they are conducted according to correct moral standards there is nothing unjust or dishonourable about them; indeed, they may even be obligatory. Yet they must not serve discord but concord. They are temporary emergency measures designed to lead to understanding and agreement. At any rate if they are to have any meaning they must aim at unity and not dissension.

d. All social structures, whether family or nation, parish or State, workshop or factory, suffer to the extent to which they lose their unity. When men begin to be at cross purposes, to be at loggerheads or to become indifferent, their vitality, efficiency, and productivity is lowered.

45. What is meant by the principle of order in social life?

Unity must be aimed at and attained in that form which suits the natural predispositions, the diverse talents and tasks of men as well as the proper domain and requirements of social life.

143

WE might put it this way: The principle of order requires that social life should not be completely uniform in its development, but should be richly diversified and graded.

1. Unity is not the same thing as monotony. A thing, an event or an action can constitute an admirable unity even where there is considerable difference and variety of parts or of participants. Many instruments of various kinds are necessary for the performance of a Beethoven symphony, yet it is one orchestra and one performance; only well-ordered multiplicity (and unified leadership) can produce unity. Order can create unity out of the most diverse things, events, activities; hence "unity of order" (Qs. 21–2).

Order prevails where everything is in its proper place, is done in the proper manner; where everything fits in as it should in keeping with its relative importance; where the one thing perfectly complements the other; where after mature consideration each is assigned his particular function in relation to the general task as well as in relation to the other partners; where it is not arbitrariness but justice and appropriateness, good will and the greatest possible consideration which form the criteria for direction and procedure, for imposing obligations and assigning duties. Briefly, when men, things, and actions stand in proper relation to one another, there is order.

2. Nowhere is there unity in the sense of complete monotony, even though at times it may appear so. Unity is always linked with order. Uniformity is not the mark of the things which God has made. We have already mentioned that in God himself, whose nature is absolutely simple, there are three persons who proceed in origin from one another and are related to each other. No creature is absolutely simple, flat as it were, without inner differentiation and tension. In every creature essence

144

differs from existence. All creatures possess powers, and all act. The powers are implanted in their nature and are consequent on that nature. Action is the employment, exercise, and utilization of a power. What has been is related to what is still to come. All visible creatures, no matter how tiny, insignificant or short-lived they may be, consist nevertheless of two essential constituents which are mutually related: prime matter and essential form.

3. Men should undoubtedly lead orderly lives. It is unthinkable that they, who are the noblest part of all visible creation, could develop and do justice to their being if they were to act contrary to this fundamental law of the universe, the principle of order in unity. It is their social duty to recognize and realize the different kinds of order in which they have been placed. These correspond to their own nature as well as to all nature, and their harmonious development and a fruitful social life depend on them. As it is then a fact, that necessary and even considerable differences prevail among men themselves and in the domains entrusted to them, the attempt to create social unity and order by bringing everything to one level of uniformity must be rejected as mistaken and unnatural. On the contrary, order and unity will be reasonable and enduring only when they are pursued and lived on the basis of diversity. History shows that many differences are conditioned by time and locality, and that they are valid only because they correspond to the outlook and the situation of certain epochs and regions. (For instance, the relationship between capital and labour does not appear in the same form always and everywhere; the restricted and the universal franchise.) The specific form in which these differences are expressed is incidental and results from the development of history; consequently it can change within

certain limits. But this does not mean society could continue to exist if it were to deny or abolish these differences altogether.

The following differences might be specially noted:

a. Men differ considerably from one another, for example, in talents and inclinations, in education and character. It is as nonsensical to expect each individual to be capable of everything, as it is to believe that these differences will disappear or even become considerably smaller in some future epoch. Every social order must be based on the fact that different individuals are endowed with different talents, that outlook and opinions vary enormously among men, that not all are capable of assimilating training and education in the same manner and to the same degree.

b. Social life, including the whole range of communities from the greatest to the smallest, embraces an abundance of functions of the most diverse nature (for example, the sociological phenomenon of the division and classification of labour). Many of these activities require a long apprenticeship in addition to basic aptitude. Undisturbed and fruitful development is assured only when functions are co-ordinated according to their relative importance.

LEO XIII (R. N., 14).

"There naturally exist among mankind manifold differences of the most important kind; people differ in capacity, skill, health, strength; and unequal fortune is a necessary result of unequal condition. Such inequality is far from being disadvantageous either to individuals or to the community. Social and public life can only be maintained by means of various kinds of capacity for business and the playing of many parts; and each man, as a rule, chooses the part which suits his own peculiar domestic condition."

146

c. The difference of functions on the one hand, and their similarity on the other, form one of the bases for the multiplicity and diversity of social groupings. The abolition of all class distinction is simply impossible. Social unity does not mean that all form up and march in step together, but that the different classes (it is significant that in the Middle Ages they were called *"ordines"*, orders) consider themselves as members of a greater whole which embraces them all, assigning to each its proper place within this whole, so that the various classes find the proper mutual relationship in which human dignity, achievements, and rights are respected.

LEO XIII (R. N., 27).

"No matter what changes may occur in forms of government, there will ever be differences and inequalities of condition in the State. Society cannot exist or be conceived of without them. Some there must be who devote themselves to the work of the commonwealth, who make the laws or administer justice, or whose advice and authority govern the nation in times of peace, and defend it in war. Such men clearly occupy the foremost place in the State, and should be held in highest estimation, for their work concerns most nearly effectively the general interests of the community. Those who labour at a trade or calling do not promote the general welfare in such measure as this; but they benefit the nation, if less directly, in a most important manner. We have insisted, it is true, that, since the end of Society is to make men better, the chief good that Society can possess is Virtue."

d. Since by social life we mean that men live together in mutual relationship, it is bound by the order of values which bind men in virtue of their nature or in virtue of a higher injunction (Qs. 25-7). This claim is widely rejected today, completely so in totalitarian societies.

PIUS XII (C. B. , 1942; C. T. S., 5).

"If social life implies internal unity it does not on that account exclude the differences between men which are grounded in reality and in nature. But so long as we hold fast to God as the supreme controller of all human concerns, both likenesses and differences find their proper place in the absolute order of being, of values, and consequently also of morality. If that foundation is attacked, however, ominous fissures appear in the structure: the various spheres of culture become dissociated from one another; outlines, boundaries, and values become blurred and uncertain, with the result that the decision between opposing policies comes to depend, according to the prevailing fashion, upon merely external factors, and often even upon blind instinct."

In particular:

i. Men do not live in community in order to be thwarted or to develop onesidedly, but for the purpose of attaining a full and complete development and perfection, and always with due consideration for others. Thus social life must aim at the complete scale of values and seek to guarantee them. Communities have no right to obscure, to suppress or to oppose values which pertain to the fulfilment of man's (supernatural) Christian life. The fact that the specifically Christian values transcend the natural (individual and social) life in no way lessens their importance; hence no community has the right to withhold them from men, to advise against them or to make their attainment difficult.

ii. The hierarchical order of values must be safeguarded. Values are not of the same rank; there are higher and lower values. This distinction is no arbitrary one but is based on the substance and the importance of the values themselves as well as on their relative importance for man's development. He who upsets this hierarchical order, placing lower before higher values, bars the way to a balanced and harmonious perfection of man. Such "value manipulations" have been carried out in a large way for centuries up to the present day, for example wherever the interests of the State, national honour, race, economic progress or business are considered and pursued as the supreme value.

iii. Closely connected with their order of rank is the urgency of values, derived from man's needs, so that material goods will be rated the more urgent, since man needs them in order to continue to exist and to act at all. (In this we include food, clothing, housing; hygienic facilities; communications; and the whole range of necessary household goods.) Considering man's life task in its entirety, however, spiritual and moral values are, in themselves, much more urgent because human development depends on them. Material goods are not thereby undervalued but merely put in their proper place. The ordered pursuit and attainment of values ought to proceed in such wise that material values will be sought and procured with a view to the spiritual and moral values, that the spiritual and moral perfection of man will not come to grief because of a want or an abundance of material goods. An excessive preoccupation with material things, whether it be due to poverty or to riches, endangers the spiritual and moral life.

Since different values represent different goals of human activity and endeavour, they inspire a multiplicity of cultural spheres, each of which is limited and independent and governed by its own particular laws. For example, in science, religion, education, law, art, and economics each sphere has its own particular task, and each has to be pursued in the most suitable manner. But, like values, the cultural spheres also form a unity. They are united according to origin and final goal. They are the manifold reflection of the infinite fullness and glory of that one value which is God himself, whose wisdom

149

and power each sphere proclaims in its own way. They are united in their immediate purpose which is to foster human existence fully, to develop and elevate it. They are united among themselves since each sphere is part of the total human good, that totality of values which is required for, and which contributes to, the whole man. It follows from this that, first, the autonomy of individual cultural spheres cannot be absolute but only relative – relative to that of the supreme value which is God, relative as a member in the "cosmos" of values (Q. 5); second, that the unity of these spheres can only be a unity of order in which each occupies the place and has the importance due to it in relation to the others; thirdly, that the community ought not to stifle their individual development but ought to guarantee and support it as far as is consistent with a reasonable general order.

e. Although in the present age the differences – partly justified, partly not – in earnings and possessions are looked on in many quarters as social barriers, yet it must be pointed out that these differences are natural and consequently necessary, being conditioned by a variety of circumstances which will be discussed further in the section on property (cf. Vol. III, Question 24). They include freedom of the human personality, diversity of tasks and achievements, diligence, and thrift. It is utter nonsense to expect unity and concord in social life from complete equality in earnings and possessions. Concord can only be attained by a just arrangement of property; not by a dead level equality, but by a differentiated and just distribution of wealth.

f. Finally we must draw attention to the peculiarities and differences bound up with a particular type of country, with race, national character, tradition and the like which have developed in the course of history and which to that extent are non-essential, but which it is impossible to disregard. Social (and especially political) unity and concord in no way demand that the various racial groups should give up their own way of life, their customs and favourite pursuits (where these do not offend against morality); on the contrary, variety reveals and enhances the worth and the creative powers of the nation as a whole.

46. How is the principle of acting true to nature to be applied in social life?

The norms and dictates of nature must be acknowledged and taken as the basis in establishing and developing all communities, and as the basis of all social schemes and decisions.

THIS principle may appear to be very general and remote, but it is nevertheless one of the most important, and it will come up again for fuller discussion (Q. 50). By demanding that natural and God-given standards be observed, it effectively combats arbitrariness, which is the worst enemy and greatest disturber of all social order.

1. Every existing community and every social activity actually carried out is always singular and unique; community in general does not exist as such ("The" State as such does not exist, but this or that State). But the individual can only be formed and developed correctly under the aspect of the general, that is, when it is so formed and developed, that it conforms to the general nation that is actualized in it. That we recognize this relationship between what is general and what is individual is shown by the following examples:
a. We pity the person who is born deformed or who is afflicted with insanity, because he lacks something which belongs to

"man". We measure him by the notion "man", which tells us that in order to be truly a man he ought to fulfil certain definite requirements and possess certain definite abilities. In this case he ought to be properly formed physically and have the use of his reason.

b. Human labour, no matter how simple, is not just a commodity even though it is looked on as such in the age of capitalism. To be valued merely as a commodity does not do justice to its nature. To be something more than a commodity is an essential note which appertains to human labour as such. All individual achievements and performances are entitled to the predicate "human labour" and therefore they should be valued according to the general norm "human labour". We see then that the general is the basis of the individual and is contained in the latter, and that the individual will develop as it ought only when the general notion is taken into consideration.

2. A social order in keeping with the times is today widely demanded, a type of community which will suit the needs and conditions of the present time. It is clear that the existing situation ought not only to be taken account of, but that it ought to form the starting point and the pivot of planning and social measures. It does not follow from this that the situation must be judged completely on its own merits and without reference to perennial ideals and laws, and that we have to ask ourselves only: What can be done? What is practicable? How can the available resources be most effectively employed? Nor does it follow that we need not ask: Is this way the right one? Can this or that be upheld according to the laws by which men are bound? Is this measure in harmony with, or contrary to, the true goals of human life?

Marxism is a typical representative of *Situationsethik:* its criterion is practicability, whether something can be attained in practice, whether something can be put into practice, whether it works; there is no need to consider it in relation to general fixed norms, in fact such a consideration is harmful and consequently must be rejected. National Socialism also agreed with this principle: "Whatever benefits the nation is right", whether it be consistent or not with the higher laws of morality makes no difference, practical advantage is the definitive norm.

Ideas of this kind are the ruin of all genuine social ethics and reform because they strip social action and social development of all fundamental (both natural and eternal) obligations. When some particular situation is made absolute to the extent that it is allowed to justify and even to demand whatever fits in with the march of events, whether such efforts, hopes or demands be right or wrong in themselves, then the individual will be at the mercy of the moment or of those who know how to take advantage of it.

Why is it wrong to hold that the morality of an action is conditioned solely by a particular situation? Because, as we have already shown, the particular situation is simply made the equivalent of what is reasonable and meaningful and right; because there is no investigation whether the particular situation is in accordance with the general norms which determine and justify it. There is no proper marriage without a prior consideration of the nature of marriage – whether it is indissoluble or only "for a time", what is its purpose, what duties it entails. If this were not to be judged according to natural and general criteria but according to popular opinion, marriage would have no stable basis, and parents and children, occupation and nation, Church and State would be the losers.

153

47. What do we understand by the principle of acting for a proper end?

In social life, too, the end does not justify the means. That is why ends and means may not be fixed arbitrarily but must be chosen and attained or applied respectively in accordance with the norms of the moral law.

ALL human action is teleological, that is, it is directed towards something which has the character of a terminus, of an end. For if a man does not act in relation to some end or object he cannot act at all (he cannot think or will or act). Acting for a proper end implies something more than this; it means that the end must be worthy of man, that the action must be fitting for man. It means in effect that man will strive for what will bring him honour and not disgrace, what will be in harmony with (or at least not contrary to) his nature, with his destiny, and with his real obligations. A robber or a murderer may set about his work with an end in view, in fact he may be very definite in his aims, but he does not act for a proper end, since he is doing something which it is not right for a man to do, and which is contrary to his dignity.

Social action is human action; hence it is subject to the general norms of the latter. Therefore, all social action ought not only to have a goal (and that of intrinsic necessity), but it must have a *proper* goal; it must be a fitting goal for man, one which he will be able to justify before God and his conscience (Q. 17). We know that there are social structures and groups which pursue their goals with fanatical zeal and with an uncanny singleness of purpose, but which clearly and even consciously oppose those goals which are proper for man (for example totalitarian states, criminal gangs (Q. 25).

When acting for a proper end both the individual and the community are bound by the following norms:

1. Man may never act contrary to his final end, either by deliberately subverting it or by putting something else in its place which he considers and declares to be the supreme good and the supreme purpose. Reason and revelation make known to man that God alone and nothing else is his true and only final goal. This automatically condemns all social structures and movements which seek to dethrone God, or to place the ultimate purpose of man (of their members, of their subjects or their comrades) in something other than God. (For example the movement of the Godless; the atheist and anarchist state, the honour of the nation and world domination as ultimate goals of the community; the pursuit of wealth.) It must be stressed particularly that such a subversion is already present where God and God's law is in fact ignored although God is not expressly attacked or an open attempt made to overthrow him.

2. In all his actions a man must be convinced that the goals he pursues as well as the means he chooses are good in themselves, or at least unobjectionable. To put it another way: Considered in its intrinsic and thus in its immediate purpose and object every action must be in accordance with the dictates of a right conscience. The first question is always: Is what I am doing now (what I am taking part in, what is being demanded of me) good or bad in itself, that is, as the matter actually stands, as it is actually happening? Have I a right to do it? Or am I claiming a right which does not belong to me? Natural – and even more so Christian – ethics recognizes actions which are right or wrong in themselves, the rightness or wrongness of which does not come from the right or wrong intention of the person perform-

155

ing the action, but from the very nature of the action itself; hence we speak of objectively good or objectively bad actions.

EXAMPLES. The intentional killing of an innocent person which does not occur in self-defence or in (a just) war (abortion; euthanasia; the shooting of hostages as a reprisal for crimes commited by others); fornication and adultery; denial of God and of the faith; cheating and calumny.

A person acts subjectively free from guilt (wholely or in part) even though the action is objectively wrong, only when he is inculpably ignorant or under strong emotion (which can have several causes: great fear, outbreaks of delirium or passion). Sufficient knowledge and free consent are necessary to render an action subjectively culpable. For the rest, it is immaterial whether the person is acting as an individual or as a member of a community (in the name of the community or in the interest of the community; in co-operation with others). The distinction between the action which is good in itself and that which is bad in itself is valid no less for society than for the individual.

3. A good end (a good intention) can never justify means which are wrong in themselves. The end does *not* justify the means. A means is that which leads to an end, with the help of which a goal is attained, an intention or plan is carried out (for instance, means of transport, means of communication, means of production etc.). Means are not sought and applied for their own sake but as instruments for something else which is the real aim. The idea is very common that we are allowed to use any means whatever provided only that the end is good, or that there are good reasons for it.

EXAMPLES. The white lie, the lie of excuse, sexual intercourse outside marriage when one is "in love", euthanasia for reasons of pity, abortion for reasons of economic hardship. In modern society this error or presumption has led to the sanctioning of the most frivolous and vile practices. They include principles such as "Right is whatever benefits the nation";

"Treaties are valid only as long as they offer an obvious advantage";
"Everyone must toe the party line".

The teaching of certain moralists concerning the role played by
good intention in the morality of human conduct, must be rejected for social life also. The highest principle of this school is that
everything depends on the intention. *What* we do is immaterial as
long as it is done with a good intention. Catholic ethics would
be the last to fail to appreciate and to deny the necessity and the
value of the good intention. On the contrary, it stresses and demands and cultivates the importance of the good intention: "Let
that mind be in you which was also in Christ Jesus" (Phil. 2:5).
But for all that it does not overlook the fact that the action or
deed itself must be good. A man should have the attitude that he
is never under any circumstances prepared to do what is wrong.

4. A wrong end (a wrong intention) devalues and perverts means
that are good. In other words, we may not pursue a morally bad
end or purpose even with morally good means. A means has
its value as derived from the end; because, and in so far as, it
serves the end. If something good or at least not objectionable in
itself is done or used for the sole purpose of attaining a bad end
or to carry out a bad intention, it loses its own value as a result
of the evil of the end (of the intention). Its value is, as it were,
cancelled out. For example, money given ostensibly to help a
poor girl, but with the real purpose of seducing her, destroys
the moral value of the gift. It is not a good, but a bad work,
not an expression of charity but of lust. From this principle,
which can lead in certain circumstances to very burdensome
and very "delicate" decisions entailing a refusal to obey authority,
the following conclusion may be drawn. No community has
the right to demand of its members (subjects) actions with
which it intends to attain immoral ends or (worse still) when

its general aims are all immoral and possibly even criminal. The individual may not support such communities or such actions. As soon as he grasps the situation so clearly that the immoral end and intentions become a certainty for him he must refuse (or at least refrain from) all co-operation and support.

EXAMPLES. Collecting funds which, though outwardly camouflaged, are in fact intended to finance enterprises that cannot be defended in conscience; contributions (and other kinds of co-operation) for organizations, enterprises, and campaigns with atheist or unnatural objectives (societies of the Godless; political parties and movements which are professedly anti-Christian and anarchist in character).

There are two possible exceptions:

i. If a man can be convinced that the support which he gives will be used for good, partial or individual ends, and that this co-operation will not further the bad general aims (for example, skilful exploitation through propaganda; consolidation of the party's position).

ii. When the only intention is to effect a moral change in the group or party and thus to convert it from its false aims. But in this case there must be a reasonable prospect of success. Naturally these prospects cannot be calculated beforehand, and hence the justification for taking a risk. At the same time taking a risk does not mean acting and hoping in an unreasonable and foolhardy manner.

48. *What does the principle of the common good imply?*

The community has the right (and the duty) to do and to demand everything that is required by its common good.

THIS principle is the logical extension of the one which we have just been discussing; because the common good, as we have said already, is nothing other than the end peculiar to the community. Hence the community acts for a proper end when it acts for the common good, when it pursues and attains that for which it exists.

The individual, having been set a goal by nature, is in duty bound to strive for it; but at the same time he is entitled to pursue his own goal and to employ suitable means to attain it. If a number of people set themselves a goal of their own free choosing everyone is at liberty to join such a community or group and thus to subscribe to its goal. But in this case the community or group also must have the right to impose obligations in relation to the goal, to take such measures as are appropriate to the goal; otherwise it would not be able to exist or operate successfully.

It might be feared that this principle gives the community *carte blanche* to impose everything and anything which it considers to be for a proper end. One may be inclined to see in it a kind of justification for totalitarian concepts of society. But these misgivings are unfounded if we recall the criteria given in Qs. 24–7:

1. Whatever is contrary to the nobility and the destiny of man may not under any circumstances be made the goal of a community, that is, be put forward as the common good. All social ends must be compatible with the basic requirements of moral living.

2. The community is competent only in matters which are necessary for the attainment of its own goal; immediately it makes claims reaching beyond what is demanded by its goal it exceeds its powers. (The State has no say in matters of religious belief; a sports club may not dictate to its members how they are to carry out the work of their trade or profession.)

3. The competence of the community is limited to the external order, that is, to whatever external activity is conditioned by the end. We can ask: how are men to regulate their external behaviour in order to attain this goal by mutual co-operation? The community can and should seek to influence the attitude (motives) of its members; but it is not empowered to prescribe legally, to impose or punish, such attitudes.

4. Each community is in duty bound to pursue its end in co-ordination with all other community ends. It pertains to its end also to uphold and to observe the social order in which it is placed. Therefore, it must observe due proportion in its demands so that it will not conflict with the other communities and especially with those which are set over it (Q. 52).

49. What does the principle of authority imply?

The community needs direction that is competent and in duty found to ascertain, lay down and make binding for its members what is required by the common good.

LET us repeat again that the whole is placed over its members or parts. (See also Q. 31.) Within a social whole this superiority has the character of authority, with the corresponding obligation of obedience (on the part of the members). The principle of authority is logically derived from the principle of the common good; because authority finds its justification in the common good (Qs. 34, 38). It is needed, constituted and empowered tangibly to define the common good, and to oblige the members to their individual share of co-operation. Therefore authority must observe carefully the four points noted in the preceding question. In addition there are the following factors:

1. Laws and regulations which have become unjust, inappropriate or pointless in consequence of a change of situation must be abolished or altered as soon as possible – provided, however, that the common good is not thereby adversely affected.

2. The citizen has a right to be addressed and to be treated in a manner worthy of a human being; this includes especially the guaranteeing of his freedom irrespective of any obligations he may have towards society (see the principle of subsidiary function, Q. 52).

3. Those in authority are in duty bound to restore their commission to the community as soon as they recognize that the commission is beyond their capabilities and that a suitable substitute is available. It is also their duty to make provision for the training of suitable persons to whom the leadership can be entrusted when the time comes. Especially where the community has to fulfil important functions and to make important decisions it would be irresponsible if those in authority were to cling to their office in spite of their obvious failure or incapability, and were to neglect training those suitable to take their places eventually. The common good forbids such a selfish attitude, as it requires that personal wishes and interests should be subordinate to it or at least should not be detrimental to it.

4. He who wields authority ought to know that, without prejudice to his position and powers, his function is to *serve* the best interests of the community as a whole. It is not the purpose of authority to prefer one man before others (although it does this), but rather to assure to the community a just order and a useful activity. Hence the person in authority must be exemplary

in seeking before all else to serve the whole (and its members). This willingness to serve must also characterize the attitude of officials in their dealings with the other members – an injunction which is addressed, for example, to civil servants and members of public corporations, but which is not always recognized and followed by them.

It would be an impossible situation if the community itself were to be completely at the mercy of the one who happens to hold authority, without any means of redress or self-defence. The community has a natural right to protect itself against illicit acts of authority and to remedy a situation where an authority carries out (or fails to carry out) its functions to the detriment of the whole. The community may not expose itself and its members to arbitrariness, oppression or brutality at the hands of any ruler; because it is – a fact which must be stressed repeatedly – a unity of order of *men* whose common but genuine human good must be promoted and achieved. It is therefore the community's concern that only honourable goals will be pursued and attained. Otherwise there is a misuse of authority which the community ought to be entitled to stop, unless it would betray its own nature.

There are many legitimate forms of redress and self-defence; yet success must not be the only criterion in deciding on their use. The different character of the various communities must also be taken into consideration. In the case of communities in which the authority is, strictly speaking, irreplaceable (as for instance the family), the higher community has the right to step in under certain circumstances. In voluntary communities there is almost always the possibility of removal or dismissal. The right to oppose the authority of the State is a very delicate and vexed question, especially in the case where terror makes the normal legal method *de facto* impossible.

50. What is the principle of organic growth in social life?

In so far as the inner structure of the community is natural in origin and character it develops from smaller to greater structures.

ON the difference between natural and voluntary communities (associations) see Qs. 27–28.

Nature shows that in growth the greater always develops from the smaller. (The plant develops from the grain of seed; first it is fertilized, then it matures, and finally it unfolds.) The parts of an organism which in the beginning are present only in the germ develop slowly in this process of growth until finally they are there in reality. The organism lives in and from its parts. To remove a part is to destroy the organism or to impair it in its activity. Unprejudiced observation of social life teaches us that the same law operates here although in another form: the family develops from marriage, the community or clan or tribe from the families, and many of these form a people or nation. Communities are therefore not all of natural origin to the same degree; some are nearer to nature than others; nearest are marriage and the family.

This principle of origin and of the corresponding development is not a human invention but is natural, that is, it is laid down by nature (and consequently by God); hence it binds in virtue of a higher authority. Modern social theories have denied this principle and have attempted to prove the opposite. They maintain that folk-lore and history show (even incontestably!) that men lived originally in greater herd-like groups and then later split up, either by mutual arrangement or by command of their rulers, into smaller communities, each with its own aims, tasks, and moral code; habits and traditions also played their part, so that the conviction gradually formed that certain communities were the earlier and more natural compared with others. A striking proof to the contrary taken from our own time is, however, the fact that every attempt, for example, to maintain and to reform a nation on any other basis than that of the family has led to the ruin not only of the family but also of the nation. Thus the nation is based on the family, not vice versa. Pointing in the same direction is the modern depopulation of country districts and the spread of urbanization, which it is now being attempted to halt because such concentrations with their strong levelling tendencies are "unnatural".

The situation is somewhat different in the case of voluntary communities. We can imagine a large community being planned and established and then organized into subordinate or member communities (general organization into branches; a trades union into industrial and regional groups); but in most cases the member communities are part of the original plan, that is, one greater community consisting of a number of smaller communities. Again, there may be smaller communities in the beginning which combine as time goes on to form a greater one. The total community can certainly attain its goal only when it is composed of a sufficient number of vigorous and efficient member communities.

What is the point of having a sports union without the individual sports clubs, a technical high school without the different branches of technical science, a consumers co-operative society without a sufficient number of shops or stores? (See the section on the principle of subsidiary function, Q. 52.)

51. *What is the principle of solidarity?*

The community as a whole and the community members belong to, and are dependent upon, each other ; therefore they are responsible for, and obliged to help, each other.

A social structure is a complete whole. We consider as such only those structures which pursue proper ends and which use no dishonest means (as for example fraud, terror, or any kind of injustice). The people who belong to it are its members. Most social structures are themselves incorporated in turn into a greater social whole. This whole rests on two facts: First, that the structure has an end which is complete in itself and in its proper domain. For example, the end of the family would not be complete in its proper domain if the upbringing of the children were to be taken over by the State. The end may be assigned by nature or it may be determined by the free choice of men. Ends laid down by nature are always complete in themselves. Those freely chosen by men receive their delimitation either from the nature of the object pursued or from the free decision of men themselves. For example, sport can be limited to football or tennis; engineering to electricity or machine tools; industry to iron, textiles, transport, and these in turn will have their various branches.

In the second place the structure should be in keeping with the end and include all those who are associated in relation to the end; because the structure must be such that it makes it possible for all to live and work together.

1. A whole lives in and from its parts, and the parts live in and from the whole. Only when the whole supports its parts and the parts contribute their share towards furthering the interests

of the whole is there a proper order. The relationship is absolutely mutual. If parts are cut off or weakened the whole is damaged or even completely destroyed, according to the importance and the function of the parts. If a part is severed from the whole, the part will lose its existence and effectiveness in that respect in which it belongs to the whole. (To play football properly we have to play in a team; a team needs a definite number and arrangement of players. A childless family lacks something which belongs essentially to a family. A factory in which some work and others idle loses the character of a working community; those who belong to it ought to have a part in its output.)

2. The members of a community are men endowed with reason and free will. Hence the mutual relationship between the whole and its parts has the character of an obligation for both sides and is subject to responsibility. The community owes certain things to the members, the members owe certain things to the community. (Children owe their parents reverence, love, and obedience; parents owe their children love, care, and education.) Community is a moral unity of order (Q. 22). It is possible for whole and parts to act against each other, but they should not do so, rather they should act for one another; in other words, it is in their power, but they have not the right, to injure or neglect one another.

3. As in every whole so also in the community there are three types of relationship (functions, obligations): the relationship of the whole to its parts; of the parts to the whole; of the parts to one another. Accordingly the principle of solidarity requires

a. that the whole should serve its members and should grant them the assistance (support, protection) which they have a right to expect from it;

b. that the members should contribute to the whole whatever is necessary for its existence and progress (sympathy, co-operation, taxes);

c. that the members should regard themselves as members and should grant one another what is due to them as members of a whole (mutual consideration for example in the club, in the factory; brothers and sisters owe one another much that they do not owe to others).

4. Communities stand to each in the relationship of greater (higher) community and subordinated or integrated member community, hence the same laws govern the relationships between communities: mutual respect, support and encouragement; obligation and responsibility of the greater community towards its member communities, of the member communities towards the greater community, of the member communities towards one another. Only in this way can there be a truly natural relationship, only in this way can communities prosper without really endangering or hampering one another, although there may be friction and tension.

52. What is the principle of subsidiary function?

Both the individual person and the member community are entitled (and indeed obliged) themselves to develop their own individuality and to carry out their own tasks; accordingly, the (higher) community is obliged to recognize, to protect, and to promote this individuality and individual activity.

WE may define this law in other words:

1. The (higher) community has not the right to hinder that development and to arrogate to itself those tasks which are

167

proper to, and within the competence of, the individual person or the member communities;

2. Both the individual and the community may (and should) themselves accomplish what they are capable of doing themselves.

This important principle has been defined by Pope Pius XI as the "supreme principle of social philosophy" (Q. A. 79). It was known before his encyclical, but has become increasingly important in recent years.

PIUS XI (Q. A., 75–80).

"It is indeed true, as history clearly proves, that owing to changed circumstances much that was formerly done by small groups can nowadays only be done by large associations. None the less, just as it is wrong to withdraw from the individual and commit to a group what private enterprise and industry can accomplish, so too it is an injustice, a grave evil and a disturbance of right order, for a larger and higher association to arrogate to itself functions which can be performed efficiently by smaller and lower societies. This is a fundamental principle of social philosophy, unshaken and unchangeable. Of its very nature the true aim of all social activity should be to help members of the social body, but never to destroy or absorb them.

The State therefore should leave to smaller groups the settlement of business of minor importance, which otherwise would greatly distract it; it will thus carry out with greater freedom, power and success the tasks belonging to it alone, because it alone can effectively accomplish these: directing, watching, stimulating, restraining, as circumstances suggest and necessity demands. Let those in power, therefore, be convinced that the more faithfully this principle of subsidiary function be followed, and a graded hierarchical order exists between various associations, the greater will be both social authority and social efficiency, and the happier and more prosperous the condition of the common weal."

PIUS XII (S. P., 24–5).

"*If the State takes over and claims for itself all the enterprises of private industry, it forgets that those enterprises are regulated by a multiplicity of rules and standards which are peculiar and private to themselves, and contribute to the due achievement of their purposes. The result is public loss, arising from the damage done to these private enterprises when they are removed from their natural sphere, which is that of private responsibility and private risk.*

A special danger arises from such habits of thought and action. It is that domestic life, the primary and indispensable cell of human society, with all its claims and interests, is thrown into the background; it is regarded as having no existence except in relation to the government of the country. Men come to forget, that they and their families have a priority over the State in the natural order of things, and that a divine Creator has endowed both with their proper rights and powers, destined both for their several functions, corresponding to the fixed exigencies of nature."

PIUS XII (Address of November 20, 1946; U. A. vol. I, p. 187–8).

"*That is why the Apostle of the Gentiles, speaking of Christians, proclaims they are no more 'children tossed to and fro' by the uncertain drift in the midst of human society. Our predecessor of happy memory, Pius XI, in his Encyclical* Quadragesimo Anno *on social order, drew a practical conclusion from this thought when he announced a principle of general application, viz: that what individual men can do by themselves and by their own forces, should not be taken from them and assigned to the community.*

It is a principle that also holds good for smaller communities and those of lower rank in relation to those which are larger and in a position of superiority. For – as the wise Pontiff said, developing his thought – every social activity is of its nature subsidiary; it must serve as a support to members of the social body and never destroy or absorb them."

EXAMPLES. An intelligent master craftsman will allow his apprentices to work independently as far as they are capable of doing so; he will attach great importance to this, encouraging his apprentices to work more and more independently and become masters themselves; we strive to procure to each family a modest home of its own, so that it may develop in its own individual way; an association which embraces several member associations will make only those general regulations which are necessary for its existence, and for the rest, it will respect and promote the individual life proper to each member. Other examples are: efforts towards emancipation of workers, of the laity in Catholic Action, of citizens in a genuinely democratic State.

It is interesting to observe that even totalitarian states, which step by step destroy the independence of individuals and of member communities would like to see their functionaries develop the greatest personal initiative in their own spheres, of course within the limits of the directives given them. The totalitarian State encourages house wardens or cell leaders to spy upon, and denounce, its citizens.

We may conclude from these examples:

Positively: Experience shows that man wishes to do independently what he is capable of doing himself, and that he is convinced that no one has the right to prevent him from doing so. As long as men are not under the influence of false slogans or under pressure from the community they regard as natural, right, and obligatory that no one should encroach upon another's domain, but should let him fulfil his duties independently;

Negatively: Individuals or communities without any desire to exert themselves and do the best for themselves are likely to be despised. Many individuals and communities resent it as improper and unjust when there is interference from above in what lies within their own province, when they are forbidden or prevented from doing what is really their affair. Every measure that bears the character of interference and suppresses tasks which are

170

proper to individuals or member communities, or transfers such tasks to where they do not properly belong, makes it difficult or even impossible to carry out these tasks, it retards progress, leads to rigidity, and works out unfavourably, at times even disastrously, for both parties.

We shall therefore appreciate the principle that both individual persons and single communities should be left to do, and take responsibility for, what is within their capacity and is consequently their proper calling.

This is the simple formulation of the principle of subsidiary function. If the competence or limits of the community are to be defined, the following questions must be very carefully examined and correctly answered: What capabilities for independent action has the individual? What communities have been instituted or intended by nature in order that this or that function may be fulfilled? What is this or that community here for? What is it to do and what is it capable of by reason of its own constitution and order?

1. God is the primary cause of all being and action. He acts in, and through, everything; everything is done in his power. But God allows his creatures to co-operate. It is true that creatures are only secondary causes, but yet they are genuine causes; they themselves act. God reveals his creative power precisely in this, that he endows created things with powers which enable them to act, and that he places the creatures so endowed just where they are able to co-operate. Nature is organically constituted. An organism has different organs for its different functions; within the whole each organ has to make its own definite contribution to the good of the whole.

2. Every creature acts in a manner proper to its nature and this natural manner of acting is likewise given by God with a

171

corresponding obligation. Creatures must work out their perfection in the manner proper to each, and must do so by activity which is in accordance with their nature. Man is an independent person with individual responsibility; it is proper to him, therefore, to act autonomously and responsibly. That implies not only that he has to account for all that he does, but also that it is in keeping with his nature and is his duty to do what he himself is capable of (and not to pass it on to others). There are many things which he must do himself, for example, live morally; other things he can and may do himself in the sense that no one has the right to prevent his acting independently as long as he is able to carry out his task.

3. It is an old principle that "God and nature do nothing without a purpose". God and nature bestow the power of independent action not in order that it should lie fallow or be set aside, but rather that it should be turned to account and used. Man's greatness is rooted precisely in this, that he can learn many things and then do them himself independently, that after sufficient training he has no longer any need for advice and help for every job he has to do. The tailor, the cobbler or the carpenter who is not competent to work on his own is a poor master of his craft. Hence Pius XI said: "It is wrong to withdraw from the individual and commit to the community at large what private enterprise and industry can accomplish." (Q. A. 79).

4. It is seldom realized that communities too among themselves ought to respect this principle. The higher community has not the right to prevent its member communities from fulfilling their obligations independently, rather it must let them do what they are capable of doing. The community is man's creation. Wherever nature allows him the freedom to do so, man must

find the way of realizing his legitimate purposes. Nature shows him the way in its law of origin and development, from lesser to more comprehensive forms of society (Q. 50). Lesser social structures do not derive their rights and their tasks from the greater social structures, but find them in nature, and consequently in themselves. It is true that the greater community is more complete, more "perfect", but for all that it is not prior in origin nor endowed with unrestricted powers in respect of the lesser communities. If God and nature apportion definite functions to a community, it follows from this:

a. that these functions can be fulfilled intelligently, well and profitably only by that community and not by other communities. The State cannot give children the upbringing which they find in the home of their parents, because God has appointed the family and not the State to be the proper place for the upbringing of children; the State has other tasks which it alone can accomplish.

b. that one of the first and most important concerns of the higher community must be to direct its energies towards enabling the member communities to become as fitted as possible for their own proper tasks; the member communities are to be so promoted and fostered that they may ever better serve the real purpose of their existence. Intelligent government will help families so that the children may be properly brought up in, and by, the family.

c. that the member communities render the best service to the higher community when they carry out their own particular tasks faithfully. Through fidelity to its own proper tasks the member community fulfills its obligation of fitting into the greater community and promoting the common good. It may, and perhaps must, assume further obligations towards the whole, provided that it always remains "true to itself". A community

173

that would undertake further tasks at the cost of neglecting its own, would harm both itself and the greater community of which it is a member.

These three principles apply to the entire sphere of community life and not merely to natural communities, although they are quite evident and obligatory in the latter case. A community which embraces several member communities must begin by finding out what the member communities can do by themselves; only then is it in a position to estimate: i. where and in how far it is obliged to help these communities; ii. what must be done to prevent the various communities from hampering either the higher community or one another; iii. to what extent it has to call on the particular services of the member communities (because the whole is capable of existing and operating only when the parts fit in with it, not by the surrender of their own function, but by fulfilling it, and anything over and above this must be subsidiary to, and by way of complementing, their own function). Consequently the (higher) community must exercise moderation. It is not entitled to extend its claims arbitrarily, rather it must recognize the limits imposed on it by nature and confine itself to its own proper functions.

5. Subsidiary function can thus be defined as the "right of the smaller social units" to pursue their own activities and to manage their own affairs. Each community should adopt that form, constitution, or structure which best suits its nature, aims, and functions. It is entitled to develop and carry on its activities in accordance with this form, manage its own affairs, create its own organs and organization. At the same time it is bound by the legitimate claims and measures of the higher community; only that is accounted legitimate which does not conflict with any natural claims and which is really necessary. If a member

community should collapse the higher community may (and in certain circumstances must) step in and see to it that the member community is put in a position by suitable assistance, and even by force if necessary, to discharge its duty. If this is not achieved and if the particular task of the member community is indispensable, then it is permissible and even necessary to entrust this task to others; they must endeavour to carry out the task as far as possible in accordance with the character of the community which is actually competent.

6. It follows that the principle of subsidiary function must harmonize with the principles of the whole (organic growth) and of the common good (Qs. 48, 50), being the highest basic principle, yet not the only one. The superior community has its own goal and its proper pattern which are not without influence on the members within the whole. The parts must develop in harmony with the whole and with their order in the whole. Hence the superior higher community has a double right:

a. of taking care of the requirements of the whole as such;

b. of thus ordering the aims of the parts so that they will stand in proper relationship both to the common goal and to one another. For no one part should push itself forward unduly, but each must have due consideration for the others. This regulating function involves in practice the danger of infringing on the proper rights and functions of the members. Larger communities are all too easily inclined to take over as many domains as possible and to extend their prerogatives more and more. But this abuse need not arise, and the danger can be averted if we remember that:

i. The whole consists not of just any, but of independent, parts and therefore must base its organization and development on the individual character and activity of precisely these parts.

ii. Men have a natural right of free association. Hence while the measure of obligation is determined by the common good, the common good ought to be based on this freedom and ought to use it to good effect. Any hard and fast regulation would be out of place, since the requirements of the common good change with the actual situation, with the acuteness of the danger, and even according to the extent to which men make use of their right of free association.

The principle of subsidiary function applies not only to some particular spheres of social living, to the economic or the political sphere, but absolutely to the totality of community life. Every community, however authoritarian in character it may be or may become, must establish its order and make its decisions on the basis of the actual or attainable efficiency of both the individuals and the member communities; thus regulations should not be made "over the heads of others" but in conformity with the rights and functions of the individuals and of the member communities.

However, the principle of subsidiary function cannot be used in the sense of the "master-in-my-own-house" attitude and by appealing to the right of independence against the endeavours for greater co-responsibility (co-determination). Each individual taking part in some common undertaking must recognize that not only he but others also are capable as persons of independent achievement and responsibility and consequently may legitimately aim at freeing themselves from their position of dependence and being entrusted, as far as possible, with independent functions. In many cases participation in management (Q. A. 65) will provide a solution. Because man is fitted by nature not only to carry out what another has planned and decided but also to counsel and make decisions either on his own or together with others, this natural aptitude cannot be simply ignored by

176

employers who need and use others in producing something by their united labour. The growing emancipation of classes formerly condemned to a position of almost complete dependence makes this problem very actual and pressing.

The principle of subsidiary function has formal significance. Of itself it reveals nothing about what functions and tasks are proper to the smaller communities and ought to be left to them. What these functions are must be learned from the nature, the aims, and the origin (whether, and to what extent, it is natural or voluntary) of the specific community. Historical and other relevant factors ought to be taken into consideration. This formal significance may be interpreted as a weakness and a defect of the principle of subsidiary function. But that would be false, although it is true that the principle is of little use on its own and without relating it to particular aims, values, spheres, and tasks. With this proviso, the principle of subsidiary function will prove its full worth and effectiveness. Its rejection will invariably lead to over-centralization, to the loss of individual rights, and to the wrong extension of power.

177

Part Three

Justice and Charity

SOCIAL life can only flourish when it is based on right and justice (not on arbitrariness and force), and when men practise charity among themselves. Wherever the popes refer to the renewing forces of society they invariably mention the two virtues of justice and charity.

PIUS XI (Q. A., 137).

"How completely deceived are those rash reformers who, zealous only for commutative justice, proudly disdain the help of Charity! Certainly charity cannot take the place of justice unfairly withheld. But even though a state of things be pictured in which every man receives at least all that is his due, a wide field will always remain open for charity. For justice alone, however faithfully observed, though it can indeed remove the cause of social strife, can never bring about a union of hearts and minds. Yet this union, binding men together, is the main principle of stability in all institutions, no matter how perfect they may seem, which aim at establishing social peace and promoting mutual aid."

PIUS XII (C. B. 1942; C. T. S., 8–9).

"This organic conception of society, the only vital conception, combines a noble humanity with the genuine Christian spirit, and it bears the inscription from Holy Writ which St. Thomas has explained (S. Th. II–II, 29 ad 3): "The work of justice shall be peace"; a text

179

applicable to the life of a people whether it be considered in itself or in its relations with other nations. In this view love and justice are not contrasted as alternatives; they are united in a fruitful synthesis. Both radiate from the spirit of God, both have their place in the programme which defends the dignity of men; they complement, help, support, and animate each other: while justice prepares the way for love, love softens the rigour of justice and ennobles it; both raise up human life to an atmosphere in which, despite the failings, the obstacles, and the harshness which earthly life presents, a brotherly intercourse becomes possible. But if the evil spirit of materialism gains the mastery, if the rough hands of power and tyranny are suffered to guide events, you will then see daily signs of the disintegration of human fellowship, and love and justice will disappear – presaging the catastrophes which must come upon a society that has apostatized from God."

PIUS XII (Address, C. M., November 1949).

" The social programme of the Catholic Church is based upon three powerful moral pillars: truth, justice, and Christian charity. To deviate, even for a little, from the requirements of these principles would have been impossible for the Church, even if thereby she had to renounce temporary propaganda successes and to disappoint the passions of the class struggle on one as on the other side. The Church has always favored those who seek the right and need help, but by principle she has never been contrary to any group, rank, or social class, and aims at the common welfare of all members of the people and of the State."

Why is it that justice and charity alone are mentioned, and not the other virtues as well? After all there are a number of other social virtues, and the so-called individual virtues are also very important for social life.

We should answer, that as social life deals with the norms and attitudes which concern the life of men as they live it together, it must consider first and foremost those virtues which take their meaning and purpose from social living and whose proper object is to establish and secure correct human relations. Justice and charity are virtues which by reason of their nature and their essential definition, refer to our fellow-man and to society. (Qs. 90, 112).

Justice and charity are the two basic social virtues. This implies that justice and charity have the widest field of operation imaginable; they are not restricted to any particular class of people or to any particular sphere of social life. Wherever men come together and have to do with one another, they are subject to the claims of justice or, at least, of charity.

Justice and charity – though charity more so, and in a higher sense than justice – are the most immediate and most important motivating forces in society. They command men to act and they take the other virtues into their service. All human endeavour flows from charity, and nature has so fashioned man that both his vision and conscience are particularly sensitive to the values of justice.

Charity – it is with Christian charity that we are concerned – (Q. 113) is so wide and fruitful that it can be expressed in many forms. It has many functions. It can move the will to translate "well meaning" into "well doing", for it is the nature of love to express itself. Charity creates and maintains peace and helps in distress (mercy). Charity warns those who have erred and the wrong doers (fraternal correction).[1] (See Lesson Five of this Part.) Justice is attended by a number of auxiliary and supplementary virtues grouped as it were around it. These virtues (also called subordinate virtues) for particular reasons lack one of the

---

[1] In order to grasp the full significance of charity we should read the "canticle of love", 1 Cor. 13, in which in a form beyond compare St. Paul enumerates the qualities, blessings and obligations of charity.

essential notes of strict justice. Nevertheless they are very important since it is their function to make men disposed to take on a wide range of obligations arising from particular circumstances, and to shoulder the various responsibilities of social life which are not strictly speaking obligatory, but which make social life attractive. St. Thomas Aquinas lists the auxiliary and supplementary virtues of justice as follows: loyalty (towards parents, home, country), respect, reverence, obedience, gratitude, truthfulness, courtesy, generosity (II–II, 101–19).[2]

That the virtues serving the direct control of the individual's interior and exterior conduct (fortitude, including courage and intrepidity; temperance, including sobriety, chastity, gentleness, modesty) are also of the greatest importance, for social life is neither denied nor weakened by the stressing of justice and charity. In the social context these virtues have indirect significance: firstly because only the man who lives an ordered life can fulfil his social obligations properly; secondly, because the personal life of the individual must necessarily affect social life either by furthering or by retarding it. Good and evil leave their mark and are not without wider influence, even though this influence may be difficult to ascertain with precision; thirdly, because the external acts of these virtues can be covered by laws and rights, thus in respect of the common good coming under the jurisdiction of the society (Q. 107).

[2] The most excellent of the subordinate virtues of justice is worship of God (II–II, 81–100) the meaning and purpose of which is to render to the Lord the service due to him. It is not specially mentioned as it has no immediate bearing on the matter under consideration.

Lesson One

RIGHT IN GENERAL

THE importance of Right was stressed by Pope Pius XII in his Christmas message of 1942:

"If social life, such as God wills it, is to attain its end it needs a legal structure for its supports, defence, and protection. The function of this structure is not to dominate, but to serve; to encourage the development and vital growth of society in the abundant variety of its aims, promoting the full achievement of private enterprise in harmonious collaboration, and protecting it by suitable and legitimate means against anything detrimental to its full expansion."

"He who would have the star of peace to shine permanently over social life must make every effort towards the restoration of a juridical constitution."

"The modern idea of justice is often corrupted by a positivist and utilitarian theory and practice subservient to the interests of particular groups, sections, and movements; the course of legislation and the administration of justice being dictated by their policies. This state of affairs can be remedied only by awakening the human conscience to the need of a juridical constitution based upon God's sovereign lordship and immune from human caprice; a constitution which will use its coercive authority to protect the inviolable rights of man against the aggression of any human power. A constitution conformable with the divine will gives man a right to juridical security, and accordingly grants him a sphere of rights immune from all arbitrary attack."

53. *What is meant by "right"?*

"Right" denotes that which is just, that which is strictly and equally due to other men.

1. THERE is universal agreement that right denotes something to which someone can lay strict claim; a thing or an achievement which must be acknowledged as his, not something which one merely wishes him or grants him, but which is his due. Hence the expression: "I have a right to this", meaning that it is my due, I can demand it. Right concerns giving, leaving or restoring to others what is their due. A right can be formulated and if this is done it is not a matter for arbitrariness or discretion. Right thus exceeds what is merely permitted or fitting; it signifies what has to be done or granted unless that which is due to others is to be denied to him or contested. In short, the object of right is that which is strictly due (Q. 57).

2. There is also agreement that right intends, and aims at, equality. Right implies that a debt should be "settled", that the *whole* debt should be paid. If someone owes £ 20 and pays back £ 12 he has satisfied only a part of the right due to the other person; the obligation to pay the rest remains. What is given back must be equal to what is given.

3. Right is an objective factor, it does not depend on opinion or attitude but rather it attaches to the thing, to the facts and factual relations. Even where something is settled by voluntary agreement, as soon as the agreement is concluded the matter is no longer at the discretion of either party. The employer must pay to the full amount the wages to which he has bound himself by contract.

54. What do we mean by title?

By title we mean the authority to make use of our right.

WE are entitled to do, claim or possess that which is our due, to which we have a right. Every legal title presupposes an objective right. Legal title is co-extensive with right on which it is based. The legal title is nowadays called "subjective" right.[3]

Thus legal title is the logical and necessary consequence of right. For it would be pointless to have an objective right which the individual is not entitled to recognize and use. The decisive point is that title is always a question of moral and not merely physical power. For if the individual were to be allowed to demand and to carry out whatever he is in a position to do by physical power, without having to consider moral rectitude and lawfulness, then brute force would become the basic principle of community life, "might is right" it would be announced, and there would be no appeal and no effective protection against it (Q. 59).

55. *Must there be Right?*

Human dignity and social order demand that there must be Right.

PIUS XII (C. B. 1942; C. T. S., 6).

"If social life such as God wills it, is to attain its end it needs a legal structure for its support, defence, and protection." (See quotation on p. 183.)

[3] There has been a lamentable confusion, indeed, falsification, of ideas ever since the sixteenth century. Right in its objective sense (meaning the just thing, what is due to others) has fallen into disuse. In its place it has been claimed that what is now called subjective right is right in its proper and original sense. Yet the contrary is the case. Right in the proper sense is what is just; whereas subjective right (legal title) is right in the derived and metaphorical sense. St. Thomas Aquinas, for example, who treats of the question of right thoroughly and in detail, undoubtedly knew what we mean by subjective right, but he did not regard legal title as right. Discussing the question: "What is right?", he enumerated the various meanings of the term "Right" (Latin: *jus*), without mentioning legal title (see II–II, 57, I). The reason is that right belongs to the category of relations (equality) whereas "title" signifies moral ability, permissibility, freedom.

THERE are many considerable errors current concerning the origin and meaning of right, its validity and scope. Only anarchists who hold that complete lawlessness would bring about ideal social conditions, would maintain that there is absolutely no need for right.

Our answer implies two important arguments:[4]

i. Right follows necessarily and immediately from the dignity of the person. For if there were no right of any kind it would be a mockery to talk of the dignity and intrinsic worth of the individual, since man would then not be able to lead a human life. Nothing would be sacred. He would be entitled to nothing.

ii. Without right, social order is unthinkable; chaos and terror inevitably reign. Ordered conditions are conditions safeguarded by right (Q. 59).

56. What is the purpose of Right?

Right is meant to serve men in the execution of their many tasks; above all their highest life's task.

See Pius XII as quoted on p. 183

1. RIGHT is no end in itself; rather it has the character of a service and of a means. It forms one of the indispensible conditions of man's capability of living a virtuous life, acting with a proper final end in view, and so attaining both his own perfection and his highest good which is God. Thus right presupposes the natural destiny and the natural ability of man in relation to his extrinsic and intrinsic goal. In virtue of his nature man is obliged to pursue the good or, more precisely, the human good (Q. 26). By doing good he must preserve and develop the disposition toward good which he has received from nature. Neither he

[4] They will be referred to again in connection with the natural law (Q. 65).

186

himself nor anyone else can release him from this obligation, and it can be discharged effectively only when the individual is able to carry it out unmolested, when he is permitted to pursue all that belongs to the God-given integrity of his life.

2. Related to this general task the life of man embraces various partial or individual tasks which either ought to, or may be, done. Right secures the measure of necessary or reasonable freedom. We call that freedom "reasonable" which is either given to man as a natural (supernatural) legacy or can be allowed him without disturbing social life. Accordingly right extends to many provinces: for example, the right to be respected protects our good name; the right to property serves a just distribution of the goods of the earth; the right to freedom of conscience is a safeguard against unwarranted interference in our lives. All these individual rights have one single aim, namely to assist man on his way to the good and thus to his real happiness.[5]

3. Men live in community and do so by reason of their nature. As we shall see presently (Q. 57) right has to do with men in their relations with one another, that is in so far as they live in community. The common good (Q. 27) implies the good, that is, the virtuous life, as the ideal which concerns and binds all, not only each one individually, but also in being the motivating reason for unity and order among men.

Hence right includes not merely a social element; it is not merely "social" in a marginal sense, but in its whole nature and purpose since its chief object is to guarantee the realization of the common good's order of values.

Thus, to put it briefly: right has a regulating function; it is

[5] Because of the importance which the good, or the end, has in our discussion of right, we might point to the intimate connections between right and morality.

to create and preserve order among men in relation to the total purpose of human life and of the human community.

PIUS XII (Address of 5 August 1950; C. D. II, 32).
"Each keeps, and should keep, its freedom of activity within such limits as place no hindrance to the common weal."

57. In which cases does the question of right arise?
The question of right arises :
i. When other persons are involved,
ii. When something is due,
iii. When what is due can and ought to be restored. [6]

1. ONLY a person and not a thing can be the subject of right, that is, can have a right; things are merely objects of rights. A right which does not belong to a person is no right at all. The subject of right is always the person in relation to another person (not in relation to himself). It is essential that this second person should be involved formally as another person, that is, as someone who as an independent partner confronts the subject of the right on the relevant level.

EXAMPLES. Buyer and seller, employee and employer, accused and judge, citizen and head of the State. In all these relationships man is a free individual, which means not only that he has a free will and is capable of personal responsibility, but also that he does not belong in some form to the other person, for example, child and parents, husband and wife, servant and master.

For in so far as men are bound together by degrees of relationship or by

[6] This question, the answer to which has already been indicated in Q. 53, is very important in order to distinguish right and justice from similar (cognate) virtues and relations, and also to have a standard with which to be able in individual cases to judge whether, and in how far, something should be considered to be right or only adequate and opportune.

being members of a household, they do not claim right from one another but show one another devotion, attachment, loyalty. This is also true of neighbours and supporters of a cause.

2. Right (that which is just) as well as justice, the object of which is rights, (Q. 89) depend on the concept of due (Latin: *debitum*). St. Thomas distinguished between moral and legal due; we are concerned with the latter (see II–II, 80). All virtues impose on man the obligation of doing what corresponds to them. Thus charity demands that a man should be charitable; patience, that he should control himself; gratitude, that he should make some return for the benefits he receives. In these and similar cases man "owes" it to himself and to his own moral perfection that he should behave as is in keeping with the particular virtue. But no one (except God) faces him as a claimant or creditor in such cases. He is a debtor to no one in the sense that he injures the clear and definite right of another person by not repaying debt. On the other hand, when and wherever it is a matter of something belonging to another person as being due to him, a new situation arises; the individual "owes" because and in so far as he is obliged to acknowledge and to return to the other person what is his, what the other is entitled to claim from him. Something is owed by right (or legally, see Q. 58) when it is the exclusive property of one (or several) or when it must be made over to him (them) exclusively.

EXAMPLES. The salesman of goods has as right to be paid, the worker has a right to his wage. This objective claim turns the customer or employer into debtors, and binds them strictly to the corresponding defrayment.

3. In the cases of purchasing and wage contacts, for example, we speak of the "equivalent value", which means that service and payment must be exactly equal if the matter is to be just. Right postulates and creates equality. It demands that everyone should

receive what is his, and should receive it not merely just anyhow but according to the full measure of what belongs to him and is due to him, or to the full value of the service he had given. Both what exceeds this amount, as what falls short of it, departs from right either by exceeding the right, or as an infringement by falling short of it. The very purpose of right is to establish and secure equality among men, and in fact that equality which they owe one another and which consequently they are entitled to demand from one another. (On the different kinds of equality and their importance see Q. 93.)

4. It must be emphasized that the three conditions which have been discussed are essential to right and must be present if it is a question of right in the true and strict sense. Hence when any one of the three conditions is absent there is right in a broader and less proper sense and therefore only a subordinate or auxiliary virtue, but not a special kind of justice. We repeat therefore:[7]

i. Parents and children, husband and wife, belong together (to one another) in such a way that they are not like other related persons, "equals". Of course, all are human persons and thus right proper may obtain among them. For example a father may not mutilate his children, punish them when they are innocent, or forbid them to profess the Catholic faith. He may not require of them to tell lies, steal, swear a false oath. But the family and the household as such are not ruled by strict right but rather by reverential and mutual loving consideration.

ii. There are many occasions when men meet one another as independent persons and when they are also in a position to make an equivalent return for what they receive; but this return has not the character of the strict debt. We may give a

[7] See II–II, 57, 4; 80, 1.

present in return and of the same value for what we have received. We may be equally friendly, candid, or generous as other
people but we should not be doing wrong by not respond-
ing in such a manner, since nothing of what is his due is taken
from the other person. Virtues such as gratitude, politeness,
generosity, candour, belong here.

iii. Finally there is the case where something is strictly owed to
another person but where there is no possibility of giving him in
equal value what is his due. Adoration, thanks and expiation are
due to God our supreme Lord, but no creature can give God as
much as it owes him. Devotion is due to parents and to our
country, but we always remain "indebted" towards our parents
and our country.

58. Is there a norm for right?

**The norm which indicates and determines what is
"of right" we call law ; natural law and human law are
especially important.**[8]

LEO XIII (L. P., 7).

"First of all, there must be law; *that is, a fixed rule of teaching
what is to be done and what is to be left undone. This rule cannot
affect the lower animals in any true sense, since they act of necessity,
following their natural instinct, and cannot of themselves act in any
other way."*

LEO XIII (S. C., 8).

*"Law is of its very essence a mandate of right reason, proclaimed by a
properly constituted authority, for the common good. But true and*

---

[8] This and the following questions are meant only to supplement the general
teaching on law; they will be treated in more detail later (Qs. 66–8; 76–7).

legitimate authority is void of sanction, unless it proceed from God, the supreme Ruler and Lord of all. The Almighty alone can commit power to a man over his fellow men; nor may that be accounted as right reason which is in disaccord with truth and with divine reason; nor that held to be true good which is repugnant to the supreme and unchangeable good, or that wrests aside and draws away the wills of men from the charity of God."

SAINT Thomas described that which is due as, "legally due",[9] in so far as it is distinctive of right and of justice, because law pronounces and determines what must be held to be a man's due; at the same time law imposes the obligation of recognizing and acknowledging this "due". Law is the norm and the measure of human conduct. It sets forth and decrees what must be done by man in relation to others (God, the community, fellowmen) so that everyone will be given his due.

The natural law, which is the primary and inescapable norm of human communities, expresses what is rooted in the nature of man or in the nature of things. (For example, material goods are in themselves capable of being equated in value: we can estimate the equal value of two horses, fields, or houses by an exact comparison.) See Lesson 2 p. 197 et seq.

In many cases men can agree among themselves on what they owe to each other (wage contracts), in others society or its authority decrees what the citizens owe to it or to one another. Agreements and decrees of this kind must not be contrary to what is due by natural law (which they are for example when services of unequal value are decreed to be of equal value,or when fraud, extortion and the like are employed); see Lesson 2.

[9] See II–II, 80, 1; 109, 3; 114, 2.

192

59. What is the relationship between Right and might?

Might is not the basis of Right, but rather Right is the basis of might. Hence might is subservient to Right.

PIUS XII (C. B., 1940; U. A. vol. I, P. 14).

"Victory over the dismal principle that utility is the foundation and aim of law, and that might can create right. This principle is bound to upset all international relations and is unacceptable to all weaker nations. This conception does not exclude the desire for the honourable improvement of conditions or the right to defend oneself if peaceful life has been attacked, or to repair the damage sustained thereby."

EXAMPLES. When someone forces another to accept unjust conditions of work and wages by exploiting the other's needy situation; when the press uses its influence to spread untruths; when someone demands exorbitant prices because he knows that the customer has no choice but to take the commodity.

PIUS XII (C. B., 1941; C. T. S., 5–6).

"Setting aside all reasonable restraint or consideration, the domination of external force and the mere possession of power override all the laws of order which govern human intercourse, those God-given laws which determine the natural and supernatural relations between justice and love in individual and social life. The conception of might as the source of right deprives both the human person and the associations which he forms with others of their natural dignity and status."

1. If might were the basis of right, then right would become the plaything of might, and would lose all genuine validity. For he who wields power could create and abolish right as he pleases; as soon as he felt himself powerful enough to subject men to his demands his will would become law.

2. On the other hand, right must be enforceable, because it concerns the external order of human relations in so far as it has to establish and guarantee due equality among men. Because of differences of opinion and especially of possible resistance (crimes, infringement and denial of right) this guarantee is only effective where might supports right, sees that right be done and intervenes in case right be not done. Thus it is customary for the constitutions of associations, societies and institutions to contain some form of penalty for negligent, disloyal and refractory members. This shows that transgressions (disloyalty, irregularity, laziness) may be prevented by pressure, and that it is the general conviction and practice that breaches of rule justly require atonement or reparation.

A variation of "might is right" is the principle of totalitarian states: "Right is what is advantageous to the people." True, it is not in so many words might that is set up as the highest norm; and the principle could be true if "advantageous" were intended in the true sense of the word and its value seen and sought in correct relation to other values (Q. 45). However, as totalitarian states claim the right to determine for themselves what benefits or harms the people, and as they are determined to enforce ruthlessly their own decisions as being right, might actually becomes the primary thing and will do away with right. What remains are sham rights for the people and the well guarded privileges of the ruling caste and their followers.

PIUS XI (M. S., 34.)

"Those human laws which are irreconcilably opposed to natural law have an innate defect which can be cured neither by compulsion nor by any external display of force. By this standard we must judge also the fundamental principle: 'Right is what is advantageous to the people.' It is true a right meaning may be given to this principle

if it is understood to mean that what is morally illicit can never be to the true advantage of the people. Even ancient paganism recognized that the maxim to be perfectly accurate should be inverted and should read: 'Nothing is ever advantageous if at the same time it is not morally good, and it is not because it is useful that it is morally good, but because it is morally good it is also useful' (Cicero, De Officiis iii. 30). This fundamental principle, cut off from moral law, would mean in relations between states a perpetual state of war amongst the various nations; in the life of the State it confuses advantage and right, and refuses to recognize the fundamental fact that man as a person possesses rights given him by God which must be preserved from every attempt by the community to deny, suppress, or hinder their exercise. To overlook this truth is to lose sight of the fact that the true common good is ultimately defined and discovered from the nature of man with its harmonious co-ordination of personal rights and social obligations, as well as from the purpose of society which is determined by the same human nature."

Bureaucratic regimes may further emphasize the unfortunate unlawful distinction of the relationship between right and might. Bureaucracy is rampant not only in all modern governments but almost everywhere where extensive (and even quite modest) administrative tasks have to be carried out. By making everything dependent on its own inquiries and decisions, on forms to be filled in, on exact adherence to official procedure, and on all kinds of other conditions, bureaucracy has taken on an importance to which it has no claim whatever. It "regulates" and rules to the point of unreason. Instead of remaining an organ of assistance and service it becomes an organ of compulsion and power.

60. Are rights lost through misuse?

He who misuses his right will not forfeit it by that fact alone; but under certain circumstances he may be restrained from the exercise of his right.

PIUS XI (Q. A., 47).

"Hence it is a mistake to contend that the right of ownership and its proper use are bounded by the same limits; and it is even less true that the right of property is destroyed or lost by its mere non-use or abuse."

WE may have rights and not use them. We may make good or bad use of our rights. I have the right to demand back a watch which has been taken from me, but I can, if I wish, renounce my right. I can use my money for good or bad purposes. Thus we must be careful not to confuse right with legal usage. There may be various reasons for not using a right: voluntary reasons (for example, renunciation out of magnanimity or the spirit of sacrifice, but also because of indolence, ill-will, avarice, hard-heartedness) and involuntary reasons (for example lack of common sense, or when someone is forcibly restrained from or deprived of doing something). Misuse in the real sense, depends on a free decision; objective misuse needs no free decision; as for instance, when a drunkard or mentally deranged person wounds or kills another with his weapon.

Right is not necessarily lost either by not being used or by misuse. A right is that which is due to a person because it is his; it does not cease to be his by the mere fact that he does not or cannot use it, or uses it unreasonably or improperly. His link with something that is his own is not destroyed by its not being used or through its misuse. In fact, there are some inalienable rights which an individual may not renounce, even voluntarily (Q. 82). At the same time right is essentially social. It concerns human relations. Besides, it is by no means a matter of indifference to social life whether and in what manner men make use of their rights (alcoholics and the insane not infrequently become a danger to the community; the spoken and written word can have evil effects). Thus social grounds as well as considerations for, and necessities of, the common good may require that anyone who misuses his rights or who is not in a condition to use them rationally should be either permanently or temporarily prevented from using them (legal disability).[10]

Lesson Two

NATURAL RIGHT AND HUMAN RIGHT

As we have already stated (Q. 59) right cannot be based on arbitrariness and power. Its validity and strength must come from itself. Its own nature must place it beyond the will and the interference of men, otherwise order and security will not be guaranteed. Thus we may inquire whether there are legal norms and legal claims which are independent of human opinion and human institutions and which bind men in virtue of a higher, a superior authority, and if so, where they are to be found? This important question concerning natural right and natural law touches the heart of social life. A correct answer ensures healthy and fruitful social life, whereas a false answer exposes the community to ceaseless trials and tribulations.

The question is as old and as universal as mankind itself. It represents the continuous search for "eternal" laws; the tenacious and indefatigable defence of fundamental rights which are independent of changing views and currents. It is both remark-

[10] A more detailed discussion of this question follows in subsequent sections where the different provinces of law are dealt with in detail.

able and significant that even its sworn opponents are for
ever being forced to fall back on the detested natural law and
to acknowledge its validity.

The Popes have continually and very emphatically stressed
the necessity and the importance of natural right. As proof of
this let the following few texts suffice; there are any number of
papal pronouncements on particular matters in which natural
right is referred to and invoked.

PIUS XI (M. S., 34).

*"It is a trend of the present day to dissociate more and more, not
only moral teaching, but also the foundations of law and justice
from true faith in God and from the revealed commandments of God.
Here We have in mind especially what is usually called natural law,
written by the finger of the Creator himself on the tables of man's
heart (Rom. 2:14, etc.), which sound human reason not blinded by
sins and passions can read on these tables. By the commandments of
this natural law every positive law, whoever may be the lawgiver,
can be tested as to its moral content and consequently as to the lawfulness of its authority and as to its obligation in conscience."*

PIUS XII (S. P., 29–30).

*"Nothing less is demanded, Worshipful Brethren, by any inter-
national understanding which is to be properly guaranteed and reasonably secure of permanence, nothing less is demanded by the need
for fruitful alliances, than a due recognition of the basic principles
of international law, and a determination to abide by them. And these
principles enjoin that each nation shall be allowed to keep its own
liberties intact, shall have the right to its own life and economic
development; further they enjoin that any pact which has been
solemnly ratified in accordance with the rights of nations shall persist,
unimpaired and inviolable."*

PIUS XII (Address of 11 November 1948, C. D., I, 20).

"There must be an express acknowledgement of the rights of God and of his Law, at very least of the natural right. This is the basis of the rights of man. Unless they are anchored to religion how can such rights and freedoms be safeguarded in one order of peace?"

PIUS XII (Address of 13 November 1949).

"The juridical order must again become part of the moral order without transgressing its limits. Yet the moral order essentially is founded in God, in his will, his holiness and being."

It is evident that in this Handbook the question concerning natural law can be put and answered only from the point of view of Catholic social ethics. We are thus referring to what is generally known as "Christian" natural rights. It is Christian because:

i. It is acknowledged in its complete rightness and validity by Christianity.

ii. Quite apart from its natural origin and content it can be completely and correctly known only with the help and guidance of supernatural Christian revelation.

iii. It is, and ought to be, considered in its relation to the Christian aims and norms of life.

PIUS XII (P. B., 1941; C. T. S., 4).

"The dictates of the natural law and the truths of revelation are like two streams, not contrary but concurrent, flowing by different courses from the one divine source. Also the Church, the custodian of the Christian supernatural order in which grace and nature converge, has the duty of instructing the consciences of men, including the consciences of those who are called upon to find solutions for the problems and duties arising out of social intercourse."

It would, therefore, be wrong to take Christian natural right as of itself belonging to Christian supernatural revelation and the Christian way of life. For in that case it would not be natural but would have to be supernatural. And it would follow that outside Christian revelation there would be no knowledge of good and evil, of right and wrong, which is undoubtedly contradicted by our experience and our conviction. But we must consider the actual situation in which men have always found themselves, and find themselves even today, when they are left to their own guidance and researches. Unless revelation and the teaching office of the Church show the sure way, natural right cannot be presented in its totality and without falsification, nor can it be correctly incorporated into the order of life as instituted by God.

The two questions which immediately follow are intended to show on what depends our knowledge of natural right, and where the "right" natural right is to be found.

61. *Who can acknowledge genuine natural right?*

Natural right can be acknowledged only by those who :

i. Acknowledge God as the creator and sovereign Lord of the world,

ii. hold that human reason is capable of knowing.

PIUS XII (H. G., 15).

"Notoriously, the Church makes much of human reason, in the following connections: when we establish beyond doubt the existence of one God, who is a personal Being; when we establish irrefutably, by proofs divinely granted to us, the basic facts on which the Christian faith itself rests; when we give just expression to the natural law which the Creator has implanted in men's hearts; and finally,

when we would attain what understanding we can – and it is a most fruitful kind of understanding – of the divine mysteries."

THOSE who deny God, or fail to acknowledge him as the creator of all things, can certainly come to a knowledge of some natural truths but not of all, and it is just those truths which matter which remain hidden from them. They lack especially the possibilty of giving the ultimate basis, the "mainstay", of the natural truths and norms of life. They will never be able to establish why it is that these commandments bind absolutely and inescapably. All reasons and sanctions which do not take the creative and sovereign power of God into account are, at the most, of a penultimate nature; they leave open the question of the why and the wherefore. Neither the consent among men and nations, nor the objective validity of values, nor the argument that otherwise the community would fall into disorder and disintegrate, is sufficient. These arguments are certainly not without weight, but they impose no ultimate responsibility. A way out of the difficulty is sought by simply calling in doubt and refusing to accept that natural right could imply or impose such a degree of responsibility.

There ought to be a natural way of knowing a "natural" right, that is, our reason ought to be able to conceive the natural meaning and the natural order of life and of the entire world. Those who deny that our nature is capable of this, and who consequently hold that the inner nature of the world and of our own soul is inaccessible to reason and remains a closed book, must deny natural right, or at least they leave it an open question (at most they will say: perhaps it is so, but we can never know!). The Catholic Church has always defended the capacity to know what is naturally good and true, and she values this capacity as a precious and indispensable gift from God.

62. Is there but one natural right?

There can only be one natural right, though in fact there are the most diverse and contradictory interpretations of what should be natural right.

NATURAL right undoubtedly means "the right of nature". And since human nature is the same in all men, the right which derives from it must be one and the same for all. However, since men's ideas of what "nature" is differ considerably and often even contradict each other, it is not surprising to find many and diverse notions of natural right. Each interpretation of "nature" is bound to result in a view of "natural right".
The following are the most important of the false views of natural right:

i. The materialist idea of natural right as advocated by Darwin, Haeckel, Büchner, Feuerbach and their followers. It is based on the materialist sciences of the nineteenth century, and blindly applies their tenets to man and human society. (The struggle for existence, natural selection, pure causal explanation of nature.) In this view man is a material being; soul and mind are mere functions of matter. There is no higher being to whom man is indebted for his existence and to whom he is responsible. This materialism is too crude to need a refutation; it fails to understand practically everything in, and about, man.

ii. The individualistic idea of natural right of the age of Enlightenment and of the age of Liberalism which followed it (Hugo Grotius [1583–1645], Thomas Hobbes [1588–1679], Christian Thomasius [1655–1728], Jean Jacques Rousseau [1712–78]; and in more recent times, in a modified form, what is called the empiricist school of law represented by German writers such as A. Merkel, K. Binding, Jellinek, Gierke, F. von List). They advocate the individual's absolute freedom and sovereignity and regard law as completely independent of morality (this was held especially by Kant), and obligation as based solely on social contract. These views are based on the false doctrine of man as a naturally good creature unaffected by original sin and consequently not in need of redemption. The social nature of man is completely neglected. Freedom is falsely understood to mean absence of restraint so that all true responsibility goes by the board. Taken as a mere total of sovereign individuals the community is denied any real value. It follows that self-interest will be expressly acknowledged and cultivated (unrestricted striving after gain and power, "elbow room", unbridled competition, the right of the fittest).

This extreme form of legal positivism denies the validity of natural right and maintains that there is no other right than that which men establish in virtue of their own authority. This form of legal positivism has been unequivocally condemned by the Popes:

PIUS XII (C. B., 1942; C. T. S., 7).

"Among these is to be counted a legal positivism which invests purely human laws with a majesty to which they have no title, opening the way to a fatal dissociation of law from morality."

PIUS XII (Address of 13 November 1949).

"Legal positivism and state absolutism with it have altered and disfigured the noble countenance of justice, the essential bases of which are law and conscience."

iii. The Marxist-collectivist idea of natural right is represented in a more or less clear-cut form by various Marxist trends; in its most extreme form it has been put into practice in Soviet Russia and its satellite states. This philosophy assigns absolute priority to the collective. Man is regarded as no more than the product of economic and social conditions. Personal immortality, the freedom of the will and all original personal rights are denied. The materialist interpretation of history, economic determinism, considers all historical development to depend on the law of necessity. The collective is the only source of right, hence it is obvious that might comes before right, that established law is not based on higher norms to which the collective and its rulers would be subject and that the Christian faith and indeed all religious belief is clearly and totally rejected (Militant Atheism, Movement of the Godless). In our view Marxist collectivism violates the nature of man and deprives it of its rights, destiny and vocation both in the individual and in the social aspects. We ought not to be deceived by the fact that Marxism contains elements of truth, that it has forcibly brought home to men the importance of history and their responsibility towards history, that it has achieved (in part directly, in part indirectly) much in its struggle for the proletariat. Its strength lies to a not inconsiderable extent in a faith in its messianic mission which is, however, completely confined to this world and is materialistic in its orientation.

iv. The moral and social teaching of the Protestant Churches treats natural law with a deep-rooted distrust, and, in fact, largely rejects it on principle. In quite recent times there has, however, been a welcome tendency among Protestant writers to recover the ancient Christian meaning of natural law. Protestant opposition to natural law is bound up with its conception of original sin and justification. Human nature is considered to be so corrupted that in religious and moral matters man is robbed of all ability to recognize and to do what is naturally right. Fortunately this negative attitude is offset to some extent by the fact that the Protestant Churches acknowledge Scripture as the word of God, and Scripture contains many natural truths which God has made known to man within his divine dispensation, for example, the Ten Commandments. Unfortunately private interpretation does not allow clear and definite pronouncements and decisions by a single teaching authority in the many and complicated cases of doubt what must be considered natural law and thus permanently binding. However, both the various pronouncements of the Protestant Churches, as also their social and ethical literature, show with surprising clarity that while natural right is doctrinally rejected, arguments are, nevertheless, frequently presented which are in reality based on natural law. For example, when general norms governing the duty of the family, of the state, of ownership, are established, which are not derived from sacred Scripture but are deduced from the nature of the family, of the state or of ownership, there is certainly an acknowledgement of natural right.

63. What do we mean by "natural" in the term "natural right?"

"Natural" denotes the essential nature of man in so far as it is the basis and the norm of human conduct.

OUR understanding of natural right depends inevitably on the correct interpretation of "nature". But as this term is used in various (at times even contrary) senses it will be necessary to examine some of its many meanings.

FALSE AND TRUE MEANING OF "NATURE"

1. We speak of nature in the sense of "God's creation" meaning the visible universe, the sun and the stars. We speak, for instance, of the process of growth and change in nature, or of order in

nature. Taken in this sense "nature" is not completely outside and beyond natural law, but it is not immediately and properly covered by the term "natural law", because in natural law we are dealing with the nature of man. Creation comes into this only in so far as man is part of it and in so far as other created things concern him, though this relationship will be primarily and essentially considered from the point of view of man and not of things.

2. Less loosely we speak of nature as the subject matter of the natural sciences, as the world of external and internal appearances which man is able to observe, record, influence or to change. It is the vast region of all that can be measured, weighed, used and "split", and in addition, everything that happens in man himself in so far as it is accessible to exact research, to the art of observation and experiment, for instance, in biology. We do not here use the word nature in this sense although human conduct in`relation to it would have to be covered by some natural right. For these observations, although they may be carried out with the most accurate of instruments, with the greatest experience and skill and may show the most astonishing results, will not really tell us what man is and what is his nature. The observations and experiments carried out by the sciences on man himself can never give us an insight into his innermost being, his likeness to God, the unity of body and soul, because such an "insight" implies a knowledge transcending the limits of experience, no matter how varied how revealing and valuable.

3. We also speak of nature as opposed to spirit. Various schools of modern philosophy describe nature as that which is not spirit, and spirit, or mind, as that which is not nature. At the same time they fail to give an exact explanation of either. If we were to start from this meaning of nature, we should arrive

at a completely false notion of natural right. Man consists of both corporeal and spiritual elements; not only the body (matter) but also, and in a certain manner even more absolutely, the spirit, the spiritual soul belongs to his nature. In the term "natural right", we use "natural" as meaning the complete essential nature of man.

4. There is also a sense in which nature is distinguished from "culture". Culture then means that which man has made of nature through labour. Thus nature means all that which is at the disposal of man to be worked on and formed and ennobled by him, and by which man shows what he can achieve especially in technology and art. This is not the meaning of nature implied in "natural right". It is too vague and ambiguous; it is not immediately, or at any rate not clearly enough, related to man.

5. Again nature is used in contrast to the supernatural, to "grace" in the Christian sense. In this context nature denotes all that which is proper to man and all that he is capable of simply as man by reason of the fact that God has created him a free, intellectual being and equipped him to act as such. The supernatural denotes the divine excellence which God has given man as a free gift of His divine love, to which man himself has no claim, and which elevates him to a mysterious participation in the divine nature and the inner life of God. This is a reality and a vocation to which no creature of himself could possibly attain, but which God gives to man, and in which God gives himself in love. This meaning of nature is correct but as yet too indefinite since it includes everything in and about man, which belongs in any way to his own specific being, life, conduct, experience, down to his personal temperament and inclinations and the social side of his nature.

6. There is finally the sense in which nature denotes an essential attribute so far as this forms the basis of a specific mode of acting and shows this mode of acting to be obligatory. St. Thomas Aquinas uses "natural" in this sense when he speaks of natural right and natural law. Catholic social ethics has followed him in this teaching which is in harmony with the Christian tradition.

But the point will need further explanation.

FURTHER EXPLANATION OF THE CORRECT NOTION OF NATURE

1. Like all created things man possesses certain basic elements and characteristics which he must necessarily have in order to be human (Q. 12). There are many things in and about man, which he does not need to have either at all or to any definite degree without calling into question the fact of his being man. He must be able to think, to will, to love, to hate and to feel; otherwise he is not man at all. But a man may be old or young, tall or short, famous or not, learned or not; he may be intensely emotional or the reverse, he may understand something of farming or mining, he may be a friend of this person or that. These things may be of importance for his whole line of conduct, but that he is a man does not depend on any of them. He can develop quite well independently of any particular one of these possibilities.

2. All the qualities and abilities with which a man is endowed are rooted in the unity of body and soul. It is this unity which constitutes man, makes him to be a man. For man is what he is because he has a body and a spiritual soul or, to put it another way, because he is endowed with reason and senses (see Q. 12). This "sentient rationality" we call the nature of man. Hence those elements and powers which are essential to man necessarily

result from this nature and are indissolubly bound up with it. Everything else in man is non-essential, it pertains to the talents or the "destiny" of this or that individual, but not to man as such. Hence in order to establish man's natural rights and claims it will be necessary to work out the basic disposition of his essential nature, and so arrive at the content and order of natural right. This is discussed in Qs. 72–4.

3. Like all created things in their own way, man also has very definite activities which are peculiar to his essential nature and are therefore "natural". He is inclined and predisposed to them by reason of his human nature and of his particular powers. To put it in another way: his essential nature is the basis and the norm of action in keeping with his being. It is the basis, that is, this action (conduct) results from his nature which is the principle or source of certain particular powers; it is the norm, the decisive measure to which his conduct must correspond, in order to be true and good.

4. Finally, man is related to everything that is above, on a level with, and below him; this is not of an arbitrary character but must be in accordance with his essential nature. As man he is incorporated into the whole of creation and into society precisely in a human manner. This also pertains to his "nature" because it is necessarily derived from it.

To sum up: "natural" in "natural law" denotes the essential nature of man in so far as it enables, assigns, and commands him to do certain things.

64. What then is natural right itself?

Natural right is that which is due to man in virtue of his essential nature; or that which man can consider and lay claim to as his own because he is man; or the

sum total of those rights which are due to man not in virtue of human institution but in virtue of his essential nature ; or man's right to do and to demand that which he is entitled to do and to demand in virtue of his essential nature.

THE immediate opposite of the notion of nature which has just been discussed is formed by *human* ordinance, enactment, authority. What is due to man by reason of his nature can be acknowledged or disregarded by man, but it can neither be granted nor abolished by him. The reason is obvious: man's nature is not dependent on the will or the action of men. It is not in their power to determine what it is that consitutes a man. This is fixed once and for all by the order of nature. It is true that men are descended from one another, and thus are the efficient cause of those they bring into existence. But it is not for them to plan and to stipulate whether what they bring into existence is to have, or to be denied, body and soul, intellect and free will, sensation and temperament; all this lies outside their power and is subject to a higher dispensation and higher laws.

Thus it is clear that natural right is something *in* man. Natural right is often taken to mean the sum of those legal axioms which summarize and formulate this right which man possesses. But it should be noted that the term natural right is then used in an improper (analogical) sense.

65. Is there such a thing as natural right at all?

The existence of natural right is so certain that it leaves no room for reasonable doubt.

LEO XIII (R. N., 5, 6, 8).

"For every man has by nature the right to possess property as his own. . . . Man precedes the State, and possesses, prior to the formation

*of any State, the right of providing for the sustenance of his body. . . .
With reason, then, the common opinion of mankind, little affected by
the few dissentients who have contended for the opposite view, has
found in the careful study of nature, and in the laws of nature, the
foundations of the division of property, and the practice of all ages has
consecrated the principle of private ownership, as being pre-eminently
in conformity with human nature, and as conducive in the most
unmistakable manner to the peace and tranquillity of human existence."*

PIUS XII *(S. P., 23–4).*

"Our learned Predecessor, Leo XIII, in his Encyclical Immortale Dei
*has explained the purpose for which the Creator of the world instituted
the authority of the State. It exists, he says, to govern the commonweal according to the prescriptions of an order of things which is
immutable, because it reposes on the universal laws and principles
which govern it. If it does that, it will help the individual human
being to achieve his own perfection in this present world, in all that
concerns his physical, mental, and moral well-being, and so promote
his attainment of his supernatural end."*

PIUS XII *(P. B., 41; C. T. S., 8).*

*"Every man, as a living being endowed with reason, has received
from nature the fundamental right to use the material goods of the
earth, though the implementing of that right is left to be more particularly determined by human contrivance and by the juridical
enactments of peoples. This personal right can in no circumstances be
suppressed, even by other rights over material goods, however certain
and admitted they may be."*

PIUS XII *(Address of 13 November 1949).*

*"Not even the most profound and most acute of juridical sciences could
establish other criterion in order to differentiate between unjust and just*

laws, between simple juridical law and true right than that which can be derived from the nature of things and of man by means of natural reason. That criterion is the law which the Creator has written in the heart of man (cf. Rom. 2:14, 15) and which explicitly has been confirmed by revelation."

1. THE actual proof is quite simple and clear. Man is designed and intended by nature to be happy and good, to act intelligently and freely, with a consciousness of reponsibility, to live in community, to make use of material goods. Man seeks by nature to preserve and to protect his life with primitive vehemence and determination. He defends himself spontaneously against attacks which threaten his life. Thus there are certain aims, arrangements, and activities which are natural to man, which belong to him intrinsically, which spring from his nature and which must be fulfilled and carried out if he is to live and develop in the particular manner proper to him. To put it another way: Much is demanded of man and much is granted him for the reason that, being specially talented and disposed, he is obliged to pursue very specific goals and activities. Man remains true to his own nature, lives "humanly" and develops to be a complete man only when he carries out the activities imposed on him by nature and observes the order of things laid down by nature. Only a development which is in accordance with nature can be called right and ordered, and it alone guarantees harmonious progress and perfection.

2. Now man is not just a thing but a person; by reason of his spiritual nature he is not an object, but a subject of right, a holder of rights. Hence what necessarily belongs to his nature and what his nature consequently demands, is due to him in virtue of natural right, as something which nature acknowledges as his. Hence he has claims in this respect which are not given

to him by men, but with which he is born and which must be acknowledged and respected by men. This argument (see also Q. 55) may be supported by the following facts and observations:

a. Even though they may differ in interpreting and establishing the fact, men generally agree in the conviction that not all right springs from human institution or agreement.

b. The very people who would deny and seek to abolish natural right scientifically are for ever having to have recourse to it.

c. It is a very significant fact that we are constantly appealing to natural rights without perhaps being aware of doing so. The following very common expressions are particularly enlightening and convincing: "That goes without saying"; "it is just not done"; "that is simply the duty of the family, of the State"; "the State has no say in the matter!" Such common usage shows clearly how everybody recognizes the validity of rights which do not depend on the favour of society but are of a higher origin.

66. Are there norms for natural right?

The norms for natural right lie in the natural law and in the eternal law of God.

PIUS XII (S. P., 12).

"This natural law reposes, as upon its foundation, on the notion of God, the almighty creator and father of us all, the supreme and perfect law-giver, the wise and just rewarder of human conduct. When the willing acceptance of that eternal Will is withdrawn, such wilfulness undermines every principle of just action. The voice of nature, which instructs the uninstructed and even those to whom

213

civilization has never penetrated, over the difference between right and wrong, becomes fainter and fainter till it dies away. Nothing is left to remind us that we shall one day have to give an account of what we have done well or ill, before a Judge from whom there is no appeal."

LAW is the norm which determines and declares what is due, and what consequently must be acknowledged as a right (Q. 58). Law is an ordination of reason, enacted with a view to the common good by him who has the care of the common good and consequently possesses the corresponding authority.[11] Every law contains two elements.

i. It points out what is to be done; thus it discloses a certain state of affairs, makes something known.

ii. It ordains that something be done, it commands, prescribes, decrees; it urges to action with an appeal which has the force of an obligation.

Human nature is the basis and the norm of natural right. But how is man to know what this nature tells him, what rights it grants him, and what duties it imposes on him? Who tells him that his nature demands this and refuses that? Law and right must coincide. Natural rights can only be based on natural laws and be known through them.

Natural law in turn raises the question of its origin and source of authority. Is the natural law sovereign, and does it bind of itself? Or is it merely the expression and the organ of a

---

[11] See St. Thomas Aquinas, I–II 90, 4; also Leo XIII (*L. P.*, 7): "On the other hand, as was said above, he who is free can either act or not act, can do this or do that as he pleases, because his judgement precedes his choice. And his judgement not only decides what is right or wrong of its own nature, but also what is practically good and therefore to be chosen, and what is practically evil and therefore to be avoided. In other words, reason prescribes to the will what it should seek after or shun, so that man may attain his last end for the sake of which all his actions ought to be performed."

higher law? Only when natural law and natural right are attributed to an authority which is absolutely sovereign and from which all obligation ultimately derives, are they firmly established and unassailable. This highest authority we call the eternal law.[12]

By showing that there is natural law and an eternal law we refute those views which seek to give another basis to the juridical order. Legal positivism (Q. 63) acknowledges only those laws which are promulgated by men themselves, laws which possess no authority higher than a human one. Germany has experienced the evil consequences of the Nazi regime's attempt to set up a so-called "healthy public opinion" as the highest norm of all right and of all juridical order. Apart from the fact that public opinion is in itself much too uncertain and vague, there is also the particularly ominous and disastrous factor that it can be put under pressure and misdirected in whatever way is desired by clever propaganda and the use of terror.

PIUS XII (C. B., 1942; 16–17).

"A constitution conformable with the divine will . . . supposes: b. clear legal principles which cannot be upset by unwarranted appeals to a supposed popular sentiment or by merely utilitarian considerations."

67. What is the eternal law and what does it mean?

The eternal law is God's wisdom in so far as it orders and guides towards an end all activities and all that happens in the universe.[13]

---

[12] St. Thomas Aquinas I–II 91, 1; 93. Since the natural law can be understood only from the eternal law, we shall first explain the eternal law in the questions immediately following, and then the natural law.

[13] This definition follows closely what St. Thomas Aquinas wrote concerning

LEO XIII (L. P., 8).

"Foremost in this office comes the natural law, *which is written and engraved in the mind of every man; and this is nothing but our reason, commanding us to do right and forbidding sin. Nevertheless all prescriptions of human reason can have force of law only inasmuch as they are the voice and the interpreters of some higher power on which our reason and liberty necessarily depend. For, since the force of law consists in the imposing of obligations and the granting of rights, authority is the one and only foundation of all law – the power, that is, of fixing duties and defining rights, as also of assigning the necessary sanctions of reward and chastisement to each and all of its commands. But all this, clearly, cannot be found in man, if, as his own supreme legislator, he is to be the rule of his own actions. It follows, therefore, that the law of nature is the same thing as the* eternal law, *implanted in rational creatures, and inclining them* to their right action and end; *and can be nothing else but the eternal reason of God, the Creator and Ruler of all the world."*

THERE are two unassailable truths from the point of view of the believer in God. First, that God's providence rules over all things created by him. Second, that nothing can exist or happen which has not been foreseen in God's plan and which does not come under God's providence.

the eternal law *(lex eterna)* especially in the *Summa Theologica* I–II 91, i;93. In developing this teaching St. Thomas himself closely followed St. Augustine. In the language of the theologians and philosophers a distinction is made between "eternal" and "divine" law, although of course the eternal law is divine and the divine law is eternal. The expression "divine law" is used to denote the law revealed in the Old and New Testament, in other words, that law which God himself gave and made known directly to men especially through his only begotten Son, Jesus Christ. (See Q. 76.)

216

This all-wise plan of God is called the eternal law in so far as it is the norm proclaiming and motivating divine providence.[14]

1. God sees all things in himself, in his own nature in so far as the latter is the eternal image of all that is or can possibly be.

2. From the infinite multitude of possible worlds God freely chooses one which he intends to make actual; he plans one of the worlds preconceived in him.

3. Such planning pertains to both the intellect and the will. The plan is the practical norm according to which the things which are called into existence are guided, that is, directed towards their several goals and towards the total goal intended by God.

4. The total goal that alone is worthy of God consists in giving glory to him, and this can be attained either by bearing mute witness to God, in an unconscious, unfree manner (as in the case of irrational creatures – all creatures apart from angels and men) or by bearing eloquent witness, knowingly and in loving devotion (as in the case of rational and spiritual creatures –angels and men). God has set each creature the immediate goal corresponding to its nature, and has given it its own proper manner of acting. He directs the world in such wise that all things are able to attain their own proper goal and by so doing contribute to the attainment of the total goal. Thus in pursuing their goals and in being faithful to their own proper manner of acting, creatures carry out the plans and the ordinances of God and obey the eter-

---

[14] We should like to mention in passing that men make a mental and verbal distinction between God's wisdom, God's world plan, and the eternal law although of course there is no such distinction in God himself. In him all attributes and activities are completely one and are identical with the divine nature.

nal law. By reason of his free will man has, of course, the possibility of refusing to obey God, of placing immediate ends before and above the total goal, and in this way of dishonouring instead of honouring God.

But it should be clear that man is not in a position to frustrate God's plans. God infallibly attains what he plans and intends, in spite of all the arbitrary and erring ways of his creatures. They can in no way surprise him, for he has seen through them and reckoned with them in his plans.

Man can of course rebel against God and against his commandments, but he may not do so. He is bound to submit to God in all things; his conduct is good only in so far as it conforms with the eternal law, whereas the eternal law is in itself intrinsically and necessarily good.

From what has been said we can, and must, draw the following conclusion, which ought to inspire all legislation and jurisdiction without reserve: All just laws have their origin from the eternal law and bind in virtue of it; no law can be just which is not in conformity with the eternal law.[15]

68. How is the natural law related to the eternal law?

"Natural law is nothing but the participation of rational creatures in the eternal law."

1. THIS answer is taken literally from St. Thomas Aquinas (I–II 91, 2). It implies that creatures endowed with reason are subject in their own way to the eternal law. Theirs is not a purely passive role, but rather they actively co-operate in the directive function of the law. Because they have reason and free will they are themselves fitted and obliged to judge and to decide what

---

[15] St. Thomas Aquinas, I–II 93, 3 esp. *ad* 2.

they must do and avoid. Irrational creatures, on the contrary, are "driven", they are inwardly bound to follow their nature, its goals and inclinations.

St. Thomas further implies that God has infused his light into human reason so that man is enabled to see and to grasp clearly certain basic truths and dictates of moral living without having to seek and to investigate (Q. 72). Besides, human reason is capable of discursive thinking, that is, from the known basic truths it is able to draw conclusions; from the more general norms it is able to infer further authoritative and directive norms for particular spheres of human conduct (ibid.).

2. Our experience shows that there are judgements concerning moral conduct which are self-evident to man, which man cannot question because they are immediately evident to him. Anyone who is in possession of his mental faculties knows without much reflection and with complete conviction that he may not do wrong; hence the evasion and excuse: "this is not really wrong;" hence the attempt to gloss over and to justify to oneself conduct which one knows very well to be wrong, but which one does not wish to discontinue.

Our experience further shows that we are continually inferring from more general norms less general ones which regulate a more restricted sphere of our moral conduct. From the self-evident axiom that we may not do another an injustice, we infer that theft, fraud, calumny are not allowed because injustice is done by them to our fellow-men. It is enlightening and significant that we do not justify their unlawfulness by saying for instance that they are forbidden by society, but rather that they are bad in themselves. This is an obvious sign that we bear within us, as it were, natural moral commandments which we must of necessity acknowledge.

3. The proof that there is a natural law, and what is meant by it, is based, then, on the following considerations:

God has so fashioned human reason that it is capable of recognizing the truth and is disposed and inclined to do so, that is, to form objectively true judgements. This ability and this inclination extend both to the sphere of pure knowledge and to the sphere of action.

All knowledge of truth and all human conduct would be irretrievably abandoned to uncertainty, to error and doubt and failure if there were no primary and universal truths immediately evident to our reason. For example how should we know and be able to state that 3 is not equal to 4 if we did not see and were not absolutely convinced that this proposition (3 = 4) implies a contradiction in terms and that what is self-contradictory cannot be true? Thus our reason *must* – and the order of creation established by God demands this – be so fashioned that it will form these first and highest principles clearly and correctly without reflection and without being able to withold its assent, that it will grasp the primary basic notions and immediately, without further reflection and without hesitation, form its first absolutely certain judgements. Immediately a man grasps the two notions "whole" and "part", he judges with unshakable conviction that the whole is greater than the part. In so far as this innate ability of our reason relates to the highest principles of action and of conduct it is called "original conscience" (Q.16, No.1). Original conscience is then the original disposition, the original facility of our practical reason: it makes known the first principles of human conduct.[16]

[16] See St. Thomas Aquinas, I–II 94, 1 *ad* 2. By "disposition", or "facility", is meant the perfection, the enrichment of a faculty. A disposition (facility) puts the faculty in a condition to carry out surely and easily that for which it is designed. Human reason is such a faculty, given and designed for the purpose of knowing,

From these highest principles of which, in the nature of things, there can only be very few, reason infers further principles and conclusions. In this process the further it moves away from the highest principles, the more difficult is its task and the more carefully it has to proceed. But we are still dealing with what are called self-evident truths, that is statements or propositions which are evident in themselves even though their universal validity and the assent to them may steadily diminish (Q. 75). For various reasons (for instance the insinuation of false motives, carelessness, deliberate aversion, passion) we may be led astray also where it is a question of well-established truths. However, so far as a judgement of our reason can, even if only with great effort, be recognized as right and valid of itself, it belongs to the natural norms of human conduct.

EXAMPLES. Many people cannot see or do not want to see that *every* lie is unlawful. And yet this follows from the "nature" of a lie as a conscious departure from the truth. Many dispute the fact that people with hereditary diseases may not be sterilized. And yet this lies in the nature of such a measure, which means a highhanded intrusion into the domain of a higher authority. That suicide and euthanasia can never be permitted is largely, and even very definitely, denied. And yet this follows necessarily from the truth that God alone is Lord over life and death.

4. We mean, then, by natural law: the highest and most general judgements concerning good and evil, right and wrong; or

that is, of grasping, of judging, of inferring one thing from another. In order to be able to do this with ease and reliability it must be disposed, perfected, by practice. For example it is difficult at first to solve arithmetical problems, but it becomes increasingly easier with practice until finally it demands practically no effort. God, in his wonderful wisdom and providence, has ordained that in order to form the most general judgements no "practice", no repeated examining and checking over, is necessary, but rather that the disposition (facility) accompanies the first "illumination" of reason so that the highest principles are present from the beginning and are ready to be employed at the first awakening of reason, and never disappear thereafter.

221

the primary natural moral truths by which man by immediate apprehension knows himself to be bound; or the norms of human conduct which are self-evident to reason, together with the general conclusions which can be inferred from them; or the dictates of human reason concerning that which man should reasonably do and avoid in virtue of his nature and because it is his duty.

To sum up: natural law is the order in human nature which has been pronounced obligatory by human reason.

LEO XIII (L. P., 8).

"*Foremost comes the* natural law, *which is written and engraved in the mind of every man; and this is nothing but our reason, commanding us to do right and forbidding sin.*

Nevertheless all prescriptions of human reason can have force of law only inasmuch as they are the voice and the interpreters of some higher power on which our reason and liberty necessarily depend. For, since the force of law consists in the imposing of obligations and the granting of rights, authority is the one and only foundation of all law – the power, that is, of fixing duties and defining rights, as also of assigning the necessary sanctions of reward and chastisements to each and all of its commands. But all this, clearly, cannot be found in man, if, as his own supreme legislator, he is to be the rule of his own actions. It follows, therefore, that the law of nature is the same thing as the eternal law, implanted in rational creatures, and inclining them to their right action and end; and can be nothing else but the eternal reason of God, the Creator and Ruler of all the World."

5. In order that this important point should be very clearly understood, we would add that the Catholic Church and Catholic social ethics hold very definitely that Holy Scripture clearly

and expressly testifies to the existence of the natural law, even though others – in particular the Protestant Churches – vigorously disagree, and seek to explain in another sense the texts quoted in its support. The two most important texts are found in St. Paul's Epistle to the Romans.

Rom. 1:26–7: ". . . and, in return, God abandoned them to passions which brought dishonour to themselves. Their women exchanged natural for unnatural intercourse; and the men, on their side, giving up natural intercourse with women, were burnt up with desire for each other; men practising vileness with their fellow-men. Thus they have received a fitting retribution for their false belief."

In this text a clear distinction is made between natural and unnatural conduct; the natural is considered and represented as ordered, the unnatural as disordered (vile). Thus sexual relations are subject to a natural law, and whoever breaks this law acts vilely because he disobeys the law of nature. The apostle has just been asserting (19–21) that "from the foundations of the world men have caught sight of his invisible nature, his eternal power and his divineness, as they are known through his creatures". Thus St. Paul speaks of a *natural* knowledge of God and expressly adds that for those who have not come to know God in this way and as a result have fallen into the vilest depravities "there is no excuse".

Rom. 2:14–16: "As for the Gentiles, though they have no law to guide them, there are times when they carry out the precepts of the law unbidden, finding in their own natures a rule to guide them, in default of any other rule; and this shows that the obligations of the law are written in their hearts; their conscience utters its own testimony, and when they dispute with one another they find themselves condemning this, approving that. And there will be a day when God (according to the gospel I preach) will pass judgement, through Jesus Christ, on the hidden thoughts of men."

St. Paul says clearly that the Gentiles, who do not possess the law revealed in the Old Testament, were nevertheless in a position to know the precepts of the law, thus to know of themselves what the law demands, and to know this only by reason of the fact that the contents of the law were written in their hearts. But what is written in the heart[17] of man is that which man is able to know of himself, what nature teaches him, and to learn which he does not need a special divine revelation.

The apostle reduces to a common denominator what was universally binding on all peoples when he says it was "written in their hearts" so that their conscience utters its own testimony; "finding in their own nature a rule to guide them". Thus they are able of themselves to distinguish good from evil. Before they received the law through Moses the Jewish people also had no law in the sense that the moral law, which was known to them in a natural way, had not yet been made known to them in a more special manner by God; this happened in the Mosaic and subsequent legislation. Prior to that the Jewish people was certainly bound by what is naturally good and right.

Placing the natural law in the human reason does not in any way mean debasing it to a mere product of reason, to something purely subjective. A law is a proposition having the form and the character of a command. As such it can only be formed and expressed by reason. But reason is related to reality, it is open and subject to reality. It seizes upon what really is; abstracts, judges, relates, and commands in accordance with what is. Hence the natural law, too, is known from human nature,

---

[17] In Semitic languages "heart" has the meaning of knowledge.

discovered and as it were borrowed from it (Q. 73–4). And this is not contradicted by the fact that the most universal principles are "spontaneously" evident to reason. Because the primary notions (the ones we first come to know), are also derived by reason from the world of actually existing things. Happily God's wise and kind providence has formed reason in such a way that at its first contact with reality it is so illumined that it cannot be deceived by illusion or subjective opinion.

It ought to be clear from our exposition that the term "natural law" means something quite different in ethics (including social ethics) and in the sciences. Within the latter there is also reference to natural laws; in fact they consider it their proper task to investigate and to discover the natural laws. But while in ethics we understand by the natural law imperative propositions which bind man in respect of his ultimate goal and the decisions he has to take relative to this, the natural laws established by natural science can only show us what takes place in nature. On the strength of sufficient observation and experiment they tell us what norms characterize the happenings of animate and inanimate nature; they tell us that one kind of union or mixture will result in another kind; that the stars follow their course as a result of certain fixed conditions; that in electricity like poles repel while opposite poles attract. These natural laws are, then, the expression of the causality and finality which God has implanted in the irrational part of his creation and to which all things are subject. In this Handbook the term natural law is always used in the ethical sense.

69. What is the first precept of natural law?

The first precept of natural law is : we must do good and avoid evil.

1. WE shall have to establish first of all that in natural law there must be a first precept. There are of course other commandments that follow this; but both our knowledge and our actions must begin with one general principle. There cannot be several principles right at the beginning since this would immediately give rise to the question of priority: which is the first? Now the remainder can be reduced to the second and third etc. On the other hand the great diversity and range both of knowledge and of action show that further principles follow on the first. They necessarily point to the first principle since they depend on it and their compass is determined by it.

Let us take as an example the precept "Thou shalt not steal!" Why not? Because we may not do another an injustice. Why may we not do another an injustice? Because it is evil, and we may not do what is evil.

2. The will is that faculty which aims at the good. At the same time it is the faculty which moves man to act. The will can only will and move in respect of the good, for it cannot deny its own proper object, since this would mean denying itself. The good is nothing else than the real so far as this is the goal of any endeavour and will. Endeavour and will aim at something that really exists, not at something that is merely imaginary. The worker does not work for an imaginary but for a real wage, for the wage actually paid out to him; the person in want seeks real, not imaginary, assistance. Evil is the contrary of good, it is that which conflicts with, and nullifies, the good. Evil offends against the basic tendency of the will. It is the lack of the good. When something is not present when it should be there is a lack of the good, and therefore evil. Thus the will is attracted by the good so far as it follows its natural designation and tendency. On the contrary it abhors and must avoid evil so far as it remains

true to its natural tendency. The will cannot go beyond the contrast "good - evil", because to act at all it cannot go outside the sphere of its own proper object. What is more, the will can never pursue evil as such. It pursues everything under the aspect of good. It is true of course that the individual can will or do something although he knows very well, and is quite conscious of the fact, that it is evil and therefore that he should not will or do it. But in all such cases he gives the evil the appearance of good and pursues it under the aspect of good. This rather striking and puzzling phenomenon is connected with the fact that on the one hand the will is free, while on the other hand it is dependent in all its actions on the reason which presents to it the object of its willing. Human reason is subject to deception and error, and the will can therefore make false decisions. But the will is never bound to submit to a judgement of reason. It can even move the reason and inveigle it into being subservient to it so that the reason will as it were turn and twist something evil until it takes on the appearance of good under the aspect desired by the will. Then it can be presented to the will as something desirable. We can easily verify this. The case is, unfortunately, familiar, of the man who is shocked at first by some suggestion because he sees that it is unlawful and perhaps even criminal, and then, giving in to the temptation, begins to lull his conscience and to find reasons for it until finally he persuades himself that it is "not so bad".

3. The precept that we must do good and avoid evil implies the statement: good is that which can be aimed at and may be done; it is the only proper and justifiable goal of willing; evil may never be aimed at or done, or can be aimed at or done only under the pretext or appearance of good. Also implied is the command that good has to be done. The will may not

remain indifferent or inactive when confronted by good; it must move towards it and seek to attain or achieve it.

The practical significance of this precept is that it obliges man to action which is both subjectively and objectively good. Because the commandment is expressed in such general terms many consider it unpracticable and useless. This is a foolish and insidious error! As experience shows, we are constantly appealing to this precept; we use it as the criterion for checking our decisions and conduct. This is shown by the type of questions we ask ourselves: Is this good? Can I therefore justify it? Why may I not do this? After all it is good!

The precept binds under a twofold aspect: First in so far as the individual may only do that which he judges to be good; no one may act unless he is convinced that his action is right; and this conviction must be honest, that is, the individual is obliged to form his judgement with the seriousness called for by the matter in question. And only then may he act. Thus the precept is the subjective norm of conscience.

Second, in so far as the individual must strive with all available means to will and to do what is actually good in contrast to what he merely considers good, what only appears good to him. Thus the precept is the objective norm of conscience. This also corresponds to the general conviction of men. We are quite conscious of the fact that our actions, in order to be incontestably right, must be right in themselves and not merely according to our own estimation. The obligation to do what is objectively good is based on the fact that the good coincides with the real, as also on the fact that the perfection of man depends on an objective ideal of the good or of virtue.

70. What actions are covered by natural law?

All those actions which must be considered naturally good and which can be known as such are covered by natural law.

HERE we encounter some considerable difficulties which must be discussed and clarified step by step.[18]

1. In many cases a person can know by himself immediately or after a moment's reflection what is good and what is evil; but sometimes it is only after taking serious counsel with himself or with others, presuming of course that he does not allow himself to be dissuaded by interior or exterior influences from forming the right judgement. A child knows very well that it does wrong when it hits or kicks another child. A boy who steals will admit straight away that he knew very well that he should not steal. We cannot be disabused of our conviction that we are obliged and justified to preserve and to defend our lives. Unless they are simply bad or deluded, parents will resist any attempt to take from them the responsibility for their children. Thus there are judgements concerning right and wrong which are much more definite than the general statement that we must do good and avoid evil, and which are nevertheless immediately evident to the reason. Whoever grasps what it means to steal will immediately form the judgement: You may not do this!

2. This "natural" knowledge extends to all those judgements which are a result of right thinking (are free from error), and of a deeper insight into the essential nature of man. Thus it extends to all judgements which are not based on human injunction, institution or habit. What is legal and valid, because it is decreed

---

[18] See St. Thomas Aquinas, I–II 94, 2; C. G. III, 129.

by men or formed by habit and custom, is no longer "naturally" knowable, because, in order to know it, we have to consult human legislation and man's way of life.

EXAMPLE. That a motorist may not run over another person is self-evident and therefore naturally known. But that he should drive on the left and overtake on the right or vice versa is known to him only from particular traffic regulations.

This is a very important point, because it gives us the criterion for deciding whether something is covered by the natural law or by human law. In cases of doubt, and they are not infrequent, we must consider whether a particular precept can be known and deduced from the natural contingency of things and events, or whether we know of it only because it has been decreed by men or because it has been adopted by custom.

EXAMPLES. Take the right of parents in the school question. Have parents the right to decide to which school they should send their children because they are the parents, or because the State has given them this right? Again, take private property. Has the individual a right to private property because he is a man, or because the State does not forbid it? Or divorce: Is marriage indissoluble in itself, or because men have accepted and established it as such?

3. Judgements concerning good and evil, right and wrong, must be incontestable. They must be supported by proper and well-established principles. The question why one thing should be naturally good and another naturally evil can be validly answered only by pointing out that human nature thus requires it. Human nature comes from God and therefore it is good. We shall then have to find out what aims are inherent in human nature and for what activities man is intended by virtue of his human nature. The designs of nature are revealed in natural

230

propensities, because man is inclined by nature to those activities which are natural to him, that is, which are not acquired from an extrinsic source, but which flow from his nature, and for which his nature fits and prepares him. Natural aims, therefore, have the character of natural good. Man must, or may, do what they demand; he must avoid what they forbid.

It is important to note that we refer only to what is naturally good, and not to all that is good. For there is good which nature leaves to man's personal choice. Thus a man is free to decide what profession he will take up, how he will arrange his work, how he will regulate the affairs of his home, whether he resides in this or that place, how he spends his leisure, and many other things. But this freely chosen good may not conflict with the aims and norms of nature. There is in particular that good which man is obliged to do by a direct commandment of God and the Church. God's commandments are contained in the Old and New Testaments. While the Old Testament lays down laws which, to a large extent, relate directly to the natural development and perfection of man, most commandments of the New Testament are of a supernatural kind not only in their aims but also in their content. They command something which in itself transcends natural powers, and which as such belongs to the realm of grace. Examples are, to believe, to be baptized, to practise charity, to attend at the sacrifice of the Mass, to take up one's cross. Much of the moral law in the Old Testament has been stated more clearly and supplemented in the New Testament.

The demands of the natural law are not to be confused with the motives from which they can, and should, be fulfilled. What is naturally good may be done from motives which are inherent in this natural good. We can obey the precepts of the natural law because the natural law prescribes them, because

231

this is the right thing to do, because we recognize natural law as the expression and the binding appeal of the divine will. But we can also fulfil the precepts of the natural law from higher motives: from supernatural love of God and of our neighbour, from faith in Christ, from the striving for Christian perfection and holiness. Actually the Christian should always and everywhere act from motives of faith. See 1 Cor. 10:31: "In eating, in drinking, in all that you do, do everything as for God's glory"; Col. 3:17: "Whatever you are about, in word and action alike, invoke always the name of the Lord Jesus Christ." There is only one ultimate end, namely, the supernatural (Q. 18, No. 5); there are many natural, particular and intermediate ends which are incorporated in, and subordinate to, this supernatural, ultimate end.

71. *For what ends and activities is man intended by virtue of his nature?*

By virtue of his nature man is intended to preserve and protect his life, to procreate ; and to prove and perfect himself intellectually and morally both as an individual and as a social being.

PIUS XI (D. R., 38).

"In consequence of this, God has bestowed upon him various prerogatives, such as the right to integrity of life and body; the right to acquire the necessities of life and duly pursue the end which God has appointed to him; the right of association, and the right to own and use private property."

THE answer is taken, not verbally but according to the sense, from St. Thomas Aquinas (I–II 94, 2), who on the basis of this threefold designation distinguishes three principal parts of

232

natural law and natural right which we might describe briefly as self-preservation, procreation, intellectual and moral development. But first of all the following points should be noted:

1. He in whom nature or God has implanted purpose and order is entitled and obliged to use the necessary means to attain this goal; he may, and must, carry out the activities which are demanded of him by this goal and by this order, that is, he can consider and assert, as individual rights granted him by nature whatever in particular he has to have or to do in order to fulfil properly the will and the task of nature.

2. It must never be forgotten that we are dealing here with man and the nature of man. Man is at all times bound to act in a specifically human manner that is worthy of him. He is at all times entitled to expect that his dignity and his individuality should be respected, unless he himself forfeits this right. Thus those natural inclinations also which man has in common with irrational creatures (for example, the instinct of self-preservation and the sex instinct) ought to be fulfilled, and be capable of this in a befitting manner.

3. Why mention this particular threefold classification? The answer is that there are in man three levels of being which are clearly distinct both in relation to the development of his nature as also to his conduct: first, the level of life: man exists, lives, grows, nourishes himself; second, the level of sentient being, with the power of creating and fostering new life of the same kind; third, the level of intellectual, rational being, which is capable of developing itself intellectually and morally and of communion with other intellectual beings, in other words which is capable of knowledge and love.[19]

[19] Metaphysics actually distinguishes four (not three) levels in man: the corporeal, the vital, the sentient, and the intellectual. Here, however, we are

A major part of what are nowadays called basic or human rights is rooted in the three main levels. In any case the extent and the significance of natural right can be shown and known from them. They disprove the view which maintains that natural law and natural right are nothing but general and meaningless formulae.[20]

SELF-PRESERVATION

It is clear both from revelation and human reason that man has the right and the duty to make provision for preserving his life. Man is not the master, but the steward and the guardian of his life. The duty of self-preservation extends not only to life itself, but to all that belongs to the natural integrity of man,

concerned with man's being in relation to his conduct. In this respect the decisive distinctions depend on the specifically different knowledge which is or is not presupposed by the carrying out of an action. For this reason the corporeal and the vital are here taken together, since knowledge is not really proper to either. Knowledge only begins on the level of sentient being, of the animal world. It may seem strange that among sentient life, St. Thomas refers only to the function of procreation and not to the whole range of passions which are undoubtedly a part of the natural endowment of sentient being, and which play such a large part in the moral life of man. (We need only think of the passions of love, fear, sorrow, delight, daring.) The explanation is that along with the instinct of self-preservation the sex instinct is the strongest and most important, since it serves the preservation and propagation of the species. Among men, too, sexual difference is the most profound and in its consequences the most important. Procreation with all its important and difficult questions represents a decisive sphere in the whole of human life. The passions were certainly not overlooked by St. Thomas. But he assigned them to the third level, since they constitute the object of the moral virtues in man and as such play an essential part in his intellectual and moral development and perfection.

[20] The following survey cannot claim to be complete. The rights mentioned in it have partly the character of entire new areas of right, and will have to be discussed in more detail where we treat of these areas in the Handbook. On basic or human rights cf. Lesson Three of this Part (Q. 78 et seq.).

thus to all those powers and members which nature has given him in order to fit him for the various tasks of life. All the faculties of mind and soul and body participate in the dignity of the human person, hence they must be judged from the point of view of the intrinsic worth of the person. The following are classified under this level as rights and duties:

1. Protection of life, of one's own life as well as of the life of others (the right of self-defence).

2. Rejection of murder in any form and from whatever reason (suicide, intentional killing of an innocent person, deliberate abortion, euthanasia).

3. Contrary to the preservation of bodily integrity are self-mutilation, sterilization, ill-treatment, acts of terror, duress, endangering life to no purpose.

4. The right to necessary livelihood: the right to work in order to live; the right to personal property for the purpose of earning and securing a livelihood.

5. Valuation and protection of labour: human labour should be valued as a personal achievement and not as an article for sale; exploitation and intolerable conditions of labour are inadmissible.

PROCREATION

According to the will of God men shall transmit life by way of procreation. In this way the human race is to be preserved and increased; hence the physical and psychological difference and the mutual attraction and complementary character of the sexes; sex instinct is intended to serve this task. The following are classified under this level as natural rights and duties:

1. The right to marry (free choice of a partner) and to beget children within wedlock.

2. Sexual intercourse outside wedlock is wrong.

3. The right of the family to sustenance, free development, and the protection of the community; the right to home and country.

4. Provision for the physical, moral, and intellectual formation of children.

5. The right of parents. Parents are primarily entitled to decide what type of education should be given to their children, to watch over its progress and to ensure its completion.

6. The duty of children to honour and obey their parents and to support them in sickness, poverty, and old age.

THE INTELLECTUAL AND MORAL LEVEL

This level comprises the large area of all that which is naturally due to man in virtue of his rationality, of his intellectual and moral destiny and vocation. Expressed in general terms this means that man has the right and the duty to follow right reason. Hence this level extends to the other two levels in so far as everything which man pursues and does must be in accordance with right reason. Three different spheres are distinguished upon this level.

1. First, the right and the obligation of personal perfection. Not only can man perfect himself, but he is obliged to do so. He must endeavour to become a good (virtuous) man (Q. 15). In this lies the primary and most important task and obligation laid upon him by God and nature. No individual can be relieved of it, and it has to be achieved by personal effort and responsibility but of course with the help and support of others. Hence man has the natural right: to investigate and to know the truth – above all concerning the purpose and the basic obligations of

his life; to act with "full personal responsibility" (Pius XII). See Q. 16; to acquire and to practise any virtue: freedom of conscience; to share in the control of material goods, to imprint the stamp of his personality upon things, to take them into his possession and to dispose of them as he thinks fit (private property).

2. The right and the duty to serve and to honour God: freedom of religion in belief and practice. The basic fact in human life is that man has his origin and goal in God, hence that he belongs to God and is in duty bound to obey him. No one can forbid him to acknowledge this fact or to act in accordance with it. Therefore every man is entitled in virtue of natural right to strive for a true and profound knowledge of God; to fulfil the precepts of God exactly as they are formulated; to live within, and in accordance with, that community which God has established as his Church, as the community of men redeemed by him; and to participate in carrying out the mission given to this Church.[21]

3. Right and duty of social life. Since men are by nature social beings (Q. 20) they are empowered and obliged by this very nature to do whatever is required for the orderly development and stability of social life, as well as whatever will make it tolerable, worthy, and secure. In this connection it is important to remember that nature, on the one hand, indicates and lays down a definite development for social life (Q. 50) and, on the other hand, appeals to men to fulfil their social duties voluntarily and to "associate" in freedom. It is no proof that it is not

---

[21] Although the last two rights do not really belong to the natural, but to the supernatural order, yet they are natural to the extent that man has the right to submit to everything which God commands. This natural right of full and absolute obedience to God embraces every general and personal order and injunction which God decrees.

dictated by nature when something ought to be freely granted or done. While not giving a complete list we mention the following: correct behaviour for men associating together: truthfulness, honesty, justice in word and deed ("Do not do to others what you would not have others do to you"); participation in decisions taken in common (the right to vote, taking part in general resolutions etc.); obedience to legal authority and to its just laws; application of the law and sharing in its advantages and burdens – in both cases "without respect of persons"; freedom of association for all honest purposes (economic, social, cultural etc.), restricted only by the genuine needs of the common good; acquisition, distribution, and use of economic goods in accordance with the needs of an orderly community life; freedom of work and profession (choice of occupation and place of work).

The Natural Rights of The Community

The rights already specified which have been established from a consideration of human nature, and first and foremost with the individual in mind, lead inevitably to the question whether, and in how far, society also possesses natural rights.

We hold that societies (communities) also have natural rights which differ according to their origin and purpose.[22]

1. The question has been answered already in so far as a number of rights have been mentioned which immediately relate to the origin, life, and development of society. Social order obviously demands that communities should possess natural rights, for otherwise there would be no natural, and consequently no firmly rooted, obligation of co-ordination and subordination,

[22] See Qs. 86, 110–11.

of recognition and consideration; social order would not be assured, and selfishness and power would dominate social life.

2. Society, that is, those people taken as a whole who live and act in an orderly manner by reason of a common origin or a common goal, holds these rights as a unity of order. They are exercised either by the whole community, for example in elections, general councils, general resolutions, or by individuals (or individual groups) in the name of the community. In this context, right is what is due to the community either from the members or from those outside the community.

3. Natural communities have a natural right in the strict sense, to exist, to operate and to develop in accordance with their individual character. The exercise of this right may be restricted, especially for urgent reasons of the common good. But the individual goals and the individual life of these communities may never be abolished or frustrated. For example it is not permitted to break up the family permanently, or to take away or estrange the children (as is the practice in totalitarian states) unless the family is obviously not fit to bring up the children. It is wrong to break up racial minorities and to disperse their members (forcible resettlement and separation of population groups; the problem of exiles).

Voluntary societies also have a natural right to pursue the goals they choose themselves and to develop their own individual life, on condition that they neither disturb nor hinder the order of social life as a whole, and especially of the natural communities. It is within the competence of human law to make provision in an appropriate form (restricting freedom as little as possible) against the endangering of the commonweal by the formation and activities of voluntary societies. It may not, however, interfere in the really personal sphere of men. For

239

example it may not prevent men from cultivating friendly and social relations among themselves.

The natural rights of natural communities are based on their natural origin and purpose, for which reason they are of an absolute nature and cannot be tampered with by men. The natural rights of voluntary societies are based, on the one hand, on the manifold possibilities of meeting, living, and acting together that are innate in our social nature, and, on the other hand, on the freedom of association and the voluntary agreement of men. They are of a conditional nature, that is, they are valid on condition that these societies do not destroy or impair the order of the community as whole, and that men remain free to join, and to submit to them.

72. *Are the precepts of natural law known to all men?*

The primary and most general precepts of natural law are known to all men; many are in ignorance and error concerning the further precepts.

1. A LAW must be known in order to be binding, for man is not in a position to do something of which he is ignorant and has not been informed. Therefore every law must be promulgated. The natural law does not really need to be expressly promulgated. God has implanted it, as it were, in human reason by so creating reason that the first precepts are self-evident to it, and from these it is able to infer others. Thus the mode of promulgation peculiar to the natural law consists in this, that God made the human reason capable of knowing the natural law.[23]

2. The first precept is known to all. It is: "We must do good and avoid evil." Here, as the facts quite clearly show, there is

[23] St. Thomas Aquinas, I–II 90, 4 *ad* 1; 100, 3; 4 *ad* 1.

no exception and no possibility of error. As soon as man comes to the use of reason, and as long as he retains it, he cannot but assent to this proposition. And this can be shown in the following manner (Q. 70): Man naturally seeks happiness; unhappiness is naturally repugnant to him. He cannot but wish to be happy; he cannot wish to be unhappy. It is true of course that he may seek happiness in false goods, but it is always happiness that he seeks. Happiness lies in the good; for the will can only be happy through what is appropriate to it, through what "agrees with it"; and this is nothing else than the good. For this reason man inevitably aims at the good if he follows his natural desire for happiness.

3. Universally known are those propositions of the natural law which are immediately and intimately connected with the first precept. They embrace the basic truths of moral living, that is, those precepts which make known to man the most important obligations, especially of social life, and protect him against the most serious and harmful lapses. In fact, man's acting according to right reason depends on these basic truths. To these norms belongs in the first place the principle: To each his own; you may not do an injustice to anyone – thus the precept forbidding murder, theft, and fraud.[24] It is almost as self-evident as the highest precept. There is also the obligation to care for our children and to honour our parents; the right of self-defence; the obligation to fulfil contracts. The second table of the Decalogue, the fourth to the tenth commandment, belongs especially to this group.

[24] Some Catholic scholars (for example H. A. Rommen, *Natural Law* [London, 1947], pp. 220 et seq.) hold that this precept: "Give everyone his own" is actually the first and highest norm of the natural law. We cannot agree, but it is obviously among the more important precepts.

241

4. Although these precepts are self-evident they are frequently wrongly applied, not because of negligence or bad will – though, unfortunately, this happens, too – but because the individual is not always able to grasp and judge the actual situation. He knows the precept and is prepared to submit to it, but he fails to see that the particular actions which he contemplates come under the precept. For example, a man may be determined never to steal and faithfully to abide by every contract, but it may not occur to him that he is in fact stealing or breaking a contract when he appropriates this thing or fails to fulfil that obligation. (Example: what in wartime used to be called "organizing things".)[25]

5. It is a different matter with precepts which man comes to know through deductive reasoning from the most general norms (Q. 70), and which have more particular applications. The further such precepts are from the primary norms, the greater the danger that in spite of intense and sustained mental effort man may fall into error, that not merely may he falsely apply the truth which he sees, but he may even fail to see the truth itself, or that the precepts are right. It must even be admitted that it is extremely difficult to state definitely how far the competence of natural law extends and where its limits lie. The reasons are:

a. At times the factual situation is extremely complicated. It is by no means always easy to recognize what is naturally right; it is often difficult to decide how a given case should be classified. For example, whether a particular wage can still be considered just, or whether it must now be considered unjust; whether a surgical operation directly or indirectly interrupts a pregnancy.

b. Original sin and its consequences. To a considerable extent reason has lost its clarity of vision and sureness of judgement.

[25] Besides the texts mentioned, see St. Thomas Aquinas, I–II, 77, 2.

This "darkening of the understanding" strongly affects the knowledge of moral obligations and their norms, since the will plays a major part therein (Q. 19).

c. The various forms of bias and confusion arising from, and often increased by, false development in doctrine and tradition, from habit, education, inclination, and the passions (anger, fear envy, hate). These cloud the judgement of men and not infrequently lead it astray. It is therefore not surprising that certain truths of the natural law have occasionally been lost sight of by individuals and groups (even by whole nations), that certain propositions which in fact may be easily inferred from the primary precepts are in many places either not at all or not correctly inferred. For example, exposing or killing sickly children; vendettas; permitting the lie of excuse; interruption of pregnancy for eugenic or social reasons.

i. The deviations from the natural law which we observe are not always the result of error, but often of conscious and deliberate disregard and neglect, or of a want of careful and serious examination. This qualification refers primarily to those nations and states which have known Christianity. Christian ethics afforded and still affords them sufficient means of safeguarding themselves to a great extent against such errors and lapses.

ii. The fact that men fall into error concerning a truth of the natural law does not prove that the truth in question does not come under the natural law, because this does not depend on what men may know, but on what is contained in, and made known by, nature.

iii. Together with the message of salvation God also expressly revealed to mankind the natural moral law, first of all in respect of its basic truths, but also in respect of many inferences. (The

Ten Commandments and many other precepts of the Old Testament; certain very definite statements of our Lord and the apostles; see Q. 68.) Besides, he conferred on the Church, together with the office of teaching, the authority and the obligation to make known and to interpret the natural law with infallible certainty. Whenever the Church declares something to be demanded by nature or to be contrary to it, it devolves on scholars to make this truth clear by showing the natural reasons and relevancies on which it rests. This has always been done, and the insight into the truth is accessible not only to the believer but to everyone who, having the proper formation, makes the corresponding effort. Considering the incalculable import of this matter, one would expect that those who are conscious of their responsibility for morality and right, even though they refuse to listen to the judgement of the Church, might at least accept the insight into the truth thus made available.

73. Where and when is the natural law valid?

The natural law is unalterable ; hence it is valid for all men of all times and everywhere.

PIUS XI (C. C., 61).

"No difficulty that arises can ever detract from the binding obligation of divine commandments which forbid acts intrinsically evil."

PIUS XII (Address of 25 September 1949; C. M., May 1950)
"In the eyes of the Church these essential rights are so inviolable that no argument of State and no pretext of common good can prevail against them.
They are protected by an insurmountable wall. As far as this wall the common good can legislate as it pleases, but beyond this wall it may

not go. It cannot touch these rights, for they constitute what is most precious in the common good."

FEW questions have been, and still are, so fiercely disputed. And this is understandable, since the whole of law is very considerably affected by it and takes on a completely different aspect according to whether it is affirmed or denied. It is only lately that this matter is again being given the importance due to it (see Lesson Three, on human rights).

1. Human nature does not change. The changes to which men are subject do not affect their essential nature but rather their individual and social character. Men may live where, when, and how they will; they may differ greatly from one another; they may progress very rapidly; their outlook may change radically; they may either be "primitive" or "enlightened", but they are and remain men. The natural law is based on human nature. It expresses the demands of this common nature of men and makes known in the form of principles those rights and obligations which are given with human nature or which can be inferred from it. Thus, since the effect corresponds to the cause, the principles of the natural law must be unalterable. Hence we are fully justified in speaking of the immutable, permanent, and unassailable precepts of the natural law.[26]

2. If the natural law is further defined, that is, supplemented by men, this in no way impugns its immutability, because such supplementation does not abolish the natural law but rather completes it in accordance with particular circumstances, and the general content and character of the natural law makes such additions necessary.

EXAMPLES. Traffic regulations help and indeed make possible the pro-

[26] St. Thomas Aquinas, I–II 94, 5–6.

245

tection of life demanded by nature. The reason why important property settlements must be specially witnessed to make them valid is to avoid uncertainty and disputes regarding property rights. When the law defines the type and degree of punishment for certain crimes it is supplementing the principle of the natural law that there must be due proportion between guilt and expiation.

There are times when a precept of the natural law may not be obeyed because it clashes with a higher precept of the natural law which takes precedence due to its greater urgency. In particular circumstances it would be unreasonable to fulfil the lesser precept since this would mean neglecting or even transgressing the higher precept. But the lesser precept is neither abolished nor altered by this. It is merely that a situation which normally comes under it is temporarily withdrawn from it because of the higher precept. It is often difficult to decide.

Here is a classical example. The natural law obliges us to return the property of another. But if one who has borrowed a revolver knows that the owner requests its return in order to shoot himself or some other person it would be neither right nor just, but wrong and unjust to return the borrowed weapon. The precept to protect human life is higher and must be fulfilled; the precept to return another's property loses its binding force as long as the situation lasts.

It can happen that a precept deriving from the natural law is in some place or at some time not known as such and consequently not binding as such. Considering such cases one might speak of the possibility of change in the natural law, but only in the restricted and conditional sense that some precepts of the natural law do not bind here or there because of inculpable ignorance. This, however, applies only for as long as the ignorance is culpable, for the obligation revives when the error is discovered and can be overcome.

3. Very important and far-reaching conclusions ought to be drawn from the immutability of the natural law.

The basic view of legal positivism that all law is changeable represents a gross and most dangerous error. It means in effect the end of all juridical order and stability.

PIUS XII (C. B.,1942). Cf. Lesson One of this Part, Introduction.

The natural law applies always and binds every community. Its validity is restricted neither by time nor place. Nations and international institutions are also subject to the natural law.

No one may carry out an order or succumb to a desire which clearly runs contrary to a precept of the natural law. There is never a case where, for example, euthanasia may be practised, a false oath sworn, a pregnancy directly interrupted, or where one may commit calumny or fraud.

74. Can anyone dispense from the natural law?

Neither individual persons nor societies (communities) can dispense from a precept of the natural law.

PIUS XI (C. C., 131).

"For there are some who consider themselves morally justified in doing anything, so long as the law of the State allows it or at any rate does not punish it; and even if their conscience forbids it, they will do these things because they have no fear of God and apparently have nothing to fear from the laws of man. And this is attended with disastrous results both to themselves and to many others."

PIUS XII (Address of March 1950 to the Catholic Press Congress in Rome; U. A. vol. 2, p. 262).

"We spoke then of the objective norms of the law, of divine natural law, which guarantees to the juridical life of mankind the autonomy demanded by a living and safe adaptation to the conditions of every era.

We fully expected that We would not be understood by the totalitarians, for whom law and right are merely instruments in the hands of the ruling circles. But it surprises us, indeed, to note the very same misunderstanding on the part of certain groups which, for a long time, assumed the role of champions of the liberal concept of life and which had condemned men simply for the error of their attachment to laws and precepts contrary to morality. In the last analysis, that a judge pronouncing sentence feels himself bound by positive law and its faithful interpretation is in no way incompatible with the recognition of the natural law; what is more, it is one of its requirements. But what cannot be legitimately granted is the notion that such a link can be forged exclusively by the act of the human legislator, from whom the law emanates. This amounts to attributing to positive legislation a pseudo-majesty which would in no way differ from that which racism or nationalism attributes to totalitarian juridical action, trampling underfoot the physical and moral rights of persons."

PIUS XII *(Address of 5 August 1950; C. D. III, 28).*

"The last word in affairs of State belongs to men for whom the natural law is something more than a mere negative norm, or a closed frontier against the encroachments of positive legislation, or simply a means of technical adjustment in varying circumstances. Not by such men as these should the last word be spoken in the management of affairs, but by those who see in the natural law the very soul of positive legislation giving it form, meaning and life."

1. THE question concerns dispensation, exemption from the natural law, and covers the case of someone dispensing himself

as also the case of someone being empowered to dispense another.[27] To dispense means to exempt from the precept, thus to declare and to authorize in the proper form that the precept will not bind here and now. Those who act with a dispensation omit to do what the precept commands, or even do the opposite; nevertheless their action is morally good and just because they are, or may consider themselves, legally exempt. Thus they do not break the law in the sense of disregarding it. Such an exemption can be granted only by proper authorities. If everyone were permitted to exempt himself from the law according to his own opinion the law would become meaningless. Those alone competent are: the lawgiver or his successor; a yet higher authority; organs or individuals expressly thus empowered.

2. The author of the natural law is God. Neither in the natural law itself nor in revelation have we any evidence for assuming that God empowered any man or any human authority to exempt anyone at any time from a precept of the natural law. All alleviations and concessions of the Old Testament were expressly and completely abolished by Christ. In cases of doubt men are obliged to keep on enquiring and investigating until they have established whether there is in fact involved a precept of the natural law. If beyond doubt this is the case, there is only one thing to do, and that is to obey!

3. In point of fact this standpoint is held consistently only by the Catholic Church, even though it implies considerable and regrettable hardship in many individual cases. But the Church keeps unswervingly and absolutely to what God through Christ has imposed on her. Certain commands and concessions

---

[27] The question of two conflicting precepts of the natural law has been dealt with in Q. 73.

which God himself gave in the Old Testament have been a subject of fierce dispute from the earliest times. (Examples: the command to Abraham to sacrifice his son Isaac; polygamy of the Patriarchs; the larceny committed at the command of God by the Israelites when they left Egypt.) The question has been asked whether God can dispense from the precepts of the natural law. But apart from the fact that whatever God, who is all-wise and all-holy, does must be right, the question is no longer of any practical significance for the Christian era – from Christ down to the end of time – since God has restored in Christ the complete validity of the order of creation. The facts of the Old Testament are explained partly by God's absolute sovereignty over all creatures (Lord over life and death: the sacrifice of Abraham; absolute right of ownership to the goods of the earth: larceny of the Israelites). Polygamy is not directly contrary to the principal natural end of marriage, since it does not render impossible, but only more difficult, the begetting and upbringing of children. We should bear in mind especially the words of our Lord to the Jews: "It was to suit your hard hearts that Moses allowed you to put your wives away; it was not so at the beginning of things" (Matt. 19:8). This does not imply a genuine exemption but rather a concession granted, as it were, under pressure.

75. *Do the circumstances in which society finds itself influence the validity of the natural law?*

Circumstances cannot impair the intrinsic validity of the natural law; but they can restrict the exercise of natural rights.

THE precepts of the natural law are always valid, even in complex and difficult circumstances. Therefore even the most

250

difficult and precarious circumstances may not entitle society to order or to grant something which clearly offends against a precept of the natural law. But there are natural rights the exercise of which depends on external conditions and circumstances, and especially on the existing economic and social situation. Hence the case may arise in which society is entitled (and in duty bound) to restrict opportunities. The case may arise when someone cannot make use of his right without violating the rights of others or of society.

EXAMPLES. As a result of unemployment it may be impossible to find work and to earn one's living by work in spite of the right to work. Government measures in time of war and other crises can considerably restrict the free disposal of one's private property, for example rationing, freezing of savings, direction of agricultural and industrial production. It is a major interference in the private life of the family when a husband or a father is called up for military service.

76. Is the natural law the only source of right?

Apart from the natural law there are the divine law and human (positive) law as independent sources of right.

LEO XIII (L. P., 9).

"For, what reason and the natural law do for individuals, that human law, *promulgated for their good, does for the citizens of States. . . . Now there are other enactments of the civil authority, which do not follow directly, but somewhat remotely, from the natural law, and decide many points which the law of nature treats only in a general and indefinite way. For instance, though nature commands all to contribute to the public peace and prosperity, whatever belongs to the manner, and circumstances, and conditions under which such service*

251

is to be rendered must be determined by the wisdom of men and not by nature herself. It is in the constitution of these particular rules of life, suggested by reason and prudence, and put forth by competent authority, that human law, properly so called, consists."

1. It follows from his divine and absolute sovereignty over all creatures that God, the author of the natural law, can promulgate other laws. And apart from the natural law God has, in fact, given men special laws which are contained in the Old and New Testaments. They are called the "divine" law in the sense of "positive" divine law. Its source is God's will as expressed in revelation and the Christian dispensation. Its object is the community of all men destined for, and subject to, God (I–II 100, 5). It stands to reason that there can be no contradiction between the natural and the divine law; God cannot contradict himself and his own actions. This divine law is also called the law of the Christian dispensation, while the natural law is called the law of creation.

2. Men also are empowered to make laws which bind in virtue of their own authority. But the latter always remains subordinate to the authority of God. These laws are no mere interpretation and promulgation of the natural law. They are independent, and distinct from the natural law. Hence they bind to that which they prescribe. The supreme and most important principle governing all human legislation is as follows (see Q. 67, No. 3): Human laws bind only in so far as they are just; but they cannot be just if they conflict with either the natural law or the divine law.

LEO XIII (L. P., 9).

"But such laws by no means derive their origin from civil society, because, just as civil society did not create human nature, so neither

252

can it be said to be the author of the good which befits human nature, or of the evil which is contrary to it. Laws come before men live together in society, and have their origin in the natural, and consequently in the eternal, law. The precepts, therefore, of the natural law, contained bodily in the laws of men, have not merely the force of human law, but they possess that higher and more august sanction which belongs to the law of nature and the eternal law."

PIUS XI (M. S., 34).

"These human laws which are irreconcilably opposed to natural law have an innate defect which can be cured neither by compulsion nor by any external display of force."

The following scheme shows how the different laws are related:

Eternal law

Natural law ———————————————— Positive law

Divine law ———— Human law

of the Old Testament ———————— of the New Testament

77. Is human law always to be obeyed to the letter?

In certain circumstances it is permitted and even obligatory to act contrary to the letter of human law.

THERE are cases in which an individual is empowered and even obliged to exempt himself from what is required of him by the letter of the law. Consequently not every transgression of a human law implies disobedience and illegality.

EXAMPLES. Traffic regulations in Great Britain require drivers to give way on the left and overtake on the right. A motorist sees that an on-coming car is driving on the wrong side of the road; at the last moment he has the presence of mind to give way on the right instead of on the left, and in so doing he prevents a serious accident. He has acted contrary to the letter of the traffic regulations. Was it right?

The superior of a monastery strictly forbids the members of his community to leave the house between 9 o'clock in the evening and 6 o'clock in the morning without his express permission. Towards midnight one of the Fathers is called to attend someone who has been seriously injured and the case is most urgent. The Father goes immediately without waiting to ask his superior's permission. Was he entitled and obliged to act thus?

In both cases we have a transgression of what was commanded by the strict letter of a human law and of a human order. But everyone will agree that in both instances the transgression was justified and completely right, and that such a self-dispensation, although materially an act of disobedience, nevertheless must not in reality be accounted neglect of duty and disobedience. In both cases the situation permitted and indeed demanded that the person in question should act as he did.

This deviation from the law on one's own responsibility is called "equity", or "*epikeia*". It is the spirit of justice which enables us to interpret laws correctly.

1. What is meant by "equity"?

a. Two things must be distinguished in law:

i. The letter: that which is expressed and indicated by the wording of the law.

ii. The purpose: that which the lawgiver intends by the law or the order. For example traffic laws are made in order that the traffic may proceed in an orderly manner and accidents be avoided. The superior of a monastery makes a rule like the one just mentioned as a precaution against inconveniences and in order to protect the good name of his house.

b. The meaning of a law is more important than its wording, because a law is made and formulated in a particular manner with the purpose of achieving a particular object. In other words, the wording of a law is meant to serve the purpose of the law. And should the case arise when literal observance frustrates or makes impossible what is intended by the law, then it would be unreasonable to stick to the letter, since this would jeopardize the very purpose which the lawgiver had in mind when he made the law. Besides, we ought to know that a human law can never command or have as its purpose the infringement of higher rights or the invalidation of obligations of a higher nature. (Take the second example: every priest is strictly bound to go as quickly as possible to the assistance of a person in immediate danger of death who is dependent on his help.)

c. Equity consists in this, that one who is subject to the law dispenses himself from what is demanded of him by the letter of the law. Thus he decides against the letter of the law and in favour of its purpose: against that which the lawgiver has formulated, and in favour of what he intended. He does this:

i. Fully realizing that he is transgressing the law. There is no question of equity where the law is unknown, or where it gives rise to doubt because of its inexact formulation, nor where someone is seeking to obscure or to misinterpret the law, but only where he is perfectly clear on what the law says and yet acts otherwise.

ii. On his own responsibility, without asking for, and obtaining, a dispensation (exemption). The very essence of equity is based on this, that one who is subject to the law takes it on himself not to obey.

255

d. Equity does not mean interpretation of the law by the rightful authority, or exemption from the law by the rightful authority, but simply and solely that a subject takes it on himself to fulfil the law according to its purpose and not according to its wording. Equity consists of the observance of a human law according to the spirit and not according to the letter.

2. How is acting according to equity to be judged?

a. The answer depends upon the one and only valid motive: those subject to the law act contrary to its wording because they desire to fulfil the purpose of the law, and because they can do so only in this manner. They are convinced that only in this way do they comply with the intention of the lawgiver. They are sure that it is the lawgiver's wish to avoid this or that evil effect which would result from a literal observance of the law. It is not laziness or disloyalty, not dissatisfaction, still less contempt which impels a person to invoke equity, but rather concern for what the law should protect, a sense of duty and responsibility.

b. Every law serves the common good of the community for which it has been made. But human limitations on the one hand, and the countless number and variety of individual actions on the other, make it impossible for any lawgiver to foresee all possible cases and to make provision for them beforehand by a general norm. Circumstances and situations of an unusual nature will always arise which must be decided on their own merits. They go beyond the scope of the general norm, and would result in completely irrational and often even calamitous consequences if the general norm were to be adhered to "at all costs".[28]

[28] See St. Thomas Aquinas, I–II 96, 6.

EXAMPLES. The regulation that no one may leave a compartment or a building by the window can certainly not still hold good when fire breaks out or when gangsters force their way in. An order to keep off the grass automatically expires when it is a question of rescuing a child who has fallen into a pond. A law forbidding citizens to cross the frontier is not binding on someone whose only way of escape from unjust persecution is by flight across the frontier. The monastic rule of silence may, and should, be broken when a member of the community is in need of immediate help or advice (in case of sickness, spiritual needs, mental depression).

c. Thus in certain circumstances equity is certainly allowed and obligatory. This is the clear teaching of St. Thomas Aquinas.[29] In fact he teaches that equity is a virtue which deserves to be highly rated. And it is easy to see the reason for this. It often demands and shows a fine spirit of personal responsibility to decide against the wording of a law and in favour of its purpose. Generally speaking, it is much easier (usually much more convenient!) to hold once and for all to the letter of the law than to make a personal judgement and decision wherever the letter becomes "tricky". The virtue of equity brings personal conscience into play. It is at once the proof and the opportunity for genuine responsibility. It is a clear refutation of the reproach that Catholic ethics teaches nothing but unquestioning obedience and leaves no room for personal responsibility.

3. When is equity permissible or obligatory?

a. Equity is permissible only in the case of human law, and not in the case of the natural or the divine law. And it must be human law in the strict and proper sense, a law (command, injunction) issued by men in virtue of their own authority. When certain precepts of the natural or the divine law are merely repeated

[29] Ibid.; and especially I–II Q. 120

or emphasized again in order that they may be better known and observed, it is not a question of human laws in the proper sense (Q. 76). Precepts of the natural and the divine law must be followed to the letter. Here men are not entitled to distinguish between the wording and the purpose, and then to act contrary to the wording in order to fulfil the purpose. The reason is obvious. These laws bind directly in virtue of the authority of God. But nothing can remain hidden and unknown to God. Laws which come directly from him are based on his infinite wisdom which has ordered all things "in measure, and number, and weight". Hence man has neither occasion nor the right to assert that God had not foreseen this or that individual case, and consequently was not able to make provision for it beforehand, so that man himself has to establish where and when the law obliges or does not oblige according to the strict letter.[30]

b. It is permissible on two conditions to apply the law of equity in respect of human law:

i. The decision must be urgent, the situation must be such that the individual has to act immediately and in this particular manner, and that the situation admits of neither choice nor postponement.

ii. When the authority competent to dispense from the law is

[30] Quite a different matter from the self-exemption discussed here is: i. The competence and the duty of the Church to determine authoritatively the import and the compass of the natural and the divine law wherever this is necessary owing to a certain vagueness in the law itself. ii. The decision to fulfil the precept which is more important here and now and to disregard the less important one in cases where several precepts of the natural or the divine law bind simultaneously (Q. 74). iii. Coming to a decision in cases of reasonable doubt which have not yet been resolved by the Church. "A doubtful law is not binding", but the individual must endeavour to resolve the doubt and must submit when the competent authority makes a ruling on the matter.

258

not available at the time; before the authority would have been reached it would have been too late. If there is time and opportunity for a dispensation it has to be obtained.[31]

c. The application of equity involves the obligation of justifying such a decision and action before the legitimate authority. A person thereby exposes himself to the danger (or the possibility) of having his way of acting disapproved of, or rejected as too high-handed and wrong. He must reckon with censure and perhaps even punishment. This "disadvantage" inevitably attaches to equity. But it is no reason for repudiating or being intimidated by it. The authority's subsequent disapproval does not retrospectively affect the morality of the action. The action was, and remains, morally right and the judgement of authority can at most be binding for the future. Equity even entitles someone who has to make an immediate decision and is unable to ask permission beforehand, to act even though he suspects or foresees that permission would be refused him if he were in a position to ask for it. Decisive alone is the situation to be dealt with here and now, and not any conjecture about the opinion of authority. The subject may legitimately presume that the authority would agree in this particular case.[32]

[31] In many cases, as for example in the rules and constitutions of some religious orders and congregations, special provision is made for the use of tacit (presumed) permission. However, someone who acts with tacit permission is usually obliged to inform his superiors subsequently and to submit to their judgement of the matter. See the following section of the text.

[32] One important qualification is, however, necessary: The human legislator is quite entitled to exclude certain things once and for all from equity, that is, to issue a law with the express proviso that equity may not be employed in respect of it, but rather that the law must always be fulfilled according to the letter. There are certain things which are so important to the commonweal as to justify such a proviso. This qualification holds good for the entire supernatural order. Thus Canon Law contains regulations of this nature. (For example

d. Those who are subject to authority may find themselves in very difficult situations and suffer considerable conflicts of conscience if, for such reasons as a lack of common sense or an exaggerated sense of its own power, the authority forbids the use of equity even where it would be quite appropriate and even necessary. The attempt should be made first of all to dissuade such authorities from their false view or attitude. If this is not successful they ought to be relieved of office or deposed because they are obviously unsuited to their tasks. If this also proves impossible, then there remains nothing else for the subjects but to act wherever they are clearly bound to do so according to the natural or the divine law, and to face the consequences bravely. Such a manner of acting has not the character of disobedience. No human authority can reassure and console its subjects simply by telling them to pass all responsibility on to itself.

EXAMPLES. In spite of the objection of his superior a priest may, and must, go to a dying person and administer the Last Sacraments to him if the case is urgent and no other priest is immediately available. Possibly contrary to the rule of her congregation and to the injunction of her superior, a nursing sister may, and must, assist at a delivery if help is absolutely necessary and no one else is available.

★

in regard to the celibacy of the clergy and the valid form of marriage.) In the natural order, on the other hand, purely human laws never attain such a binding force that an exception would not be permitted or even obligatory in particularly urgent and serious individual cases. For example, a government decrees in the strictest form that *everyone* residing within its frontiers must report to the authorities and have himself registered. It threatens with the severest penalties anyone who harbours or assists a person who has failed to report. Nevertheless we may be permitted or even obliged in conscience not to report or to assist someone who has failed to report. (For example those persecuted because of their religious belief or their race; an underground movement against unjust oppressors.) Here we are dealing with a law which is partly unjust in consequence of the existing circumstances.

No authority has the right to forbid a tenant to share his flat freely with a poor homeless person who would otherwise be on the street. (Of course the authorities can prevent it by force!)

Lesson Three

FUNDAMENTAL HUMAN RIGHTS

JURISPRUDENCE and especially the constitutions and international organizations of the present day (for example the United Nations) do not refer so much to "natural" rights as to "basic", or fundamental "human", rights. We should not take the two expressions as meaning quite the same thing, since the lists of fundamental human rights contain matters which do not belong to natural right, and on the other hand, they omit or falsify matters which undoubtedly belong to natural right. At any rate the question concerning fundamental human rights has, for well-known and understandable reasons,[33] assumed such importance that it must be discussed. In this Handbook we shall confine ourselves to the social aspect of the problem. Thus we are concerned with estimating and showing to what extent such rights must exist, in what they consist, who grants and guarantees them, what validity they claim, whether they can be abolished or changed by human authority.

Discussion of the question is rendered more difficult by the fact that it may be approached from two different angles. Elementary human rights may be determined in two ways:

[33] We need only recall that in totalitarian States men are deprived of their rights and enslaved, that whole sections of the people are banished; the horrors of total war, religious and racial persecution. It is, to put it mildly, grotesque to find the constitution of Soviet Russia referring to "immutable basic rights".

i. From the point of view of natural right, taking natural right as the basis;

ii. From the purely positivist point of view, taking human agreements and declarations as the only basis.

The differences are significant enough to merit particular attention (Qs. 80–81), but first of all we should like to review briefly the history of fundamental human rights.

A History of Fundamental Human Rights[34]

On 15 June 1215 the English Barons exacted sign and seal for their feudal liberties, which were set down in the famous *Magna Charta Libertatum*. These guaranteed among other things freedom of the Church in England, freedom of the person, the right to legal trial in criminal cases, protection of widows and orphans, protection of private property as well as the restriction of feudal dues demanded by the king. In the course of the seventeenth and eighteenth centuries these rights were extended to the English middle classes and further developed in the "Petition of Right" (1628) and in the "Agreement of the People" (1647). Under the influence of the Republican followers of Cromwell the transition took place from privileged estates into democratic foundations of the modern State. In 1679, Charles II supplemented this settlement by the *Habeas Corpus* Act. In the "Bill of Rights" (1689) Parliament established its rights in relation to the Crown. Free elections and freedom of speech in Parliament were assured; cruel punishments were forbidden.

In 1620 the Pilgrim Fathers landed on the North American coast. Before leaving the *Mayflower* they signed a document in

---

[34] We are indebted to *Geschichte der Grundrechte* by Alfred Voigt (Spemann-Verlag, Stuttgart, 1950).

which they pledged themselves in obedience to their king to found a colony for the glory of God and for the spread of the Christian faith, in which they would live and work with equal rights for the common good. From this pact the American liberties gradually developed to become those irrevocable norms of public and social life which found expression in the constitutions of the North American states during the War of Independence, and which were supplemented in 1791 by the "Bill of Rights". The effective legal institution which watches over the observance of basic rights is formed by the Supreme Court.

On the continent of Europe the ideas of equality and liberty won recognition in the French Revolution and were formulated in the *Déclaration des droits de l'homme et du citoyen* of 26 August 1789. Article I: "All men are born free and with equal rights and they remain so. Differences of social standing can be justified only by virtue of the general weal." Article 2: "The purpose of every political association is the protection of man's natural and inalienable rights. These rights are: liberty, ownership, security, and resistance to oppression." In 1795, and again following the Napoleonic era, France received a modified constitution which served as a model for most European constitutions in the subsequent 150 years.

The "Constitution of the Russian Soviet Federated Socialist Republic" of 10 July 1918 begins with the declaration of the "Rights of the working people" and abolishes private ownership of land, banks, and the means of production, for the purpose of collectivization. In order to "guarantee" freedom of conscience the Church is separated from the State and education from the Church. Only those have a right to vote who earn their livelihood by productive labour which benefits the whole community. The constitution of 1936 is the first to contain a section on "fundamental rights" in which the right of citizens to work, holidays, old age pensions as well as equality before the law and inviolability of the person are acknowledged as an unalterable law.

In the Italy of Mussolini fundamental rights were completely abolished in favour of the Corporative State. The highest maxim was the benefit of the nation as understood by Fascism. In Nazi Germany this system was brought to perfection. By emergency orders and by revoking a number of articles of the constitution the National Socialist regime removed all obstacles to dictatorship. "You are nothing, the people is everything" was the argument used to brush aside the individual's fundamental rights, which in themselves contradicted the |*Führerprinzip*. Laws were arbitrarily abolished, or even enacted and the corresponding punishments imposed retrospectively.

Disregard for the rights of citizens was followed naturally by disregard for the right of nations and minorities which had developed since the French Revolution and which gave rise to international arbitration courts and organizations. After the collapse of the Axis powers the United Nations Organization (UNO) was established. The preamble to the Charter declared that the peoples of the United Nations are determined to demonstrate anew their faith in the fundamental rights of man, in the dignity and the worth of the human person, in the equal rights of men and women, of great and small nations, and that these nations intended to promote social progress and a better standard of living in greater liberty; to this end they would practise tolerance and live together in peace as good neighbours. According to Article One, the purpose of the organization is, among other things, the collective encouragement of "respect for human rights and for fundamental freedoms for all without distinction as to race, sex, language, or religion". The United Nations General Assembly meeting in Paris on 10 December 1948, adopted "The Universal Declaration of Human Rights".

78. What is a fundamental right?

A fundamental right is a right which forms the foundation and support of other rights.

FUNDAMENTAL rights are those rights from which juridical order takes its beginning, from which it results, on which it rests, in which it finds stability and support. The quality, scope, and security of juridical order depends, then, on the quality, completeness, and stability of fundamental rights.

The very term "fundamental rights" shows that there must be other rights that follow these, that are dependent on, and supplementary to, them. These subsequent rights cannot claim to be of equal importance since they are not as firmly rooted, and have not the same validity.

At the same time the term "fundamental right" does not of itself imply that we are here dealing with a natural, inalienable, and inviolable right. For example in a particular constitution the term may imply and intend nothing more than that a certain right is considered unassailable within the community, that it may not be altered as long as the constitution is not changed. It is essential to observe carefully what is intended in each case.

79. What is a universal human right?

A universal human right is a right which is given to man in virtue of his human nature, and which therefore must be acknowledged by all men.

As opposed to "universal" there are "particular" human rights which are limited to a particular time and place, as they are valid only within certain communities. We are not here concerned with these.[35]

---

[35] The notorious "emergency laws" of totalitarian States are something

In our reply the term "universal human right" is equivalent to natural right, the latter to be taken in the strict and proper sense (Q. 64). This gives a clear and general basis for all national and international legislation and jurisdiction. For it follows necessarily that this right must be valid always and everywhere and must be acknowledged and observed by all men. But the other case is also possible, namely, that only that is held to be a universal human right which peoples and States by mutual agreement acknowledge and declare to be such. A number of States agree to consider certain rights as universal human rights and undertake to put them into force either for all time or until a new agreement is made.

80. In what manner do basic human rights originate today?

Basic human rights originate today mostly by way of agreement and common declaration.

1. It is significant that the decision taken on the basis of an unanimous or majority vote has, according to modern opinion, a creative and binding character. Men do not therefore merely declare that certain natural rights are herewith acknowledged as the basis of juridical order, but rather they constitute and declare rights in virtue of their own authority: this or that must be considered a fundamental human right because we – the United Nations, Parliament – have decided this and have so agreed.[36] The line of argument and explanation are purely

different again. Through these, sections of the people are exempted from the body of existing law, and this is usually done in an arbitrary fashion and in violation of the natural law.

[36] At the beginning of its first draft the United Nations commission for the declaration of human rights spoke of God as the author of these rights; but this draft was later altered, and the agreement and authority of the United Nations substituted.

positivist, they are based on the "general will" (Rousseau), on the rule of the majority. No doubt this is due to the mentality of our times, which have turned away from God and no longer have any perception of genuine natural right.

2. In spite of this defect two points should be noted: First, by means of actual agreement and legal expression, accompanied by the corresponding guarantees, proper bases of law have been created which are at any rate supported by a strong human authority. Second, examination of the basic human rights declared in this manner shows a large measure of agreement with natural right. Much of the content of natural law has been elevated to positive law. This fact supports the claim of the Church's social ethics — that nature's laws are written into the hearts of men, and that the basic moral truths are self-evident, or can be inferred by men.

3. As against these advantages there are the following defects and dangers:

i. It is to be deplored that mankind is no longer prepared to acknowledge God as the author and guarantor of right, as fundamental rights are thereby deprived of their only true sanction. Opinions, power, and the will of men are substituted for God; the sanctity and effectivness of right are surrendered.

ii. Important rights are all too easily overlooked (either from want of discernment or purposely for "tactical" reasons) and not included in the declaration (because of self-interest; out of consideration for the views of one or the other world-power; or because the defeated nations did not participate).

iii. Here human agreement cannot guarantee that the rights which have been declared to be such are in reality genuine fundamental human rights; it cannot guarantee that liberty has not been falsely restricted, or that a false tolerance has not been practised (for example, certain "concessions" and exceptions may be made in favour of totalitarian states).

iv. Fundamental human rights established in this positivist manner remain valid only as long as the partners to the contract abide by their agreement and are prepared to carry it out. When new agreements are being drawn up some very unfortunate and disturbing changes may take place.

81. *When can we speak of a proper promulgation of fundamental human rights?*

We can speak of a proper promulgation of fundamental human rights when there is acknowledgement of what nature teaches and commands.

PIUS XII (Address of 21 January 1950; C. D. III, 18).

"When the individual man is recognized by all in his true stature as the image of God gifted with inherent rights which no merely human power may violate . . . ."

NATURE is the immediate work of God and not of men. Clearly and with incontestable certainty it makes known the mind of its Creator. Hence the rights it grants carry the highest sanction which cannot be legitimately overruled. For this reason the interpretation of fundamental rights as natural right lays a solid foundation which does not depend on human agreement but is sufficiently strong and effective in itself, and rests in itself, that is, in the will of the Creator who arranged nature precisely in this way.

Men are thus obliged: i. to study nature carefully in order to find out what nature grants and demands of them; ii. to acknowledge and observe natural rights. These may be promulgated anew by human authority, but acknowledgement and acceptance is thereby presupposed; it does not establish the rights in the first instance; iii. to apply natural rights correctly to a changing situation, or to change the situation so that natural rights can become effective.

Regardless of whether they come about in the first or the second way fundamental human rights are not to be confused, or identified, with existing international law. The latter contains all agreements and usages which are made or recognized among nations. It goes beyond what is demanded by human rights and may also be contrary to human rights.

In this Handbook fundamental rights are understood to mean universal human rights granted by nature.

82. What are the characteristics of fundamental rights?

Fundamental rights are inalienable, inviolable, binding in themselves, and independent of human consent and legislation.

1. THE individual is not entitled to renounce a fundamental right, for he has not himself issued this right. He as well as others are bound by human nature. It is wrong for example to commit suicide, to inculpate oneself falsely, to renounce parental right.

2. We may not be deprived of fundamental rights; they may not be infringed upon. Being the work and gift of God, nature may not be subjected to human interference; it ought to be, on the contrary, subject to reverent protection.

3. For fundamental rights to be binding there is no need of human injunction (although an injunction may serve to call to mind and "underline" the natural law, because the laws of

nature precede all human laws. They are binding in themselves and by the authority of God who has established goals and claims of nature. As soon as fundamental rights are recognized as such we are by that very fact obliged in conscience to acknowledge and to realize them. In cases of doubt we may be excused in conscience. As far as Roman Catholics are concerned such doubts are removed when the Church clearly states that a natural right is involved or an action is contrary to nature. Thus, for example, the Church has declared that sterilization on the grounds of hereditary disease is contrary to nature.

4. That which is binding in itself does not need to be expressly made obligatory by some other authority. It is independent of human consent or rejection. But this characteristic deserves to be specially mentioned because totalitarian States in particular make all right dependent on themselves. They only recognize "positive" right, that is right granted by themselves; and in this connection they are the most consistent adherents of Legal Positivism. Under the pretext of freedom men have lost their liberty increasingly wherever positive right alone has obtained. Nature cannot be denied and violated with impunity.

83. Do these characteristics pertain to all fundamental rights without exception?

These characteristics pertain to primary fundamental rights without exception, but to derivative fundamental rights with certain limitations.

1. Not all fundamental rights are equally close to nature. We distinguish among them two groups:

a. Primary fundamental rights which correspond directly to the natural goals on which depends the rightness of human life decisively and inescapably. Without the recognition and actual granting of these fundamental rights the existence and the basic obligations of human life are not possible at all (Q. 84).

b. Derivative fundamental rights presuppose original fundamental rights and result from them by way of deductive reasoning. They, too, are part of the rightness of human life, but not with the same degree of necessity (Q. 85).

This distinction would be differently interpreted by the positivist school which considers those fundamental rights as original or derived that have been declared to be such. However, an interpretation according to natural right cannot be discarded even by this school. It is realized that nature cannot be passed over wherever fundamental rights are honestly and objectively sought, uninfluenced by prejudices and political power. In fact the natural relationship between primary and derivative fundamental rights is so evident that it is to a large extent tacitly acknowledged even by those who have deliberately attempted to exclude natural right from their deliberations.

2. This distinction concerns not only the origin but also the validity of fundamental rights. Primary fundamental rights are absolutely valid, everywhere and always, as they stand, in respect of their entire content, and without qualification. But individuals may, from higher considerations, have to face the loss of certain fundamental rights. The individual may for example have to risk his life for the defence of his country, or he may forfeit life as a result of a grave crime (capital punishment). Derivative fundamental rights are conditionally valid. There are cases when exceptions may be justified or even required. This may be due to: i. particular circumstances having changed a situation; for example illness or injury justify operations which it would never be lawful to perform on a healthy person.

271

ii. social circumstances preventing the use of a right which is in itself legitimate, for example when the acquisition and use of private property is limited.

No fundamental right, therefore, can be abolished or restricted at will. Limitations are justified only where they are really necessary and to that extent alone. And in that case care must be taken particularly that the common good will not be seriously affected or endangered (for example, interference in the economic structure and in private ownership through which deficiencies in material goods may become worse instead of being eliminated). But derivative or conditional fundamental rights, too, never cease to be guiding and obligatory norms. Conditions ought to be created in which all fundamental rights can be guaranteed to all men.

84. What are primary fundamental rights?

Primary fundamental rights are:
1. **the right to maintain one's life;**
2. **the right to pursue the ultimate end of life (God and man's own moral perfection) in such wise that it can be obtained;**
3. **the right to fulfil obligations with personal responsibility;**
4. **the right to live as a man among fellow-men;**
5. **the right to marry and to provide for and bring up children;**
6. **the right to acquire, possess, and use private property.**

ONLY some additional remarks will be necessary as the explanations have already been given, especially in Q. 71.

1. It may be asked why it is that precisely these rights are considered as primary fundamental rights. The answer must be based on a consideration of man from the point of view of his essential destiny and characteristics. Man is a rational, sentient being, created by God and social by nature. As a rational, sentient being man possesses his own human life as the most natural good which does not derive from himself but from his Creator. As long as, and because, that life exists it deserves and requires to be preserved. Man also has the ability to act and develop as man. This is the most immediate and most characteristic expression of his humanity, that is, a primary endowment of nature. Man is thereby enabled: i. to acknowledge truth and to do good, because only through that which is true and good can man become perfect; ii. to take personal responsibility for his entire conduct; iii. to rule over, to perfect and utilize for himself irrational nature.

2. As a rational, sentient being created by God man has the inalienable and inviolable right to acknowledge and to worship God, to seek him as his ultimate end, and to fulfil God's commandments. This also is a primary right, since it is based, on the one hand, on God's creative and sovereign power, and on the other, on man's complete and absolute dependence on God. As a fundamental right it extends to everything that man must do in order that he may find God.

As a rational, sentient being who by nature is social, who has been sent into, and obliged to, social life in virtue of his nature, man may, and must, demand: i. to be respected as a man among his fellow men and to be fitted into social life; ii. the possibility of finding the natural complement and development of his person; iii. to have the care of those who belong to him as his offspring.

273

It follows that attacks on primary fundamental rights undermine the foundations of law and are indeed "crimes against humanity".

85. What are derivative fundamental rights?

Derivative fundamental rights are those which spring from primary fundamental rights by deductive reasoning.

1. MAN has the ability: i. to penetrate ever deeper into the goals and orders of his human nature, that is to say, to examine and to find out what powers nature has given him and what tasks it has set him; ii. to infer one thing from another. For example when he observes smoke he infers that something is burning; iii. to recognize fundamental truths in virtue of which nature actually makes possible and guarantees genuine human living in the first instance. Important in this connection are first and foremost the following principles:

Nature intends man to develop himself so as to reach that perfection which is proper to him and for which he is designed.

Nature gives man the right to the means that are absolutely necessary for reaching in a humanly worthy manner the goals which it has set him.

It is something entirely distinct if man discovers further rights by deductive reasoning from the natural bases and relationship of right, or if he creates additional rights in the strict sense, that is, using his own discretion and according to circumstances decides what is proper and may be declared lawful. In the first case we are dealing with a fundamental right, in the second case with positive law.

2. Human nature, and consequently primary fundamental rights, are by no means narrow, but on the contrary extra-

ordinarily wide. A great number of further rights can be derived from them. Besides, there is no end to what man is constantly discovering about his own nature. New conditions especially arising from intellectual, economic, and social development afford him new insights into the manifold possibilities which God has bestowed on man as a natural gift. Hence it is not surprising that the list of fundamental rights is increasing as time goes on. Some rights are not sufficiently known at one moment or the situation did not call for their being specially emphasized. Thus, for example, if parents are free and able to send their children to the type of school acceptable to them, this part of parental rights does not need to be specially mentioned and assured. And if with good will and personal effort everyone could find work and a home without difficulty it would be superfluous to make a special point of emphasizing the relevant right.[37]

86. Can we also speak of the fundamental rights of society (community)?

Since there are natural rights of society (community) we may also speak of fundamental rights of society.

1. THE question has been answered already in substance (Q. 71). Ours, unlike former ages, is much concerned with the fundamental rights of society. The reason is that society

[37] Individual derivative fundamental rights will be discussed elsewhere. Let it suffice here to draw attention to some compilations of fundamental rights. *Declaration of Human Rights* drawn up by the United Nations Commission for Human Rights, published 1948. *The Charter of Human Rights and Obligations of San Sebastian* (Spain), 1948. It is based entirely upon the Catholic standpoint. *The Rights of Woman and Child*, Proposals of the International Union of Catholic Women's Leagues, 1949. *Declaration of Rights*, drafted by N.C.W.C. in 1947.

possesses both a value of its own, and natural rights, and it is both necessary and proper to underline this, if only for the sake of truth. Moreover, the views, conditions, and complexities of our time demand that the community should be acknowledged in its full significance and at the same time kept within its proper limits. Extreme individualism caused the disintegration of society in the past, while the "rediscovery" of society occurred in our socialist age. There are great dangers to society in the different forms of collectivism.

In considering the fundamental rights of society we are not dealing with the fact that individual persons with their fundamental rights come into contact with one another and have to show consideration for one another. We have in mind rather the community as an independent reality like the family, the profession, or the State.

2. While having due regard to the difference between natural and voluntary communities, there are certainly three general fundamental rights of society: i. the right to exist and to make use of the means necessary for existence; ii. the right to carry out its own proper tasks independently, and to develop in a natural manner; iii. the right to take its proper place within and to receive assistance from the social structures as a whole.

87. Are there supernatural fundamental rights?

There are supernatural fundamental rights in so far as the rights bestowed by Christ are inalienable and inviolable.

By supernatural we mean that which belongs directly to the Christian dispensation. It is not made known to men in a natural way, but through the Church from supernatural divine Revelation in the Old and New Testament and from tradition and the body of faith.

From these sources of faith it is quite clear that there are supernatural rights. It is clear from the fact that in these very sources tasks and powers are transmitted, and directives are given which in the strictest form bind to very definite things. But he whom God himself puts under obligation in such wise receives at the same time from God himself the right to fulfil this obligation.

As these rights and obligations cannot be derived from nature they do not possess the character of fundamental rights in the ordinary sense, because the latter are of natural origin and character. But under an aspect which is decisive for the order of right they are equal, and even superior to, natural rights. Rights which God himself grants claim the most absolute and most unrestricted validity. They are inalienable and inviolable. This follows from God's absolute sovereignty. Man is absolutely and in all circumstances bound to obey God, especially when God calls him to everlasting life and endows him with grace.

Although the rights granted by God must be considered inalienable and inviolable, it is possible to distinguish within the supernatural order those which are of primary importance. Other rights have been granted by God or can be derived from them. They may be called supernatural fundamental rights. The denial or violation of these is a grievous fault committed against Christ and his salvation.

The ultimate goal of supernatural fundamental rights is the Kingdom of God on earth and in heaven, the honour of the triune God in the community of the redeemed. God has granted the necessary rights and powers both to the Church as God's people made holy in Christ, and also to men called to

277

salvation and to the Church, in order that they may fulfil his will, and that they may be able, through his grace and guidance in this life, to work for their perfection in the next life.

Supernatural fundamental rights of the Church

The right to exist to the end of time and to spread over the whole earth.

The right to govern independently her own organization and all matters entrusted to her by Christ.

The right of worshipping God in the form which he has laid down.

The right to guard, expound and proclaim the natural and supernatural truths necessary for salvation.

The right to lead all men to the fullness of life in Christ. (Sacraments, preaching, commandments, education.)

The right to use such material aids as will guarantee the fruitful fulfilment of her mission. (Property; support from the natural communities.)

Supernatural fundamental rights of the individual

The right to believe in Christ and to confess this faith before men.

The right to follow Christ. (Loyalty to his commandments; voluntary acceptance of the evangelical counsels.)

The right to belong to the Church of Christ, to share in her means of salvation and to observe her commandments.

The right to co-operate in making the world more Christian.

These rights may be summed up in the right to be and to live as a Christian. In this everything is contained which Christ called us to be and to do.

88. What protection is there for fundamental rights?

Fundamental rights are protected in a number of ways. Church and State are obliged to look after their external protection.

PIUS XII (*Address of 5 August 1950; C. D., III, 26*).

"*Besides, there are rights and freedom of action possessed by the individual and family which the State is at all times bound to defend and which it cannot set aside on the pretext that the good of the community is at stake. We have in mind, to give but a few instances, a person's right to his honour and his good name, to worship the true God, the natural rights of parents over their offspring and their education. The fact that some Constitutions have recently acknowledged this truth is a happy augury which We greet with joy, seeing in it the beginning of a renewed respect for the rights of man as they have been decreed and established by God.*"

1. Two facts are quite certain; first that fundamental rights are in need of effective protection, since both private and social life depend on them absolutely. If fundamental rights are violated or denied, human life ceases to be bearable and worthy; everything becomes fluid and stability of right disappears more and more.

2. Second, fundamental rights are nowadays especially threatened and endangered by all totalitarian ideologies. Fundamental rights as such are protected by the divine sanction inherent in them, by our conscience and our sense of right.

Fundamental rights have natural origin and natural validity (Qs. 81–2). They carry their own guarantee (God and nature), which is more lasting than any possible human protection. This is why individuals and communities are obliged not only to make use of their basic rights but also to defend them. Examples are associations of parents for the protection of denominational schools; the protest of the Church against encroachments on the part of the State.

Effect, proof, and guarantee of this inner sanction is the important fact that the human conscience is instinctively roused, the natural sense of right rebels when fundamental rights are attacked and overruled. But incitement, fear, or the prospect of personal advantage may warp our judgement or at least cause us to be silent. Hence it happens, for example, that certain fundamental rights are claimed for a political party and for members of the same social class but denied to others.

3. The Church makes no arrogant claim but merely fulfils her duty when in order to protect fundamental rights she declares that in this or that case a fundamental right is involved, and in what sense; when she raises her voice to warn the world to respect fundamental rights and make them effective; when she uses her spiritual power (excommunication) against those who violate a fundamental right.

It is true that genuine fundamental rights, belong to the natural order of life. But they are of such decisive importance for eternal salvation (the Kingdom of God and its purpose in the world) that the Church must speak and act when they are being jeopardized or abolished.

4. States ought to consider it as one of their principal tasks to establish and guarantee a genuine juridical order. But this is not possible without acknowledging and observing fundamental rights. Legislation and the administration of justice ought to be rooted in fundamental rights, and in the first place aim at right being carried out effectively. Some states have listed fundamental rights in their constitutions and declared them to be binding. It

is the violation of fundamental rights which has led to the setting up of an international organization for the protection of human rights. (See the historical survey at the beginning of this Lesson.)

5. There are also national and international voluntary organizations for the protection of fundamental rights. Such organizations are to be welcomed if they do not attempt to represent everything imaginable as a fundamental right,[38] since they serve as a constant reminder and warning to the public. At the same time it is still more important that men and communities should mutually acknowledge and respect their fundamental rights, and that the whole of life should be sustained by, and bear witness to, a profound regard and reverence for fundamental rights.

Lesson Four

THE VIRTUE OF JUSTICE

EXPERIENCE shows that men often and easily forget their obligations in justice, and frequently commit injustice, even flagrant injustice. We know that man will keep unflinchingly and unerringly to what is just only when he is animated by a genuine and constant will to be just. Hence there is need of a strong attitude of mind and an unswerving line of conduct to guarantee that justice be done and injustice avoided. This attitude is called the virtue of justice.

---

[38] A recent example is the recommendation by one organization that "euthanasia by request" should be adopted as an universal human right.

89. What is the virtue of justice?

It is that virtue which has right for its object and disposes us to render to everyone his due.

1. MAN is by nature capable of doing good, if he so wills he can act justly. But this natural capability of doing good is, in fact, too indefinite; it extends to the whole orbit of moral obligations, extensive, many-sided, and changing as they are; it is too uncertain, since man is insufficiently attuned to, and inwardly poorly disposed towards, his various obligations. Good ought therefore to be more deeply rooted in man. He ought to be so well versed in doing good that he will, as a matter of course, pursue the good and make it his "second nature". This stable habit, an abiding disposition to will and to do only what is good, which goes beyond mere ability, is called virtue. It is not a free gift of nature; rather the individual himself must acquire it by deliberate and repeated practice.[39]

What is true of the moral sphere is also true of other spheres

---

[39] Besides the acquired, there are the infused moral virtues. They are of a supernatural nature and have their origin in sanctifying grace (Q. 18, No. 5). They correspond to the theological virtues (faith, hope, charity), which are likewise infused along with sanctifying grace, and they govern human conduct in so far as it is subject to reason enlightened by faith. We might also say that they govern the conduct of man as the "child of God made holy by grace" (see St. Thomas Aquinas, I–II 63, 3–4). For in accordance with the injunctions of revelation, and as followers of Christ, we assume new and higher obligations. Our natural obligations will be seen in the light of the supernatural; they ought to be discharged from supernatural motives. As a consequence natural standards must often be set aside. They do not lose their validity, but they will be superseded. Thus for example it is in keeping with natural justice that an injustice should be redressed; yet according to supernatural teaching we should suffer injustice patiently and return good for evil. Hence a man may be obliged for our Lord's sake to renounce voluntarily the satisfaction and atonement due to him. The supernatural love of God and our neighbour often requires us to put charity before justice, and instead of insisting on justice to exercise mercy.

of human conduct. Man engages in the most diverse activities, professions and arts by reason of his natural disposition, ability, and talent. But no man is born a master. He has to develop his abilities in certain directions; he has first to acquire skill and facility. (Unskilled and skilled labour; the apprentice, the trained hand, and the master craftsman; training in sport; facility of touch in drawing or in playing a musical instrument; the born and the trained orator.)

2. Acting justly is a particular category of human conduct. For instance being moderate in eating and drinking is something different from being brave in the face of danger, or from preserving one's equanimity in both good and ill fortune. Acting justly is a matter of the will. In order that the will may everywhere and always decide spontaneously in favour of what is in accordance with right, it must be inwardly disposed towards right and ever ready to do right. The will receives this readiness through the virtue of justice which is, as St. Thomas Aquinas says, no more than a "readiness, according to which each has a perpetual and constant will to render to everyone his due."[40] Man can therefore be said to have the virtue of justice only when by constant practice he has reached the stage where he is at all times and in every respect really inclined and anxious to render to everyone his due.

3. Because right is a matter of such consequence it is most important for men to possess the virtue of justice so that they may fulfil the manifold and often irksome demands of right, not with a bad grace and merely externally, but willingly and spontaneously, honestly shrinking from doing an injustice. Hence the acquisition and the cultivation of the virtue of justice rank

[40] St. Thomas Aquinas, II–II, 58, 1.

among the most important aims of education. The virtue of justice is necessary above all to those who by reason of their position or their profession are servants of the law. (Legislators, judges, those in authority; but also parents, teachers, managers, foremen.)

90. What are the conditions required for the virtue of justice?

As in the case of right so also for the virtue of justice three conditions are required.

THE essence and the function of the virtue of justice consists in giving willingly to everyone what is his right. Hence the virtue of justice must fulfil the same conditions as right. These conditions have been sufficiently discussed in Q. 57.

91. With what is justice concerned?

Justice is concerned with exterior things and actions only.

1. IN all virtues an interior and an exterior act has to be distinguished. Initially, good must be willed, inwardly consented to, and striven after. The next step is to realize the good through actions, to perform exterior actions which will correspond to the interior ones.

EXAMPLES. Patience requires us first of all to control our anger inwardly, and then to control ourselves in our exterior behaviour. For example, a temperate man will not desire more than agrees with him in eating and drinking.

2. In the case of all other virtues, with the exception of justice, the exterior act is but the continuation and natural conclusion, of the interior act. The value of the exterior action depends entire-

ly on the interior act. The orderly interior act produces and releases the orderly exterior act. He is a continent man who keeps his interior desires under discipline. He will preserve his self-control in actual indulgence. But in the case of justice it is different. For justice is directed towards other people; it regulates the mutual relations of men in so far as each renders to the other what is due to him. This is done by way of exterior actions,[41] and exterior actions correspond to the exterior good with which they are concerned.

EXAMPLES. Interior liberty can neither be given to another person nor taken from him, exterior liberty can be thus bestowed; yet the restriction or suppression of exterior liberty indirectly also affects interior liberty, though the latter cannot be touched directly. Buying and selling occurs through the exchange of articles of equal value, or by exchanging a corresponding sum of money for an article. In both cases we have exterior actions and exterior goods. Life, health, physical well-being, honour, property, decent housing conditions are exterior goods which are attained or harmed by exterior actions.

3. The interior act of justice is therefore determined by the exterior act. The just man is he who fulfils just demands as they come from outside. He can fulfil them only by performing the exterior actions due to the other, or by giving the other those exterior goods which are due to him, and this again can only be done by exterior actions. Thus exterior actions and exterior goods are the standards for deciding whether a person is just or unjust in his intentions.

EXAMPLE. When we want to buy something we first ask what the article costs. Having learned the price we know what we have to pay. We shall be acting in justice only when a certain amount is being paid. Our intentions are therefore just only when they submit to the exterior proportional value between article and price.

[41] St. Thomas Aquinas, II–II 58, 5; See Q. 37.

Nevertheless the exterior act is also in the realm of justice the outcome and effect of the interior act. Man acts from an interior readiness to give or to render what he owes exteriorly. The circle is thus complete: the precept of justice is both intended and realized.

Our diagram shows the balance:

Exterior goods and services

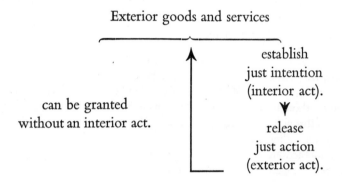

can be granted
without an interior act.

establish
just intention
(interior act).

release
just action
(exterior act).

This balance between the interior and exterior act explains the peculiar fact that we may fulfil the demands of justice exteriorly without having the interior disposition and intention to be just. In such cases there is a perfectly correct procedure from a purely legal point of view; everyone retains, or receives, what in fact is his due, and human law and justice must be satisfied with that. From the moral point of view, however, the decisive element is missing, namely, the intention to be just.

EXAMPLES. The employer who pays wages because he is legally compelled to do so, and not because he considers the workers' claims to be just. There is the person who restores some valuable object he has found merely because he has been observed and cannot do otherwise. There is the person who pays compensation for damage he has caused merely because a court of justice has sentenced him to do so.

Exterior goods and services can be restored only by those who are in a position to do so. For example, sickness; loss of property through theft; eviction from home; acts of God may result in complete inability to repay. And so it can happen that a person may interiorly act justly and yet may not be able to meet his obligations exteriorly. Of course, apart from special cases, obligations are not thereby removed but only deferred.

92. Why do we speak of "even-handed justice"?

Because justice preserves the balance between too much and too little; in the case of justice this balance depends on the matter involved.[42]

1. A man's conduct is virtuous when it is in conformity with right reason, that is, when a man acts in conformity with the moral law, as his reason dictates. It is peculiar to the moral virtues[43] to preserve the mean between two opposites, between too much and too little. For virtue is the standard for the right

[42] St. Thomas Aquinas, I–II 60, 2; II–II 58, 10.

[43] While the theological virtues have God himself, the ultimate goal of life, for their object, the moral virtues relate to the means needed to the ultimate goal, by which we understand many of what are called intermediate goals also as outward goods. That which in itself is not worth attaining but serves a necessary purpose is defined as means or instrument (thus a football is merely the means of a game; a bicycle is merely a means of transport). But an intermediate goal is that which possesses a value of its own and therefore may be striven for, for its own sake, without necessarily representing the highest and ultimate value. Science, virtue, art, and true culture are such intermediate goals, since they are something more than mere means to an end. Since justice has to do with external goods and actions it belongs to the moral virtues. It is one of the four cardinal virtues which are so called because moral living as it were hangs and turns on them as a door on its hinges (*cardo* = hinge). Thus the cardinal virtues are the chief supports of morality (see St. Thomas Aquinas, I–II 61, 1-3).

conduct of men. But standards can be disregarded either by going beyond them or by not going far enough. Fortitude preserves the balance between cowardice and foolhardiness, generosity between meanness and extravagance, friendliness between flattery and quarrelsomeness. It is for reason to establish by means of prudence where the correct mean lies for each individual person and in each case. Hence the "mean" of moral virtues is called the rational mean, *medium rationis*.

EXAMPLES. Moderation requires on the one hand that a man should eat and drink sufficiently to sustain life and to keep fit (lower limit), and on the other hand, that he should not eat or drink more than agrees with him. How much that may be differs from one individual to another, while age, profession, health, sickness, and other circumstances must also be taken into consideration. Thus each one must find out what amount is reasonable and right for him and for those entrusted to his charge. We may say that parents act "unreasonably" when they force a sick child to eat as much as a child that is quite well.

2. Justice, too, preserves the mean between what is too much and what is too little. If somebody sells articles valued at 5s., he acts justly if he charges 5s. If he charges 6s. he overcharges the customer. If he charges 4s. he renounces part of his right. As far as this part of his right is concerned he may be influenced not by justice but by other considerations (for example, kindness, compassion). The example shows that in the case of justice the "mean" is based on the thing, on the relation of real equality between what is demanded and what is given. Hence we speak of the *real* mean *(medium rei)*. Reason can merely take note of, or at most calculate, in what the equality consists, and this calculation is independent of the view both of the person who charges and of the person obliged to pay. It is a question of material, objective equality. Whether the person who buys a

watch is rich or poor, a friend or an enemy, does not in itself affect the price of the watch. In this connection wage negotiations are often very instructive. First the capabilities of the person seeking work are examined and established. Then on the basis of the expected service the wage is determined (equality of service and remuneration). If the worker does more he must be paid more; if he does not reach the stipulated quota his pay is reduced accordingly.

93. Which are the subdivisions of justice?

Justice is subdivided into general or legal justice and particular justice; the latter is subdivided into commutative and distributive justice.

PIUS XII (C. B., 1942; C. T. S., 7).
"The legal structure has also the noble and arduous task of securing harmonious relations between individual citizens, between various associations within the State, and between their members."

THIS subdivision of justice represents the traditional Catholic moral and social teaching since St. Thomas Aquinas. What is meant by social justice will be dealt with in Qs. 110–11.

In this division we are dealing with the kinds of justice taken in the proper and strict sense, and not with the auxiliary or supplementary virtues such as obedience, veracity, devotion, generosity. That means that not only commutative justice but also legal and distributive justice have right as their proper object, i. e., that which is due to others (Q. 57, No. 2). Hence all three kinds are concerned with genuine claims and obligations in justice. It is wrong to limit strict justice to commutative justice, and to consider legal and distributive justice as justice in a metaphorical sense.[44]

[44] See St. Thomas Aquinas, II–II 58, 5.

The three kinds mentioned are not on a par with one another, rather justice is first divided into general and particular; the particular is then subdivided into commutative and distributive; thus:

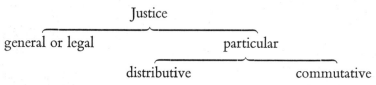

Justice

general or legal   particular

distributive   commutative

The differences and connections will be explained more fully in Q. 94 et seq. Here we are concerned with showing the reasons why this subdivision is necessary and correct.

1. Justice concerns and regulates man's relations with other men. They may be individuals or a community, that is, the social whole of which he is a part and a member. Both have to be considered; otherwise the reality in which the individual lives is being missed.[45]

2. The individual as such has his own special good (private good), his own right; the community for its part has its own proper goal, the common good. This common good is not equivalent to the sum total of the individual goods, but con-

[45] What we have written previously (Q. 21 et seq.) concerning the reality of the community is at this point of decisive importance. We ought to bear in mind that the community is men related to one another and living together in a definite order. If the community is regarded as an impersonal, let alone unreal, entity, nothing can be "due to it", because an impersonal, and much less an unreal "whole", can claim nothing as its own. On this assumption it would be necessary to have recourse to a so-called legal fiction, as is frequently done by modern jurisprudence. On the other hand if we take community to mean a unity of order of persons, they may very properly be owed something. At the same time it is clear that in respect of what is due to the community we are dealing with an entirely new factor compared with what is due to the individual as such.

stitutes an independent good, i.e., different from private good not only in degree and size but in its essential character (Qs. 24–5, 29). It is a good common to all the members so that each as a member of the community can claim his proper share. If he receives what is due to him, this share becomes his own private good. From this emerges first the fact that the community has its own good, namely, the common good; second, that each individual has his own good, that is, private good. This is of two kinds: i. as good due to him as an individual; ii. as good due to him as a member of a community.

3. Virtues are specified and specifically differentiated by what is called the formal object, that is, not merely the number and diversity of things covered by the particular virtue, but rather the special aspect under which all this is comprehended and ordered. Each new independent aspect implies a new function and a new virtue.[46] Since justice has for its object what is lawfully due, there must be a different form of justice wherever there is a new good lawfully due, for that requires in each case very different functions of justice. Now there are two goods above all which in consequence of their essentially different character establish two specifically different forms of what is legally due, namely, the common good of the community, and the particular good of the individual. Thus general justice and particular justice

---

[46] As an illustration we give the following example: What we regard as money and property may be considered; i. in so far as one person owes it to another, in which case it is the object of justice; ii. in so far as one person gives it to another as a free gift, in which case it is the object of generosity; iii. in so far as one person uses it to relieve the distress of another, in which case it is the object of mercy. The same thing may thus be covered by different virtues according to the aspect under which it is considered, and according to the motive. The aspects and motives mentioned differ one from the other to such an extent that each demands a particular virtue in order that the corresponding work may be done.

differ as two distinct virtues and not merely as two functions of one single virtue. The particular good of the individual (private good) is legally, however, of a completely different kind according to whether the individual has a claim to it as a private person or as a member of the community. For it is precisely this fact, that the individual may claim something as his own, at one moment as an individual person and at another as a member of the community, that differentiates also what is his due. For this reason particular justice cannot be but one virtue, but must consist of two distinct virtues.[47]

A. COMMUTATIVE JUSTICE

94. What is commutative justice?

Commutative justice is that kind of justice which impels man to render to his fellow men who are his equals the full amount of what is their due.

1. COMMUTATIVE justice regulates the rightful relations between individuals; thus it equalizes the claims of individual persons who enjoy equal rights. Since it regulates principally, though not exclusively, economic relations it is also called exchange justice (in industry, commerce and trade).

EXAMPLES. One person sells, another buys; one lends, the other borrows; one man does a job, another pays the wage.

2. Commutative justice embraces a large area. It extends to all goods and services which one person owes, or may owe, to another: life (murder, manslaughter); bodily integrity (bodily

[47] The explanation which follows begins with commutative justice, not because this is the highest form of justice but because it is easier to understand.

injury, rape); honour (calumny); property (theft, robbery, embezzlement); wages (withholding the agreed wage).

3. Commutative justice is not confined to individual persons in such wise as not to concern the community, or individuals in relation to the community. It may very well extend beyond mutual dealings between individual persons, as happens when dealings take place between an individual person and a community, or between individual communities. (For example when the state leases or buys land, pays its officials, runs commercial or industrial concerns; the transfer of property or wealth from one community to another.)

95. Why "commutative" justice?

Because service is exchanged for service on a basis of strict equality (of value).

PIUS XI (Q. A., 47).

"It belongs to what is called commutative justice, faithfully to respect private ownership, and not to encroach on the rights of another by exceeding the limits of one's own right of property."

1. THERE is an equation in the strict sense where two goods or services are perfectly equal when measured or weighed against one another. We are not and cannot be concerned with the persons who wish to exchange one thing for another, but rather with comparing the value of one article or service with the value of another. One person must give or restore the exact amount that the other offers, demands or is deprived of. At a horse fair we are not interested in the name of the farmer who wishes to sell a horse, but rather in the value of the horse. In order to establish what restitution must be made in case of theft we inquire

293

what has been stolen and what is the value of the stolen goods. This absolute equality is seen most clearly when we deal with figures; hence we speak of numerical, arithmetical equality (numerical and quantitative equation).

$$5 = 5; \ 8 = 3 + 5; \ 21 = 3 \times 7$$

6 working hours at 3/- per hour = 18/-.
One suit of clothes = 5 or 6 pairs of shoes
(according to the quality of each).

2. The following should be noted:

a. When it is not a question of material but of higher goods it is very difficult to estimate what has to be paid in accordance with the demands of commutative justice (remuneration for intellectual or artistic services; compensation for bodily injury, rape, wrongful imprisonment). The difficulty lies in the fact that there is no standard scale of measurement with which to calculate higher goods or services in terms of material goods. Only values of the same category allow of direct comparison with one another, and only material values allow of being expressed in number and quantity.

b. A man can commit an injustice only of his own free will and only against his will can he suffer an injustice. This principle applies first and foremost to the moral order, but also, on a broader plane, to the juridical order, because in giving judgement the judge must also consider the degree of responsibility (negligence, wrongful intention). Unintentional harm or damage caused to others, for example through inadvertency or as a consequence of some unfortunate accident, is not an injustice in the true sense, although it may involve liability for the damage. Nor is acquiescence in losses, actions, or treatment, necessarily an injustice (for example a girl who allows herself to be abused;

294

a worker who works for less than the standard rate without being compelled to do so).

c. The violation of commutative justice can lead to direct legal action to enforce the return or replacement of the thing involved: right of action.

96. What is the particular function of commutative justice?

The particular function of commutative justice is the return or restoration of other people's property, also called restitution or compensation.

"RESTITUTION" means to put someone again in the possession of his property; to restore to a person the thing that belongs to him, or another thing of equal value. One can only give back that which belongs to a person but which is not at the time in his possession (as for example borrowed or stolen goods). If the goods no longer exist, or if one person causes damage to another without personal gain, then restitution can only take the form of compensation or damages.

Restitution has a twofold basis:

a. The other person's property, and the damage caused to the other person. What is another's property must be returned to the owner; any damage done must be compensated.

b. Not only unlawfully acquired goods belonging to others but also property that may have come lawfully into our possession must be returned (for example, things found, borrowed, stored, inadvertently taken).

c. It is also a part of rendering another his due that we should not damage the property of another or seek to dispute his right to what is his, or what he has a claim to.

97. Is restitution obligatory?

We are bound, in conscience, to return other people's property and to compensate for any damage we may have caused, and we must do so as soon as we can, unless it has been otherwise agreed.

1. JUSTICE belongs to those virtues which it is absolutely necessary to practise in order to live a morally good life. But justice demands that everyone should be allowed to retain, or should be given back, what belongs to him. Therefore whoever refuses to give back or to compensate, or does so only in part, or wrongfully delays doing so, acts unjustly. The gravity of the injustice committed depends on the value of the goods involved, as also on the material circumstances of the person who has suffered the damage. The ability to make restitution is also a factor, for example in deciding how much must be restored and how soon (see No. 2). At any rate the obligation to make restitution binds in conscience (also in the case of small things and slight damage). The reason has already been stated, namely, that the demands of justice are necessarily bound up with the ultimate goal of life. Whoever seriously offends against justice acts contrary to his ultimate goal, since he prefers created things to the uncreated good. The saying of our Lord applies to him: "You must serve God or money; you cannot serve both" (Matt. 6:24).

2. The time for making restitution has to be determined according to the following two rules:

i. Unless difficulties arise for which we are not responsible we must abide by agreements made (wages to be paid at the end of the week; salaries at the beginning or at the end of the month; rent and lease contracts; payment of bills; payment of interest and instalments). Any considerable postponement through one's own fault is an offence, in certain circumstances even a grave offence, against justice. The gravity of this offence depends on how much the other person is dependent on what is due to him (for example, workers and employees usually cannot afford to wait long for their wages; many people letting houses and land depend on the rents for their livelihood; sometimes a tradesman cannot work if the tools which he has lent or which have been stolen from him are not returned).

ii. Property that is unlawfully held must be restored immediately. Damage caused must be repaired immediately, because the other person has a right to have at his disposal at all times what is his, unless there are lawful reasons to the contrary. If restitution is not immediately possible, then what is feasible at the time must be done, and the rest as soon as possible. Those in debt should live frugally until the whole debt has been discharged in order to be able to meet their obligation. The debtor should restrict himself to a simple way of living in keeping with his status as a debtor. In certain cases even further restrictions may be called for depending on the size of the debt and the material circumstances of the person who has suffered the damage.

iii. There are various reasons which may wholly or at least in part, or for the time being, excuse a person from restitution. For example, if the owner or the person who has suffered the damage waives his claim; inability as a result of illness or of being conscripted to the armed forces, or loss of one's own property (through fire, acts of God, failure of the bank, theft).

iv. The person who has the other's property in his possession or who has caused the damage is the one to make restitution or to repair the damage. The obligation passes on to the heirs in so far as the inherited property (not that which is otherwise acquired) has to be used to meet it.

98. *Is commutative justice subject to the regulations of human law?*

Human law is entitled to make enactments directly or indirectly affecting commutative justice.

STRICTLY speaking the standard of commutative justice is based on equality in quantity and value of goods and services (Q. 95). This equality is independent of state enactments and is based on the nature of the thing involved or on voluntary agreement and mutual consent (see II–II 57, 2). But commutative justice, too, is not outside, but within, the common good. Hence it also must operate in such a manner that the common good can be properly and surely attained.

1. The common good demands first of all that what is naturally right should be observed; hence it requires that men should respect and establish among themselves the equality of *quid pro quo*. In this respect it is for human law to protect the work of commutative justice by guaranteeing individual persons the possession and use of what is theirs, as also by punishing offences (theft, fraud, calumny).

2. Taxes and other assessments imposed for the purpose of the common good at least indirectly affect commutative justice. They are continually causing changes, necessitating limitations, and restricting the possession and disposal of property. Fixed prices, tariffs, state monopolies, exercise an indirect influence.

3. The common good requires and justifies that that be done which will guarantee concord and peace in justice. But in the

domain of commutative justice, cases arise not infrequently which make it difficult to gain a proper perspective and judgement of things and circumstances, so that in the absence of a regulation in law the situation remains obscure and uncertain; that leads to quarrels and dissensions which are sometimes quite serious. This danger can, and must, be warded off.

EXAMPLES. The law relating to the rights of property of married women; regulations governing the validity of wills; right-of-way; regulations governing the legal form of wage contracts.

B. DISTRIBUTIVE JUSTICE

99. What is distributive justice?

Distributive justice is that kind of justice designed to distribute advantages and burdens equitably among members of the community.[48]

THE common good or the good of the community as a whole, concerns members of the community in a twofold manner:

i. All must co-operate in preserving and furthering it. Each member of the community must contribute his share towards making it possible for the whole to live and act in an orderly and profitable manner.

ii. It is there for all and it should benefit all.

Distributive justice is concerned that common advantages and burdens are not arbitrarily given to, or imposed upon, this or that individual or group, but rather distributed "fairly", that is, as is proper for the whole in relation to its parts. That is why it is called "distributive" justice.

[48] St. Thomas Aquinas, II–II Qs. 61–63.

1. Distributive justice affects the strict right of the members of the community. It affects things which are due to the members because they belong to the community, and because the community has an obligation towards them. Hence the community has to make a just distribution of advantages and burdens, for its members can claim that what is there for all, or what has been achieved by all, will not be withheld from them, and that they will not be called upon to shoulder more than their due share of the burdens.

2. The right of the members is not a "right in the thing" *(jus in re)*, but a "right to the thing" *(jus ad rem)*, the right that a definite share of the common good will fall to them, will become theirs. If these shares are not granted to them the members can take legal action, not directly for the thing, but against the community or its representatives.

3. Distributive justice belongs to man's equipment in virtue; for anyone may be called upon to fulfil many of its requirements (Q. 101). It is particularly necessary, however, for those who govern a community or who administer or distribute common property.

That we are dealing with rights in distributive justice is shown by comparing it with generosity. A man is free to decide what person or persons he wishes to help with his own private means, and to what extent. That is generosity. If, on the other hand, someone wants to reward several people, he has to take his standard from their merits. That is distributive justice. Hence we speak of a just or unjust reward, but of prudent or imprudent charity, of opportune or misplaced help.

100. Is equality also necessary for distributive justice?

Distributive justice establishes a true but proportionate equality.

EXAMPLES. i. Children in a family are not all given exactly the same food, clothes, education, but rather what is in each case appropriate; which depends on age, sex, state of health, talents, inclinations, even industry. But each child receives what is due to him in relation to the others.

ii. Somebody who is commissioned to distribute £1,000 family allowance among ten families in accordance with their needs can not simply give each family £100. He has to discover how the families differ in their needs. These depend on a number of circumstances such as the number of children, the income of the father, health or sickness in the families, how long they have been in need, the cost of living in the place where they live. Again each family receives what is its due; what is due to it in proportion to the others. It has a right to this on the basis of its situation and of the sum to be distributed.

iii. Profit shares will be calculated according to the circumstances of the interested parties: level of income, working time lost through own fault, number of service years, exceptional achievements. Everybody shares not merely anyhow but in a just form.

Our examples show:

1. The shares in the advantages and burdens can be very unequal, and yet be proportionately equal.[49] This proportion is based on the inequality of the persons, that is, on the unequal condition of the members conditioned by the whole (Q. 101).

---

[49] For example one person may pay £10 income tax and another £20, and yet both pay 3% of their income.

Or: With an income of £200 . . . . . 3%
£200 to £500 . . . 5%
£500 to £1000 . . . 8%

in accordance with greater productive capacity and the greater importance of the security guaranteed to all.

Hence we speak of proportional equality, which is nevertheless a kind of genuine equality:

$$\left. \begin{array}{l} \frac{2}{5} = \frac{4}{10} \\ \frac{A}{3} = \frac{B}{9} \end{array} \right\} \text{ each receives what is appropriate and due to him}$$

2. If we look at the matter carefully we can see that there are two matters to be considered in distributive justice:

i. The relation of the persons to one another, or of their services (service, capacity, ability);

ii. The proportion of goods and burdens in respect of persons. It is a different matter whether £400 is to be distributed in equal shares between two families, or between four families. In the first case each family receives £200 = the half, in the second case each family receives £100 = a quarter.

3. The example shows that quality or achievement is decisive in distributive justice; quality or achievement is peculiar to the persons in so far as the latter are members of a particular community, and, consequently, have rights and obligations in respect of that community. Thus first of all we have to belong to a community. If it is a question of appointment to certain definite tasks, then we have to possess the particular suitability in keeping with the purpose and character of the community and of the tasks. In short, we have to fulfil those conditions which are required by the community for the particular function or assignment. Thus the important thing is to know whether, and how far, rights and obligations are based on the fact of membership of this particular community.

EXAMPLES. Members of a football team can claim the right to play in a match, not because they hold high positions in their private professions, and not because they have good voices, but because as proficient players they can guarantee a good performance by the team. Appointments to offices must be made according to the standard of suitability for the particular office. Children's allowances should be regulated according to the number and age of the children, and the sufficiency or insufficiency of income. Honors and decorations should be awarded according to service and merit.

4. The proportional equality of distributive justice is usually more difficult to determine than the simple arithmetical equality of commutative justice. The reason is obvious. We cannot directly compare thing with thing and service with service, but have to consider the relation of the members to the whole (what they achieve or can achieve for the whole as compared with the other members), and their difference from one another in this respect. Only when this has been established is it possible to determine or calculate precisely, possibly in figures, the proportional amount due to each. Distributive justice has, nevertheless, not only a rational, but also a real mean (Q. 92), since it has to evaluate actual, objective situations, for instance, what this or that individual has actually done for the common good; who is in fact suitable.

101. What is the function of distributive justice?

It is the function of distributive justice :

i. **To decide what is just ;**

ii. **To distribute justly in accordance with this decision ;**

iii. **To protect the rights of community members effectively.**

THE distribution, from which this kind of justice derives its name, is just when each one in the community receives what he is entitled to in proportion to the others, and when no one is burdened more than he should be in proportion to the others (Q. 100). St. Thomas emphasized that the distribution of common goods should be made cautiously with consideration for the general good which must not be endangered.[50] It is senseless and irresponsible to distribute so much that the community can no longer continue to exist and be effective (for example, to destroy the capital basis of a business).

1. Before the distribution can be made it must be established how high the shares are which are to be allotted to the members of the community. Thus a judgement is required to determine what is just for the individual members. Our rational faculty has to make this judgement, but it is subject to the command of the will, the impulse of justice, which disposes man to exclude all considerations that might falsify the judgement, and thus to be guided solely by real claims. Those who have to decide what is just in the individual case must be animated by the will to be just. That applies especially to judges whom Aristotle, for that reason, called a "living embodiment of justice". Judges normally make their decisions according to written or common law. However, if this law clearly conflicts with the natural law, or obviously works out to the detriment of the common good, judges ought to have the courage (and the liberty) to pronounce judgements which conform to the natural law and do not injure the common good. If situations arise where the existing law cannot be applied without causing obvious injustice, then the law must be changed without delay; and in the meantime the judge should obviate defects by having recourse to the natural law.

EXAMPLES. Strictly speaking it is unjust to overcharge. Yet it may be justified for grave reasons (if the business will go bankrupt otherwise; in

[50] See St. Thomas Aquinas, II–II 61, I ad I.

order to keep the business going and solvent; the problem of the black market). Penalties which were fixed by law in times of crisis and as such were considered just, may become very unjust in normal times (the penalty of death or hard labor for desertion at the front or during training at the home base).

2. Distribution follows upon the judgement and the decision as to what is just in relation to persons and things. In the case of some offices we speak of investiture, appointment, assignment; in the case of laws and regulations we speak of application and execution. It is clear that distribution must be in accordance with the judgement and decision. Those persons especially who exercise distributive functions only are not competent on their own initiative to change the judgement or to circumvent or delay its execution, unless of course such powers have been granted to them (Qs. 102–103).

3. Distributive justice also has the very important function of ensuring that within the community the liberties, rights and advantages of the members are preserved and safeguarded,[51] that that which belongs and is due to the members is not taken from them or curtailed or encroached upon under any pretext or through advantage being taken of a position of power. The danger can come from the community as a whole as well as from the members. Distributive justice guarantees that the principle of subsidiary function (Q. 52), according to which members are empowered to do what it is possible for them to do by reason of natural rights or of rights in positive law, will be respected and applied. Hence the preservation of distributive justice offers effective protection against totalitarianism, absolutism in industrial and cultural realms, against unjust taxation.

---

[51] St. Thomas Aquinas, *De div. nom.* 8, 4.

102. How do we offend against distributive justice?

We offend against distributive justice above all by "respect of persons".

1. "Respect of persons" is synonymous with unjust preference or discrimination. Advantages and burdens are apportioned with no regard for those considerations which should alone be decisive. Wrong standards are applied and wrong means are employed. Prejudice and favoritism are the results.

EXAMPLES. When offices, honors or financial aid are not apportioned to those who are suitable, deserving or in need (the only valid criteria), but instead to relatives (nepotism), to those who are of the same way of thinking, to members of the same party who are "politically reliable"; when bribes are accepted; when a judge allows his judgement to be influenced by partiality or dislike, by social or political (party) considerations (People's Courts); when tax officials turn a blind eye in the direction of their friends. In all these cases there are misplaced and false reasons at work; distribution is not determined by objective considerations.

2. "Irresponsible judgement" is another widespread fault which is often very frivolously committed. Without sufficient grounds and on the strength of misunderstandings and misinterpreted indications somebody suspects or accuses another, magnifies and misrepresents his failings, attributes to him things which the other did not mean or do, or at any rate not in that way. Usually personal motives are the cause; envy and jealousy, resentment and pique, trying experiences; also class prejudice, political views, and party politics.

103. Is the obligation of restitution demanded by distributive justice?

Whoever offends against distributive justice is bound to restitution if at the same time he offends against commutative justice.

THIS answer represents the view generally held in Catholic ethics today. To substantiate it, it is argued chiefly that restitution means putting a person again in possession of what is his, that is, restoring that which belongs to the other but which has been unlawfully withheld or taken from him or damaged. Hence the obligation of restitution presupposes first that the other person has a clear, strict and individual right to the thing, second, that the injustice should be righted fully (numerical or arithmetical equality; Q. 95, 1).

These two conditions are fulfilled only through commutative justice. Hence it is through commutative justice that the obligation of restitution is established. But it may happen that someone offends directly against distributive justice, yet in so doing, at the same time damages another person in his lawful possessions or rights. In that case he has "indirectly" offended against commutative justice and is therefore bound to restitution.[52]

[52] Fr. Faidherbe O.P. holds that he has shown in an essay published in 1934 (see bibliography), that the view put forward above and generally held today is not the only one which is supported by traditional teaching. St. Thomas Aquinas and important later theologians (Cardinal Cajetan, D. Soto, John of St. Thomas) had taught otherwise, namely, that whoever offends against distributive justice was bound to restitution because and in so far as he has offended against distributive justice. Fr. Faidherbe supports this thesis with weighty arguments, and theologians who have commented on his essay (Ramírez, Palacio, Renard, Tonneau) are in complete agreement with him. I also hold his view to be correct, but up to the present day it has not been generally accepted. According to Fr. Faidherbe, this is the position:

With regard to the obligation of restitution, two factors have to be distinguished:

i. Which kind of justice is obliged to carry out restitution, that is, to restore the balance? The answer is that this function is proper to commutative justice alone. And in this sense restitution is the function of commutative justice alone. For restitution is only possible when equal goods or burdens are being confronted; restitution means to restore an equal value.

ii. It is quite a different matter to ask how the obligation of restitution arises and

EXAMPLES. A judge who through gross negligence does not punish a guilty person adequately, so that individual persons or the community suffer serious loss as a result, is bound to make good this loss; his culpable negligence would be at the same time the cause of the loss. Civil servants who by making a consciously unjust assessment, undertax some and overtax others, ought to make good the loss suffered by the latter, for everyone has the right not to be deprived of his property without necessity or just cause.

why and when we have to make restitution. In this case the answer is that a person must make restitution whenever and wherever he offends against strict justice, in other words as often as he acts unjustly in the proper sense, whenever he unlawfully takes, withholds or damages what belongs to another, denies it to him or will not acknowledge his right to it. Now since there is a threefold sense in which something may belong to another person (Q. 93), there is also a threefold source of the obligation of restitution. This obligation can spring from all three forms of strict justice.

With regard to distributive justice the following should be noted:

i. Whoever distributes unjustly what is common property is bound to restitution because he has not made a proper distribution, because he has disregarded and falsified the objective proportion between those entitled to a share. By virtue of his distribution he has culpably prevented from becoming theirs what is their due.

ii. In order to calculate how in such cases damages are to be made good, the proportion has to be considered in which the claimants were involved or in which the debtors were to be assessed; for only in this way can we arrive at the claim and thus at the compensation.

iii. This consideration will result in the absolute figure of the owed damages, and it will then be for commutative justice actually to carry out restitution.

EXAMPLE. A family complains that it has received too little in a distribution of allowances which has to be made according to definite regulations. The investigation must begin by inquiring whether the person responsible has made a just distribution. If it is established that this is not the case, the question arises, by how much, in relation to the others, this family was disregarded. A definite sum will be the result. The unjust distributor therefore ought to replace this amount. He is obliged to do this because he has defrauded the family through his unjust distribution.

308

C. UNIVERSAL OR LEGAL JUSTICE

104. What is universal or legal justice?

Universal or legal justice is that virtue which disposes the human will to render to the community what is its due.[53]

1. SINCE man is socially inclined, and can attain his natural perfection only as a social being, the community is necessary to him. But this community cannot develop in an orderly manner unless its members live in accordance with its nature, that is, unless they render it that service which is necessary for its existence and proper development. Hence the community must have the right to demand from its members whatever it needs in order properly to fulfil its function. On the member rests the obligation of acknowledging and fulfilling these demands.

2. Although men are aware that they are indebted to the community for a great deal, and that the community can neither exist nor prosper without their willing incorporation and co-operation, experience shows nevertheless that often they are reluctant to do their duty by the community. They are much more inclined to satisfy their own private interests than those of the common good, and particularly so when no personal advantages but at most only disadvantages seem to accrue to them from their co-operation in matters of common concern. Nor is it always easy to decide what the community needs and whether it should be better done in this way or that way. Often personal opinions must be set aside. We have all at some time

[53] St. Thomas Aquinas II–II 58, 5–6. In what follows the adjectives "universal" and "legal" are always used to signify the same kind of justice.

or other heard these endless discussions about the necessity and the particular wording of laws, the level of subscriptions, competence of managements, suitable investments of dividends.

105. What is the object of universal justice?

Universal justice is concerned with the common good in so far as this establishes legal demands on the members of the community.

1. Every virtue has its own proper object which is specifically different from that of other virtues. The common good differs not merely in degree and extent, but essentially, from private good. It has an essentially different character (Qs. 25, 94). Therefore it constitutes a special virtue.

The common good ought to be regarded not as something merely good and worth striving for, but as that particular good appertaining exclusively to the community.

Seen in this way the common good gives rise to definite services which it is owed from its members. These are legal, not only moral claims, which are part of justice or constitute a virtue which ought to be classified among the kinds of strict justice.

2. The common good is concerned with all the members of the community. That is the first reason why this virtue is called "universal" justice. A second reason is the comprehensive range of this virtue which directs all other virtues to the common good (Q. 107).

3. Common justice is more generally known as "legal" justice. It is so called because it is for the law to declare as binding the demands of the common good and to enforce them. Law is the

norm of right (Q. 58). Hence wherever a law obliges us to perform a service which is necessary in the interest of the common good we are concerned with a legal debt (ibid.), with something to which the members are bound by law. The legal regulation changes an action perhaps otherwise voluntary into an obligation in law.

106. What is the concern of universal justice?

Universal justice is concerned both with that which is prescribed by positive law, and, especially, with that which the natural law commands.

1. Communities have two kinds of goals. The first is based on human nature and comprises the goals proper to man and to human nature as such. There are duties which are right and proper in respect of every man because he is a man. The natural law imposes these obligations on all men. The second kind is based on the particular character of each specific community. They are the objects which confront a community because it has to exist and operate here and now. These objects find expression in human, positive law which prescribes what ought to be done in the interest of the common good (Q. 27).

2. The historical aims of communities can never invalidate the aims of nature (Qs. 46–47). It is particularly important to note that natural obligations are always and everywhere valid even before they have been expressly repeated and affirmed by positive law, and even when they are disputed and pronounced (with presumptuous authority) not to be binding (Qs. 72–76).

3. Accordingly we may distinguish a twofold function of universal justice, a natural function or a function in natural law

which must hold good for everyone, since everyone is a member of the greater community of mankind, and a positive function or a function in positive law which holds good within that community to which the individual person and the individual community belong by reason of their particular historical situation. The latter claims obedience to just human law.[54]

107. What human actions come under universal justice?

All external actions come under universal (legal) justice so far as they are prescribed by law in respect of the common good.

1. The internal act of universal justice consists in willing the common good. Man acknowledges the common good as an obligatory norm of his conduct. He is disposed and determined to do whatever the common good dictates by way of obligations and sacrifices.

2. The common good may make external acts of all virtues necessary. Thus the external acts of all other virtues are the field directly covered by universal justice. This virtue directs the acts of all the other virtues to their goal. It motivates and commands the acts of all other virtues and elicits them after the manner of an efficient cause. External acts of all virtues may be related to the common good, since they may as such become important for the order of the community. They must be related to it if they

[54] There are scholars such as Horváth, who recognize not only this double function, but a twofold kind of legal justice: a natural kind, the norm of which is the natural law, and a positive kind, the norm of which is human law. They argue that natural law and human law differ in essence, and that consequently rights and obligations based on natural law are essentially different from rights and obligations based on human law. We need not go into this question here, since in practice it is of no decisive importance provided that the totality of both natural and positive rights and functions are admitted in practice.

are necessary for the community, and if the latter accordingly prescribes them or forbids what is opposed to them.

EXAMPLES. To meet great danger is a matter of courage. In public crises (war, rebellion, natural catastrophes, defence against crime) the individual is, or may be, obliged to expose his life to danger. Strictly speaking this is (and remains) a function of courage, but on account of the common good it becomes an obligation in justice towards the community. In a food crisis brought about through failure of the harvest, blockade or some such circumstance, rationing imposes restrictions which in themselves come under the virtue of temperance. Income tax obliges one to give up a fixed sum of money to the exchequer, which means that an act of commutative justice is made a legal obligation.

3. An external act is often directly commanded by the natural law. We are obliged to help a person in mortal danger even at the cost of personal sacrifices where we are in a position to do so without putting ourselves or our family in the same danger (for example by material assistance, and so by foregoing certain material advantages). Thus in many cases a special injunction on the part of the community is not necessary in order to establish a legal obligation. Rather the obligation arises from the claims of human nature which result from the existing situation. The natural law commands us to respect the "human" element in man. It commands us to cultivate the values, to pursue the goals, to abide by the norms and considerations in human society which are proper and fitting among men. For example natural correctness demands that men will not insult each other or make life difficult for one another, that each will respect the human dignity of the other, that they will co-operate in establishing and preserving social peace (abstaining from whatever will disturb the peace: untruthfulness, subversive views and party strife, unjustified and harmful strikes).[55]

[55] The function of universal justice in natural law is particularly important in connection with the right to private property.

313

108. In what sense is equality established by universal justice?

Universal justice establishes a just balance between the demands of the community and the services of the members in accordance with what is regulated by law.

1. Objective equality is an essential characteristic of strict justice. Common justice binds the members in respect of what the community has to demand in the interest of the common good. Hence it establishes an objective equality, since it is concerned with the objective necessities and with the obligations that can be objectively defined. Law determines the form and the extent of the obligation of members towards the common good. Hence whoever fulfills what is required of him by law renders to the community its due, and does so equitably, since he renders the service to which he is obliged.

2. This is true in the first place of positive law which can determine the service exactly. In the case of the natural law it is often very difficult to determine the service and its extent, which the individual has to render in order to bring his conduct into line with the natural requirements binding here and now. For example who can state exactly how much of one's accomodation or financial means may have to be surrendered in a general emergency, or to what extent the individual must help in averting or rectifying a great catastrophe? It is true that the natural law, in so far as it deals with outward obligations, omissions or transgressions, is binding not only in conscience, but also before human society. Courts of law are therefore empowered in certain serious and "obvious" cases to deal with and to punish crimes against humanity. Of course the court ought to be impartial and free from bias and must consider all incriminating and exonerating circumstances. Generally we

314

ought to decide and act in conscience according to the dictates of the natural law. A man is not bound in virtue of a human law since such a law does not exist. Unfortunately we usually take our obligations in natural law all too lightly, although these are much more serious and more fundamental than obligations in positive law. And so the excuse that some matter is not forbidden "by law" is often a shallow and dishonest evasion.

3. Catholic moral teaching regarding the obligation of restitution is similar to that on distributive justice (Q. 103). Offences against universal or legal justice involve restitution only when there has been at the same time an offence against commutative justice. Universal justice binds in respect of the common good; it commands above all obedience to just law. Failure to fulfil an obligation, imposed by law, towards the common good, is undoubtedly an offence, possibly a serious one. Yet since what is due to the community on the part of the members is not confined to material goods (the actions of all virtues may come under universal justice; Q. 107), and since there is no calculable equality between what is due to the community and what is due to the members, an obligation of restitution does not result from an offence against universal justice alone. It may, however, be the case of an offence against commutative justice, that is, in conjunction with, and as a result of, offences against the common good, and in that case an obligation to restitution arises. (For example bribing the tax-collector to reduce or to overlook just taxes.)[56]

[56] If the obligation to restitution may result not only from commutative but also from distributive justice, the same must hold good for common or legal justice, since it also deals with what is due in law (Q. 105, No. 3). In the light of the afore-mentioned essay by Faidherbe we should argue that offences against common or legal justice involve restitution on this account, and not only because of an indirect offence against commutative justice.

4. Since human authority sometimes imposes unjust and very considerable burdens on its subjects, and indeed wrongs them, the obligation of restitution frequently ceases. The individual need only take on those sacrifices in respect of the community which are really necessary in accordance with distributive justice. The common good of an impoverished people, for example, does not justify extravagant enterprises.

109. What are the functions of universal justice?[57]

The functions of universal justice are :

i. To dispose the human will towards a due acknowledgement of and active co-operation in the common good.

ii. To make us capable of and inclined to loyalty towards nature's principles of right; that is to respect the aims, values and obligations inherent in human nature (general aims of humanity, human rights).

iii. To strive after and bring about the development of the personality in harmony with the claims of the community (integration of the self into the common good).

iv. To command and encourage members not to make demands which cannot be granted by the community, or which are unwarranted under particular circumstances (thrift, being content with a modest way of living; patience when conditions cannot be immediately changed).

[57] We shall now summarize what we have so far pointed out, stressing especially the great importance of this kind of justice, and thus arriving at the part of the book dealing with social justice.

v. To bring about social peace by establishing a just and fruitful balance between the common and the private weal (overcoming social disparities).

FOLLOWING Aristotle, whose teaching he further developed, St. Thomas Aquinas held universal justice to be the highest form of strict justice and the most important virtue in the purely natural order (see II–II 58, 6–7). He argued that just as supernatural Christian charity directs everything to God, the ultimate goal of life, so universal justice, too, directs everything to the common good (to the total human good), and thus to the proper development of the human person, which can only be attained in society.

D. SOCIAL JUSTICE

The term "social justice" is of comparatively recent origin. Its present significance is largely due to the great encyclical of Pius XI, *Quadragesimo Anno*. Nowadays we refer less frequently to universal or legal justice than to "social" justice.

"Social" is, indeed, more suggestive than "universal" and more meaningful than "legal". But there are many people who consider the traditional threefold division of justice no longer adequate to cover and regulate all the very different forms of modern society. New social classes have given rise to problems formerly unknown. Tremendous progress and changes in economics and politics are said to require new considerations and decisions to the extent that the traditional teaching on justice has to be supplemented by a fourth kind, namely, social justice. The new factors in modern society are industrial development which has created an antithesis between capital and labour; the proletariat and the problem of deproletarianization; laws to protect workers and give them the right to form unions; the modern state which is something quite different from the "political community" of former epochs, and which from the beginning has tended towards expansion of power and omnipotence. It is maintained that to stress the modern State's obligation of legal justice is dangerous because it uses law and right not in the service of the general weal but for its own lust for power. A further reason is said to be the progressive development towards larger economic and political units for which former small-scale standards no longer suffice. Therefore it is said that international interdependence influences the situation at every point so that the relation of the social whole to its members (parts) has to be newly defined. It is often argued that the "State" is ceasing to be a community sufficient in itself and can survive only as part of a greater whole, unless it is to disappear altogether.

No one will deny that these facts are true and must be duly appreciated. There is no sense in trying to hold on at all costs to traditional systems. On the other hand there is no reason for departing from the tried principles of ethics. It is not the number and diversity of problems peculiar to a particular age which is decisive, but their essential differences. More important than the dispute concerning the division of justice is first, to show as widely as possible where and why there are obligations in justice; second, the firm resolve to fulfil these obligations in their entirety.

PIUS XI (D. R., 71).

"For it is to be noted that besides what is called commutative justice there is also a social justice to be observed, and this imposes obligations which neither workers nor employers may evade. It is the function of social justice to require of each individual that which is necessary for the common good. Consider a living organism; the good of the whole is not being properly secured unless arrangements are made for every single member to receive all that it needs to fulfil its own function.

318

Exactly the same is true of the constitution and government of a community: the common good of a society cannot be adequately provided for unless each individual member, a human being endowed with the dignity of personality, receives all that he needs to discharge his social function. If social justice has been observed, therefore, the national economy will bear fruit in the shape of an intensive and thriving activity, developing in a peaceful and orderly manner and manifesting the vigour and stability of the nation; very much as a regular, full, and productive activity gives evidence of good health in a human body."

110. What is social justice?

Social justice is not a new and independent kind of justice, but merely a new term for legal and distributive justice taken together.

PIUS XI (Q. A., 88).

"To that end all the institutions of public and social life must be imbued with the spirit of this justice, which must be truly operative, must build up a juridical and social order pervading the whole economic regime. Social charity should be, as it were, the soul of this order, an order which the State must actively defend and vindicate. This task the State will perform the more easily, if it frees itself from those burdens which, as We have already declared, are not properly its own."

PIUS XI (Q. A., 110).

"The public institutions of the nations must be such as to make the whole of human society conform to the needs of the common good, that is, to the standard of social justice. If this is done, the economic regime, that most important branch of social life, will necessarily be restored to right and healthy order."

319

THE German economist, H. Pesch, S.J. (1854–1926), held that social justice was merely a common term for legal and distributive justice. Later authors agreed with him. Some, however, now hold that social justice is a distinct fourth form of justice which had hitherto been incomplete. According to this view there are four forms of justice: universal, commutative, distributive and social. However, universal (legal) justice is rarely mentioned by this school.

We agree with the first-mentioned view. It is not a question of a new virtue, but rather of a new term for those two forms of justice which regulate the relation of the whole to its parts and of the parts to the whole, both of which directly concern the common good and consequently the order in the community. "Social justice" reveals new aspects and functions of universal and of distributive justice. Of course, the inner structure of the virtue of justice as a whole is not modified, but its individual forms are recognized more clearly in their mutually complementary function and in their relation to modern conditions. Thus social justice deals both with what is owed to the common good by individual members and what is due to the members out of the common good by the community. The decisive moral problems remain the same. Whose are the goods? To what extent may we dispose of them? Why ought they to be distributed in a particular way? Where and how should common good precede private interest?

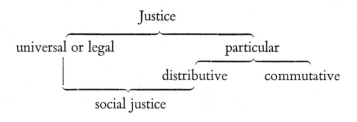

Justice

universal or legal   particular

distributive   commutative

social justice

1. We should have to assume new virtues only if there had been a proper, hitherto neglected, "formal object". On the other hand if the individual problems with which a virtue is concerned have merely become more numerous and more complicated, if due to particular historical circumstances it has merely become more difficult to view the whole field covered by a virtue, and to define obligations as they arise, that would not necessarily suggest that hitherto existing classifications of virtues were incomplete. Basically no more and no less than three relations constitute and direct social life: the relation of the whole to the parts, of the parts to the whole, and of the parts to each other. These relations may take on particular forms in individual cases, they may change considerably in accordance with the general development, but basically they neither increase nor diminish in number.

It follows from to this threefold relation that there is a threefold aspect of legal dues and obligations, and it is this difference in what is due that alone determines the subordinate forms of . justice.

It is widely held that social justice is economic justice and that its function is to direct economic matters. To this we reply that the material objects with which economics deal, do not give rise to independent criteria within justice. They come within the scope of all three forms of justice and are dealt with by each of them according to the particular aspect of what is owed by them.

2. It has been claimed that the proposition "to each his own' is but a principle of particular (individual) justice, whereas the principle of social justice implied that the social order, or the common good, must be maintained. We consider, however, that "to each his own" covers all forms of justice. "His own",

cannot without danger of falsification be confined to the individual. The social order is preserved and guaranteed precisely by granting to both the community and the members what is owed to each. For the community as a whole that means its order; the will to serve the common good is therefore synonymous with the will to serve the social order. The whole can only exist and develop when it is properly ordered.

3. It is important to note the difference between the function of natural law and of positive law in legal justice (Q. 107). The function of natural law is always directed by the aims and the will of nature. It guarantees that those matters which are not covered and regulated by positive law should not be overlooked and neglected. It keeps legislation "elastic" by constantly holding the natural up to the positive order. It also takes care that room is left for the pursuit and realization of the total human good in accordance with new possibilities and conditions.

4. An increasing progress in technical, economic and political development means that we are approaching a situation in which the full content of the common good (Q. 26) can be achieved and guaranteed only in a system no longer confined to the individual state. The system obtaining up to the present is proving increasingly inadequate, since modern political structures are of themselves less and less able to create the conditions and fulfil the demands of this total human good.[58] Accordingly very important functions of both legal and distributive justice – thus social justice – will have to be solved on a more comprehensive and higher plane. New forms of the relation between the whole and its members are developing. Social structures which today still possess, or appear to possess, the character of total

[58] A more detailed treatment of this highly important question will be given in in a later volume of this work.

communities will in future largely have to adopt the character of branch communities. Basically, however, social relations of the whole to the member, of the member to the whole, of member to member, will remain unaffected. But one particularly urgent concern of present–day social ethics will have to be considered and attended to more intensely then ever. We shall deal with it in the following question.

111. Why has the term "social justice" been introduced?

"Social justice" emphasizes:
i. the duty of member communities towards the higher total community and towards each other;
ii. the duty of members to adapt themselves to social development.[59]

1. MEMBERS of a community may be not only individual persons, but also communities which belong to a higher social whole. Such member communities have definite obligations towards the higher community which only they can fulfil; they have rights which must be respected or granted by the higher community (Qs. 51–2). Member communities must, therefore, seek to become aware both of their own status and of their importance for the higher community, and to develop accordingly. In so far as their goals and functions are not determined by nature (Qs. 26–7) the common good can claim special consideration, as, in certain circumstances, when the necessity arises, very definite things may have to be done without delay, and considerable restrictions on this or that member community

[59] See Nell-Breuning, *Wörterbuch*, iii, col. 33 et seq. Father Nell-Breuning S.J., was, as far as we know, the first to work out these relations clearly and in detail. His exposition seems to us, however, to leave it open whether or not social justice is to be considered a new and fourth kind of justice.

may have to be imposed. The member communities are mutually related not only as independent units, but also as parts (members) of the same higher community. In this latter respect they owe each other not only toleration but also self-restraint and support in accordance with the particular importance each of them has for the common good. It is, for example, not right when associations devoted to sport or social activities claim support to such an extent that men are diverted and kept away from higher obligations, or when forms of entertainment claim so much in subsidies that educational requirements get less than their fair share.

2. The present age has demonstrated the changeable character of society. We are always being presented with new obligations towards the common good. For example, there will be differences where there is an agricultural or an industrial economy; in times of peace or war; on account of movements of population. Willingness to serve the common good implies the readiness to serve society in accordance with existing necessities, to create the appropriate legal basis in good time, and to make the unavoidable sacrifices demanded by the times. Certainly, to think and to act socially in the true sense is not to cling rigidly to tradition, but to take account of living realities. In this sense the term "social justice" emphasizes new factors in so far as modern development has shown more clearly than ever the instability of society and the changes to which it is subject.

Lesson Five

CHARITY IN SOCIAL LIFE

IF social life is to proceed along orderly and fitting lines, justice must be accompanied by charity. That is common experience, as everyone must admit. What kind of charity is meant here? How does it operate? How is it related to justice?

LEO XIII (S. C., 40).

"It is, however, urgent above all, that charity, which is the main foundation of the Christian life, and apart from which the other virtues exist not or remain barren, should be quickened and maintained. That is why the Apostle Paul, after having exhorted the Colossians to flee all vice and cultivate all virtue, adds: 'Above all things have charity, which is the bond of perfection'. Yea, truly, charity is the bond of perfection, for it binds intimately to God those whom it has embraced and with loving tenderness causes them to draw their life from God, to act with God, to refer all to God. However, the love of God should not be severed from the love of our neighbor, since men have a share in the infinite goodness of God and bear in themselves the impress of His image and likeness."

LEO XIII (R. N., 21).

"But, if Christian precepts prevail, the respective classes will not only be united in the bonds of friendship, but also in those of brotherly love. For they will understand and feel that all men are children of the same common Father, who is God; that all have alike the same last end, which is God Himself, who alone can make either men or angels absolutely and perfectly happy; that each and all are redeemed and made sons of God, by Jesus Christ, 'the firstborn among many brethren'; *that the blessings of nature and the gifts of grace belong to the whole human race in common, and that from none except the unworthy is withheld the inheritance of the Kingdom of Heaven.* 'If sons, heirs also; heirs indeed of God, and co-heirs with Christ' (Rom. 8 : 17).*
Such is the scheme of duties and rights which is shown forth to the world by the Gospel. Would it not seem that, were Society penetrated with ideas like these, strife must quickly cease?"*

1. "Charity" (love) has different meanings; it may denote:

i. the natural inclination or impetus inherent in every creature to attain its proper goals (goods) and thus its natural perfection. Ancient wisdom speaks of a *pondus,* a law of gravity in nature according to which all things strive after (love) their own perfection and desire peace (St. Augustine). ii. The first stirring of the sensual appetite towards a recognized particular good: love as passion, that is, as a basic emotion. Whatever is seized by the senses immediately awakens pleasure in our sensual faculties.

iii. The pleasure which the will takes in Good as such. The first contact of the will with the Good, its immediate inclination towards all being presented to it by the reason as good. Under this aspect love (charity) is the root, the beginning and the inevitable condition of all endeavour, of all decisions and activity. Desire, joy and even denial, envy and hate spring from it. It precedes any intention and choice of means. However important (and at times fatal) love, both in the sense of "the gravitation of nature" and of passion, may be for social life, it is love in the sense of an intellectual and voluntary power and habit which is decisive in the sphere of morality. It is that love which follows on intellectual knowledge, and which in its turn quickens and fructifies this knowledge. Man can only love what he knows, but love spurs him on to ever deeper and more comprehensive knowledge; because love will not be satisfied with a mere general or superficial knowledge. Rather it desires to learn the personal secret and personal endowment of the loved one (see St. Thomas Aquinas, I–II 28, 2).

2. The will may turn its pleasure towards:

i. *Things.* A real, objective value which is striven for because, and in so far as it is necessary or useful, because, and in so far as it contributes to the perfection of a person (knowledge, virtue, power, prestige, wealth). Thus it is by no means a question of material values and goods.

ii. *Persons.* Another person may be the object of desire. This kind of love presupposes equality or at least similarity in intellectual nature. It can only exist between persons, and only love for another person deserves to be called "love" in the full and proper sense. Strictly speaking, we cannot "love" an animal.

The other person may be loved for his own sake, that is, the one who loves wishes the other person well because he is worthy of it and the one who loves wishes to see and make him perfectly good and happy. This is benevolent, disinterested, unselfish love.

The person may be loved from self-interest. The one who loves is attached to the other because the other is useful to him, because the one who loves expects something from the other person. This is a self-seeking love, but not necessarily selfish in the bad sense.

Where two or more persons are drawn together by mutual sympathy there arises the love of friendship. It is characteristic of true friendship that each desires to serve the other, to give himself and what is his to the other in a complete and voluntary self-surrender. One person becomes the other's other self. Naturally the highest degree of this altruistic love is reached when one person makes a complete self-surrender and receives a complete self-surrender from the other without being himself in any way enriched interiorly by it, as in God's love for his creatures.

3. There are several forms of mutual love among mankind:

i. Purely personal affection (marriage, family, personal friendship). The direct and exclusive motive is the other person because of his or her personal qualities or natural ties. This love brings the highest possible gain not only to the person who loves; in its radiating influence it can be of the greatest importance and bring blessings to many, even to entire nations and epochs.[60]

ii. Love for general reasons. Its motive is human nature, the identity and similarity in nature, goals and tasks; one person loves another (or all others) because he is a human being. This love is the condition for natural social justice which has to fulfil its claims wherever the good of human nature has the character of something that is owed. This applies especially to the most fundamental and noble goods of nature (Q. 71). But love of mankind in general is also the driving force behind many works of charity which are not carried out in the name of Christian charity (welfare work, social service). It is undoubtedly very important in social life.[61]

iii. Social charity.[62] This is the love which exists between members of a particular community, and which is based on the common good as the unifying goal, or on common membership of the same community. Its object is the well-being of all

[60] We shall have more to say about this kind of love in the section on marriage and the family in Volume Two.

[61] See the encyclical *Mystici Corporis Christi* of Pius XII.

[62] The term "social charity" appears in Q. A., par. 88, alongside the term "social justice". It is not easy to determine whether the Pope meant what is here presented as social charity, or whether he had in mind Christian charity in so far as this supplements social justice and moves it to action (Q. A., par. 137). At any rate what is meant here by social charity is no new discovery of our time. Aristotle and St. Thomas Aquinas referred to the love that exists between members of the community, and that is based on the common good (St. Thomas, II–II 26, 8). See here also Nell-Breuning, *Wörterbuch*, iii, col. 36.

members organized and living together in community. Love of the common good as a goal worth striving for precedes social justice which considers the common good as something that is owed as the basis of right. It need hardly be pointed out that great blessings are the result of social charity, for the more the common good is deliberately advocated and striven for as a good, the more will its members be prepared to fulfil their obligations towards the community, and the more closely will they be united among themselves.

iv. Christian charity. This belongs to an essentially different and higher order, the supernatural order of grace and salvation. It is the basic force in the redeemed world, in the lives of individuals and society.

112. What is Christian charity?

Christian charity is the supernatural virtue of the love for God in so far as it extends from God to our fellow men.

Love for God and for our neighbour are one and the same virtue. It is supernatural and is infused by God into man, that is into his will, together with sanctifying grace. Its immediate or principal object is God himself, the triune God, as the highest good and the ultimate aim of man. God is loved for his own sake, because of his infinite goodness.

Christian charity is defined as a "theological" virtue because it has God himself for its object, origin and aim.

The second object of this love is the rational creature on whom God has bestowed his grace and who has been destined to share in the divine nature (2 Peter 1:4) and to enjoy the vision and the love of God in the next life. This love turns from God to his children, the image of God. They are loved "in God". God is the motive of love for them. In God they become "our neighbours".

113. Why is this charity called "Christian"?

It is called "Christian"

i. because together with grace Christ has earned for us, and bestowed on us, the power and the virtue of charity;

ii. because he himself has practised this charity in an eminent degree and has proclaimed it the supreme precept and the hall-mark of his followers;

iii. because we are called upon and obliged, for this reason, to love our fellow men "for the sake of Christ".

PIUS XII (*Address of 12 October 1947; C. M., December, 1947*).

"*Charity is a word sometimes loosely used to signify any sort of benevolent and philanthropic activity, but for you charity has a sacred, consecrated meaning. Charity is different from any other human love because it is the replica of Christ's love for man. 'A new commandment I give you, that you love one another: that as I have loved you, you also love one another.' That is charity. St. Paul writes to the Romans: 'Receive one another, even as Christ has received you to the honour of God.' ... The doctor is said to love the sick; yet what is it in the sick that he loves? Surely not the disease. No, he loves health that he hopes to restore to the patient.*

Charity means that you love each other thus with a view to bringing God more and more into the lives of each other so that, linked together as so many members by the spirit of Divine Love, you may co-operate in forming a body not unworthy of the Divine Head."

ORDER in the world and among men has been founded once and for all by God himself upon Christ the Son of God become man. Salvation has been won by Christ on the cross. For this reason all God's gifts of grace bear the sign of the one and only Mediator and Redeemer, Jesus Christ. They are Christ's grace.

1. Charity is love for our fellowmen redeemed by Christ: it is fraternal love in Christ. Christ not only proclaims but is also the motive of this love. We love our fellowmen because of Christ, because in them we encounter Christ. "What you did to the least of my brethren you did to me."

2. Charity extends to all men in two ways:

i. All are images of God, called to be children of God;

ii. All have been redeemed and are at least potentially members of Christ's mystical body.

3. We can appreciate both the importance and the difficulty of the precept of charity from the fact that Christ placed charity in the foreground of his life and teaching. Man will be judged in so far as he has followed this commandment. The religion whose ideals are self-renunciation and the cross upholds not the easiest but the most difficult commandment as our standard of judgement.

In recent times the obligatory character of charity has come to be doubted. It is argued that charity is not really a precept, since "love" could not be commanded, but must show itself and be given voluntarily. However, Christ himself spoke quite definitely of the precept of charity: "This is my commandment, that you should love one another as I have loved you." Without any doubt he meant by this not only the external acts of charity, but love as a sentiment, as an act of the will. Again, a voluntary act of the will can be commanded and be made a matter of obedience without ceasing to be a free act. Moreover, the motive of charity is in no way affected, weakened or excluded by the precept. Charity derives its character from its motivation. Charity is charity only because, and in so far as it allows itself to be guided by the motivation that is proper to it. This motivation effects the abandonment that is peculiar to charity. This is not in any way changed or destroyed by the precept.

114. What is the influence of charity on social life?

Charity has an immeasurably wide, profound influence for good on social life.

1. CHARITY urges us to seek truth and to pass it on to others. Error and ignorance are major obstacles to right living in general, and to a right social order in particular. It is a perilous situation when ignorance is spreading to all levels of society and affecting vital questions, and when in addition cleverly camouflaged false views deceive the people who no longer have any certainty or solid principles to fall back upon. Man can only be saved by the truth. Charity urges us to take pity on those who have become uprooted, in the first place by spreading among as many as possible the way of truth. The spiritual works of mercy include instructing the ignorant, giving counsel to those who are in doubt. Charity is persevering and unselfish in the service of truth. It urges us not to shirk the trouble involved in seeking the truth and endeavouring to understand it better. Charity fires our zeal and knows how to find the right word which leads to the truth (sermon and lecture; apostolate of

press, radio and television; private conversation; a mind open to all truth).

2. Charity leads us to honour our neighbour and to the deepest understanding of his needs. Another person is most clearly seen when loved. Christian charity makes us see our fellow "in God", as God's image and child, as well as "in Christ", as one redeemed by his blood and sanctified by his grace. There can be no higher vision and standard. The value of man, which is the starting point of any social order, cannot otherwise be illuminated more effectively. Theologians, among them St. Thomas Aquinas, refer to the *mutua inhaesio,* that is the union of those who love each other. Charles Williams wrote of it as "co-inhesion". It is the attainment of a genuine unity of thought, purpose and action. Men no longer treat one another with the indifference of strangers. Charity gives us the deepest understanding of the individuality and of the situation of our fellowman. It makes us see, and sensitive to, his needs.

3. Charity alone can overcome that selfishness which is the greatest obstacle in any society. Charity "seeks not its own". Since supernatural charity is bestowed on man as a consequence of sanctifying grace it has a healing power. It heals the worst human sickness which is a false attachment to our own self. Nature has inclined man to seek at least more readily his own interest rather than that of another or what is in the common interest. Original sin has distorted this natural, and in itself, normal inclination and turned it into a terrible obsession with the ego which is expressed in many ways but always to the detriment of our fellowmen and of the community (Q. 19). Christian charity is the only effective counter-force, since it alone can produce the proper motivation and spiritual aids. It is only when God and Christ are seen in every human being that

opposites can be overcome in a higher unity and with divine assistance.

In recent times the Popes have insisted on the necessity and the significance of sacrifice and penance for society. It is super-natural charity that supplies strength for sacrifice and penance.

PIUS XI (C. C. C. 1932, 16).

"But to prayer we must also join penance, the spirit of penance, and the practice of Christian penance. Thus our divine Master teaches us, whose first preaching was precisely penance: 'Jesus began to preach and to say, Do penance' (Matt. 4:17). The same is the teaching of all Christian tradition, of the whole history of the Church. In the great calamities, in the great tribulations of Christianity, when the need of God's help was most pressing, the faithful, either spontaneously or more often following the lead and exhortations of their holy Pastors, have always taken in hand the two most mighty weapons of spiritual life: prayer and penance. By that sacred instinct, by which unconsciously, as it were, the Christian people is guided when not led astray by the sowers of tares, and which is none other than that 'mind of Christ' (Phil. 2:5) of which the Apostle speaks, the faithful have always felt immediately in such cases the need of purifying their souls from sin with contrition of heart, with the sacrament of reconciliation, and of appeasing divine Justice with external works of penance as well."

4. Charity informs all other virtues and moves them to action. St. Paul calls charity the "bond of perfection". Charity affects and gives life to every other virtue, since it directs all virtues to God, the highest goal of life, and since it makes men act always "from love of God". All virtues are in the service, under the command and urge, of charity. Charity inspires generosity and friendliness, patience and contentedness. It also takes care of our natural sentiments and obligations of love, making sure

that both the love of men in general and social love do what they are intended to do (Q. 116).

5. Charity is the source of social progress. This is meant in the narrow sense of progress in social thought, regarding capital and labour, the production and consumption of goods, etc., in social legislation, in the structure of society, in social institutions. There are many particular reasons which lead to new attitudes and new measures in the social field; for example, the conservation of the power to work, economic stability, dangers to the health of the nation, self-aid by whole classes (the struggle of the wage-earners), even concern for the national defence potential.

Real social progress of mankind is, however, primarily due to the great champions of Christian charity, to their exhortation, their example and action.

115. How does Christian charity differ from justice?

The virtues of charity and justice differ in regard to their object, motive, and the form of obligation which they impose.

1. JUSTICE deals with what is due, with what is due to others, with that to which others are strictly entitled. Charity is concerned with the good in so far as it perfects the other person and is voluntarily given to him, so far as the one who loves wishes the other well and likes him. The object of justice is what belongs to you; the object of charity is what belongs to me and is freely given.

2. Justice looks upon my neighbour as a person who confronts me with a claim. That is implicit in the nature of a settlement that is due. Charity looks upon my neighbour as an equal, as one united to me in God and Christ.

335

3. Obligations in justice derive from a claim which can be objectively substantiated and exactly defined. They can be enforced when there is a refusal to carry them out (legal action). Obligations in charity derive from an attitude of sympathy, from the fact that in every fellowman we see God and Christ who are worthy of all love, and in whose likeness we grow through the practice of charity. Hence of its nature charity has no mean (we can never love enough, and, of course, we can never love too much). It must be given freely from attachment to God (and to the good); it can never be enforced. There is a precept of charity, but no enforced act of love. Such an act would lose its validity as a sign of love through the very fact of compulsion. There may be transgression against the order of charity, just as there may be prudence or imprudence in works of charity and mercy, but of charity itself no excess is possible.

116. *What significance has charity for justice?*

Charity cannot replace justice, but presupposes it. It inspires the loyal fulfilment of the obligation of justice. It is particularly effective wherever justice is not enough.

PIUS XI (Q. A., 4).

". . . as though it were the task of charity to make amends for the open violation of justice, a violation not merely tolerated, but sometimes even ratified, by legislators."

PIUS XI (Q. A., 137).

"How completely deceived are those rash reformers who, zealous only for legal justice, proudly disdain the help of charity! Certainly charity cannot take the place of justice unfairly withheld. But, even

though a state of things be pictured in which every man receives at last all that is his due, a wide field will always remain open for charity. For justice alone, however faithfully observed, though it can indeed remove the cause of social strife, can never bring about a union of hearts and minds. Yet this union, binding men together, is the main principle of stability in all institutions, no matter how perfect they may seem, which aim at establishing social peace and promoting mutual aid."

PIUS XI *(D. R., 689).*

"But charity does not deserve the name of charity unless it is grounded in justice. Therefore the Apostle, having said that 'he who loves his neighbour has done all that the law demands', goes on to explain that 'all the commandments, Thou shalt not commit adultery, Thou shalt do no murder, Thou shalt not steal . . . *and the rest, are resumed in this one saying:* Thou shalt love thy neighbour as thyself.' *According to the Apostle, then, all our duties, even those to which we are bound in strict justice, such as the avoidance of murder and theft, are reduced to the one commandment of true charity. It therefore follows that a charity which defrauds the worker of his just wage is no true charity, but a hollow name and a pretence."*

PIUS XII *(S. P., 16).*

"The first (of these errors) disastrously wide-spread in our day, consists in losing sight of that kinship and love which ought to bind human beings to one another. Such love is called for by our common human origin; it is called for by our common possession, whatever race we belong to, of the reasoning faculty by which man is distinguished. And it is further enjoined on us by that sacrifice of Redemption, which Christ our Lord offered to His Eternal Father for the salvation of souls."

1. CHARITY imparts to all other virtues their true and ultimate value. This does not mean that good (virtuous) actions are worthless without charity, or that charity can replace the other virtues. There can, however, be no *supernatural* moral virtues without the supernatural love of God and neighbour, since they are infused together with charity. The natural (acquired) moral virtues are directed to the supernatural ultimate goal by divine charity (the love of God and neighbour), and it is this that makes them virtues in the full sense of the term, because it is of the very nature of virtue to make man and man's actions good in relation to the ultimate goal (St. Thomas Aquinas, I–II 65, 2). It is a blatant error to think that charity could dispense with the obligations of justice, rendering justice superfluous or lessening its importance. The opposite is true. Charity seeks the good in all its forms. But right is undoubtedly an eminent good. Without right and justice *no social order is possible*. Conflict and discord abound everywhere where justice is perverted and right violated.

EXAMPLES. It is wrong for someone to give alms instead of paying his debts, or paying workers a just wage. We may not lie or steal "out of charity". Interruption of pregnancy (abortion) and euthanasia are never allowed because they are unjust in themselves, not even out of compassion or on what are described as "humane" grounds.

2. Charity impels men to fulfil obligations of justice faithfully. Man can, and should, be just from motives of charity, that is, because he loves his fellowmen, because he sees God and Christ in them and for that reason is ready, and does everything in his power, to uphold and to grant to them what is their due.

Christ himself has said: "Do to other men all that you would have them do to you" (Matt. 7:12). Charity has, therefore, an eminent function in social justice, since it is the latter's function to create conditions which are in accordance with the will of nature and of the Creator, and since charity is particularly concerned in the attainment and guaranteeing of such conditions.[63]

3. Justice covers and orders only very definite legal relations. It can only consider the facts, because it is concerned exclusively with preserving, granting or re-establishing equality among men in what is due. Special circumstances are taken into consideration only in so far as the amount due is dependent on them. It is neither the function of justice to relieve distress, nor is it in a position to do so. On the contrary, whenever the law is upheld in a narrow and rigid manner, men invariably become hard and indifferent. That is why charity must prevail among men, otherwise social life would become unbearable, and those who are most in need of assistance, the poor and the suffering, would be neglected.

Charity begins where justice ends. It is those who are hard pressed and in need of help who are particularly cared for by charity; it is then that charity turns into mercy (Q. 124).

It is frequently said that some matter binds not in justice but "only" in charity. (Help for a poor person; for one in the depths of despair; encouraging a despondent person; counselling the perplexed, etc.) Thus the impression is given that obligations in charity are not to be taken too seriously, at any rate not so seriously as obligations in justice. (It sounds almost of no consequence: "only in charity", but "not" in justice!)

Strictly speaking obligations of charity rank higher than those of justice, even though in general the latter must be fulfilled

---

[63] "Justice begins with inequalities and ends with their adjustment. Charity begins with the adjusted conditions and thence proceeds to unequal, proportionate acts." (Horváth). In support of this see St. Thomas Aquinas, *Ethics*, viii, Lect. 7.

first. The rank of the obligation depends upon the rank of the virtue. Charity is the first, the highest and greatest of the virtues.

The expression "only an obligation in charity" implies nothing concerning the rank and seriousness of the obligation, but merely concerning the form, especially in regard to the restitution to be made. Legal claims can be drawn up and taken to court. To disregard them is to commit an offence for which one might be made liable. Tokens of charity may be expected or considered expedient and even obligatory. Whoever neglects them does not offend against justice and cannot be legally assessed although a grave offence may have been committed in the sight of God.

Is there a right to charity?[64] Both the Old and the New Testament are familiar with the precept of charity. Thus charity can be covered by law and obedience, but does it become thereby a kind of right? It is always only the carrying out of an act which is covered by the precept. The precept, for instance, demands that acts of love of God and of neighbour should be carried out. The precept also states who is to be acknowledged as a neighbour, and how far charity has to extend. Finally the precept may define in general the amount of help to be given. Nevertheless, all that does not affect the essence of charity. An act of charity is only present where the individual himself freely wills and acts from the motives of charity. Even though he may have been told a thousand times to love God and his neighbour, he can make an act of charity only when he surrenders himself to God the supreme Good by a free act of the will, and when he wishes to be good to his fellowman because he sees God and Christ in him. The "works" of charity always retain their own character, as a token of inward, freely granted, sympathy. There

[64] See Q. 113, p. 330.

is right which can be consecrated and glorified by charity; but there is no right to charity. The obligation of charity is of prior origin, higher rank and stronger than the obligation of justice.

117. What are the necessary qualities of charity?

Charity must be universal, ordered, practical, in keeping with the situation, merciful.

THESE qualities will be explained in the subsequent questions.[65] It is clear that charity needs to be particularly effective in situations which can only be overcome by intense charity. Hence in many respects the obligation of charity is not always equally great and equally pressing.

118. When is charity universal?

When it excludes no one, but embraces all men and seeks as far as possible to help every one.

As we know, Christian charity extends even to the love of our enemies. It overcomes natural resistance and antipathies, even hate and all other wrong. It has this power from its supernatural motives and from the efficacy of grace.[66]

There are many reasons why one person excludes another from his love. In our time universal charity needs to be particularly effective in the relations between different social classes. Charity extends to every man regardless of social position, income, economic independence or dependence. It is opposed to

[65] It is not the task of this book to answer all questions connected with the nature and effectiveness of charity. Readers are referred to the sections on charity in the general catechism.
[66] Sermon on the Mount.

the class struggle, the division of mankind into separate camps (employers and workers), the evaluation of men according to their material means, racial and religious discrimination.

119. When is charity ordered?

When it is guided by right standards.

IT is true that charity embraces all men, but this does not mean that all must (or may) be loved to the same degree and in the same way. There is an "order of charity". It is important to inquire into this order of charity, since practical decisions depend on it, or are largely influenced by it.[67]

1. Three considerations determine the order of charity:
i. The worthiness, natural ties and needs of our neighbour.
ii. The scale of values (goods).
iii. The urgency of particular needs.

2. It is a fact that the individual cannot expressly love all his fellowmen for the simple reason that by far the most of them are completely unknown to him. With the best will in the world he is able to help only a few, not all those he would wish to help, and not always even those whom he feels obliged to help. The human will and ability are limited, whereas God's power and God's will are infinite.

3. The order of charity is regulated by the following principles:
i. Since God himself or the divine good *(bonum divinum)* is the object and the motive of charity, a fellowman is all the more

[67] See St. Thomas Aquinas, II–II 26. The answer shows among other things how much Christian ethics appreciates and cultivates the naturally good aspects and obligations of life.

worthy of being loved the holier and more united to God he is, the more he grows in grace as a child of God. The more holy he is the more entitled he is to be loved. (Christ as man, the Mother of God, the saints in their degrees of perfection.) We do not begrudge those so blessed the riches which God has bestowed on them, and we show them all the honour of which they are worthy.

ii. Under the subjective (affective) aspect charity begins "at home", with the person himself who loves, that is, with the natural motives and obligations of charity (family ties, community, fellowship, gratitude). It is by no means wrong, but quite natural that we should love more intensely those with whom we are more closely united (love between husband and wife, parents and children, friends).

iii. The status of our neighbour in the (natural or supernatural) community is sometimes an important factor in regard to the common good. General considerations may require us to give special assistance to those whose activities are necessary for the common good, even though this means withdrawing such assistance from relatives or from those intimately connected with us in some way.[68]

EXAMPLE. Someone is confronted with the alternative of saving either his sick brother or a sick priest from certain death by a blood donation. He decides to help the priest because here and now (for instance in a war or during religious persecution, or on the mission fields) the people cannot possibly do without the priest.

iv. The scale of values and the priorities of needs must also be taken into consideration because charity cannot devote itself indiscriminately to the good, much less can it do just as it

[68] See St. Thomas Aquinas, II–II 32, 9.

343

pleases with the good. Where the need is greater, help must be given more quickly and generously. Spiritual needs often require particularly speedy and effective support. Intellectual values deserve to be given preference over material and physical values, although in times of emergency and crisis they often assume a secondary place (a scholar may be obliged to abandon his research work for a time in order to look after the sick, or to do manual work in order to earn a living). No one may act in a manner which conflicts with his moral integrity. We may never do what cannot be reconciled with the natural and the divine moral law. In Christian language, we cannot have charity at the price of sin by offending God. We may never comply with someone else's desire at the price of our own immortal soul.[69]

In view of these observations it is not surprising that great complications can arise in particular cases and that an individual may sometimes be in doubt and may have to consider carefully how to do his duty.

On this point Father Nell-Breuning comments: "The same order which we deduce by reasoning can be discovered in most issues of practical life by the common sense of ordinary untrained minds." (*Wörterbuch,* iii, col. 48.) We would add: the ordinary untrained man (like everyone else) who really loves

---

[69] True self-love and love of one's neighbour can never be opposed irreconcilably. By making even the greatest sacrifices for his neighbour, even by renouncing many things for his neighbour's sake to which his love for God urges him (taking part in prayer), a man will serve and benefit himself and his own salvation. For all good done in the right spirit redounds to the doer. "In learning the difficult lesson of how to forget ourselves and spend ourselves in the service of others, we are really consulting our own highest interests, we are learning the wise art of loving ourselves rightly, the unselfish service of our own perfection!" (W. Bardon, O.P., *What happens at the Mass* [Clonmore and Reynolds, Dublin], p. 11.)

his neighbour and allows himself to be guided by this love. Because, as St. Thomas Aquinas says, the virtuous man judges all that concerns virtue with a spontaneous and reliable sureness.[70] By reason of his inner assimilation to the good, to virtue, he has the right sense also of the manner in which virtue must be practised. He makes his decisions willingly and aptly in accordance with what is required by the virtue.

120. When is charity active?

When charitable sentiments are translated into charitable deeds.

THE appeals of Holy Scripture; the example of Christ. Genuine love is communicative; it impels towards giving, helping.

1. Charity does not wait until the law commands, or threatens to command, before it acts; it anticipates legal enactment.

2. Fear of the future, of what might happen, of possible upheavals, is not a motive of genuine charity. Whoever acts (helps, concedes greater rights) merely from fear, is motivated by self-interest, by the desire to be "covered" in good time, but not by sympathy and disinterested readiness to help.

3. Charity immediately turns to whatever tasks it can accomplish. Because big things may be beyond its power, or because the general situation cannot be quickly remedied, it will not allow itself to be put off from dealing with smaller tasks. It does whatever it can. Big deeds are made up of many small ones.

[70] For example, in his commentary on the *Ethics* of Aristotle, Book III, 10 (Marietti edition, No. 494).

345

121. When is charity in keeping with the situation?

When it does what can best and most effectively be done here and now.

EVERY situation is unique. Sometimes it can be got over or at least alleviated by a kind word. Sometimes there are more ways than one of dealing suitably with a situation (for example, poverty can be met by direct assistance or by providing employment). Charity seeks and finds a way, or *the* way, in accordance with the situation and overcomes it as effectively as possible. (Words of sympathy are no help for a homeless person; it might not be wise merely to give money to someone who is able, but too lazy, to work.)

Our great example is the charity of God and Christ. By sending his Son and through the Redemption wrought by him, God did just that which the world needed. Christ's miracles were always suited to the particular circumstances which he encountered. He healed the sick, fed the hungry, restored to the widow her only son. In the parable of the good Samaritan it is not the priest or the Levite who practise charity, but the Samaritan, who does what has to be done here and now.

Doing what the situation demands applies to the individual situation as it exists from one person to another (one family helping another – neighbourly help). It also applies to the existing historical situation. We have to enquire into the goals, forces, and decisions necessary so that the existing situation may develop as it should in the sight of the Lord of history. Our basis is the firm (supernatural) conviction that neither events and upheavals, nor social ideas and movements, however unacceptable, are accidental and immaterial for our future. What cannot be approved by reason enlightened by faith must in spite of its insufficiency and even irrelevancy be appreciated in its historical significance and be taken seriously according to the measure of its influence. For right decisions are also, and in fact sometimes very substantially conditioned by it. Even mistakes are taken into account in the plan which divine Providence actualizes in the world. They serve not only truth but also the purification and trial of the world.

122. When is charity merciful?

When it takes pity on others in their needs.

EXAMPLES are God and Christ. The history of Christian charity in its many forms. (St. Vincent de Paul and Father Damien are among many others who looked after the sick, sacrificed their lives, ransomed captives, tended lepers.)

1. Mercy is not a special virtue. It is the virtue of charity directed towards those who are suffering want and are in need of assistance. Mercy demands and reveals especially the unselfishness of charity, because it helps in situations where we frequently have to practise greatest self-denial and where we may expect the least return. Mercy presupposes compassion; we must be moved by the other's misery – open our hearts and souls to it.

2. The Church has the right freely to practise works of Christian charity. Voluntary charitable activities may only be restricted where just laws are infringed or where obvious abuses are detected. Christ has proclaimed active charity as his precept, and has bound both the Church and the faithful to this precept. In this respect the Church has full liberty. By virtue of her divine right she may perform works of Christian charity and consequently may do everything that is necessary for this end. (She may acquire and manage property, set up and maintain

charitable organizations, collect for charitable purposes. She may also establish or approve religious confraternities and associations devoted to charitable work.)

3. By "voluntary" charitable activities we mean those that are carried out either by the individual faithful or by associations expressly formed for this purpose, such as religious congregations, parish societies, hospitals. These activities, like every other public activity, are bound by the general laws of public order, but apart from that they ought to be free; they ought not to be subject to legal regulation, coercion or interference from public authorities. The natural limits of these charitable activities are infringement of the right of others or neglect of other obligations. (For example, if someone gives away in charity the money with which he should have paid his bills; or if he stints his family in order to make contributions to charitable social works.) In consideration of the common good the State and public authorities may demand that just laws should be observed (for example, concerning the acquisition of wealth, wills, certain rates and taxes, registration of societies). Where there are abuses which might be harmful to the general public, the public authorities may, and sometimes must, first issue a warning, and then stop the abuses.

If the charitable activities of the Church herself or of the organs commissioned by her create the impression that disadvantages are resulting for the common good, then the right way of dealing with the matter is not by force, but by open and peaceful discussion. The State and the municipalities are bound to acknowledge the immense blessings of the Church's charitable activities, which are one of the most valuable factors contributing to the common good.

123. What does charity guarantee to social life?

Charity guarantees true, stable, and lasting concord in society.

1. PEACE, as St. Augustine says, is "the tranquility of order". According to St. Thomas Aquinas, order is "unity arising from the harmonious arrangement of many things".[71]

2. Justice is necessary so that peace may reign among men. Hence the saying of Holy Scripture: "Peace is the work of justice" *(opus justitiae pax)*. Unless each gives to others what is theirs, unrest and dissension are inevitable. But justice alone is not enough; we have stated our reasons in Q. 116.

PIUS XII (C. B., 1942; C. T. S., 8–9).

"This organic conception of society, the only vital conception, combines a noble humanity with the genuine Christian spirit, and it bears the inscription from Holy Writ which St. Thomas has explained (S. Th. II–II 29, 3): 'The work of justice shall be peace'; a text applicable to the life of a people whether it be considered in itself or in its relations with other nations. In this view love and justice are not contrasted as alternatives; they are united in a fruitful synthesis. Both radiate from the spirit of God, both have their place in the programme which defends the dignity of men; they complement, help, support, and animate each other: while justice prepares the way for love, love softens the rigour of justice and ennobles it; both raise up human life to an atmosphere in which, despite the failings, the obstacles, and the harshness which earthly life presents, a brotherly intercourse becomes possible. But if the evil spirit of materialism gains the mastery, if the

71 See St. Thomas Aquinas, C. G. 71; I, Q. 65, I. Pius XI refers to these sources in Q. A. 84.

rough hands of power and tyranny are suffered to guide events, you will then see daily signs of the disintegration of human fellowship, and love and justice will disappear – presaging the catastrophes which must come upon a society that has apostatized from God."

We have already quoted St. Thomas Aquinas[72] on this point. We have to distinguish between:

i. Interior order: in the soul, among the faculties of the human spirit; this is "inward peace", or simply "peace" (pax).

ii. Outward order: the order among men, real understanding, agreement between two or more people; it is called "outward peace", or concord.

Inner and outward order, peace and concord mutually condition each other. A man who is without inner peace (dipsomaniacs, people who are domineering, moody) creates disturbance and discord in a community. External discord (quarrels, dissension) hinders and mars inner peace. Inner peace may be preserved in spite of external disorder and temptation provided a man possesses sufficient inner strength (as the saints have in time of persecution and in prison; wives or husbands who have put up with each other's moods; nurses who remain cheerful in spite of the everlasting complaints and grumblings of patients). Those who lack inner peace may be able to "get

[72] See Q. 44, footnote (St. Thomas, II–II, 29). The matter is important enough, especially in connection with the pastoral ministry, to be mentioned again in the section on charity. It belongs to the pastoral office to guide and to urge men i. to preserve, or to regain, inner peace, and strengthen it; ii. to become disposed and capable of appreciating and fulfilling their obligations for the sake of external peace. But it is also part of pastoral duties to point out, at least in general, the necessities and obligations of external peace, since here also we are dealing with genuine divine claims which the Christian may not ignore, for they belong to Christian responsibility (Qs. 10, 19).

along" together with other people but they cannot live together in a finer, deeper human manner. Their concord lacks a really sound basis, and is preserved only by considerations of mutual advantage or convention, by compulsion and external force.

Man becomes ordered in himself by fixing his will on God, his ultimate goal, and by subordinating all his other faculties to his will. This order is the effect of the supernatural love of God. It surrenders the human will to God, the supreme Good. It alone overcomes the inner conflict in man which resulted from sin.

Man is coordinated inwardly in the right way with his fellow-men when he loves them in God and in their relation to God. Our neighbour is "rightly" seen and "rightly" loved as a child of God. This love is but supernatural charity. It brings about that inner harmony of human wills which remains firm and is able to stand up to every storm, because it is rooted in God and sanctified in Christ. Charity thus creates unity of hearts and souls in Christ: "There was one heart and one soul in all the company of believers" (Acts 4:32).

If external peace (concord) is to be genuine and lasting, it must be rooted in the hearts of men, it must grow out of inner peace and there find its permanent support.

Thus we see once again that social order has need of Christian men, men living Christian lives, if it is to correspond to the will of the Creator, and to prove equal to every situation. Indeed, Christian charity alone can establish and guarantee social peace. This is obvious in the case of smaller communities, especially where men live permanently together (families, neighbours, places of work), where thoughtfulness for others is ever necessary and demands repeated self-denial, patience and generosity. But it also holds good for larger communities, nations, and international organizations. Only when men come to recognize in faith

351

that they form a "commonweal under God" (I–II, 100, 5), and draw the logical conclusions from this fact will the peace of the world be assured.

PIUS XI (Q. A., 137).

"Yet this union, binding men together, is the main principle of stability in all institutions, no matter how perfect they may seem, which aim at establishing social peace and promoting mutual aid. In its absence, as repeated experience proves, the wisest regulations come to nothing. Then only will it be possible to unite all in harmonious striving for the common good, when all sections of society have the intimate conviction that they are members of one great family, and children of the same Heavenly Father, and further, that they are 'one body in Christ, and everyone members one of another', so that 'if one member suffer anything, all members suffer with it'. Then the rich and others in power will change their former neglect of their poorer brethren into solicitous and effective love; will listen readily to their just demands, and will willingly forgive them the faults and mistakes they may possibly make. The workers, too, will lay aside all feelings of hatred or envy, which the instigators of social strife exploit so skillfully. Not only will they cease to feel discontent at the position assigned them by divine Providence in human society; they will become proud of it, well aware that they are working usefully and honourably for the common good, each according to his office and function, and are following more closely in the footsteps of him, who being God, chose to become a carpenter among men, and to be known as the son of a carpenter."

124. *Which other fruit of charity is important for society?*

Joy is important for society as a further fruit of charity.

1. Joy is, like peace, an effect of charity. Both possession and expectation of the beloved makes a man joyful. In Holy Scripture peace and joy are numbered among the fruits of the Holy Spirit (Gal. 5:22). But they are there to be understood in a special sense, as supernatural blessings which are bestowed on the individual who acts in the power and under the influence of the Holy Spirit (See I–II 70, 1).[73] That joy is something honourable, permissible, and necessary is clear especially from Scripture, which calls on us to rejoice and be glad. See, for example: John 15:11; 16:24; Rom. 12:15; 2 Cor .13:11; Philip. 4:4; 1 Thess. 5:16; 1 John 1:4.

2. There are many kinds of joy:

Inner and outward joy: The former fills the soul and heart of man. It may show itself outwardly, but need not do so. The latter consists of certain attitudes and signs which in themselves indicate inner joy, although the individual who shows outward joy is sometimes not at all happy inwardly (a "cheerful disposition", laughter). Outward joy is often caused by games, company and dancing, wit and humour, down to very dubious or even sordid pleasures.

Genuine and false joy: The former is the (reasonable) joy in goodness. It is pleasing to God. Its field is by no means as narrow as is often thought. It embraces not only the joy in spiritual and moral goodness, the joys of family life, joy in one's work and profession, but for example also enjoyment of a good book, play or film, or sport. By false joy we mean deceptive joy. It has various forms and degrees: There is enjoyment of what is wrong (illicit sexual intercourse; maltreatment of another person). Immoderate joy (false exuberance, going "mad"

[73] "Joy" is in our context used in a general sense.

353

with joy). Simulated joy is also false. (A person pretends to be happy although inwardly he is unhappy; sometimes a person simulates joy in order to delude others and lead them astray: this is sinful joy.)

Spontaneous joy, and joy deliberately sought. The former is its own reason without having to be specially sought and provided. It simply accompanies and attaches to human action so far as this is not painful or is not felt to be so (for example, joy in the success of some work; joy in, and resulting from, the faithful performance of one's duty, joy in the presence of a loved one; the peace and joy of a good conscience). The latter is expressly sought. Someone intends to make himself or others happy. (He "causes" them to be joyful.)

EXAMPLES. Thinking of happy events and incentives in order to overcome sadness; going to the theatre to be cheered up; giving a present in order to show one's affection and make the other happy. Those little things which are often unnoticed by the world around us, and which are likely to bring "a little sunshine" into the lives of people, particularly of those who are sorely tried and the despondent (little attentions such as a kind word, a visit to a sick person; we may also pray for joy for ourselves and for others).

3. The importance of genuine joy for social life may be easily seen from its good effects:

Joy stimulates. It lends wings to the will, it widens our hearts, as Holy Scripture says (Isaias 60:5). When a man is happy everything comes easier to him, he usually works better and with more enthusiasm.

Joy dissolves or lessens tensions and conflicts among men. It makes men more affable and more ready to listen to one another. The happy man is more ready to admit another's points of view, to forget and forgive, to settle differences with others. He finds it easier to put up with the inevitable inconveniences or hardships of social life, and in general he creates an atmosphere about him in which men feel better. One of the reasons why the social conflicts of the present day are so bitter and ruinous is that they are carried on with a bitterness and doggedness which purposely avoids almost any spontaneous and "good-humoured" meeting of the opposing parties.

4. This valuable asset of joy can only be preserved and increased if whatever kills, suppresses or deprives us of genuine joy is energetically and persistently counteracted.

The real enemy of joy is not sorrow,[74] but peevishness and discontent (illhumour, ill-feeling, irritation, spite, anger). It has a paralysing and sometimes disastrous effect on those around us, and nips in the bud any expression or even feeling of joy. It becomes especially mischievous and unbearable in those who wield authority, because the frigid atmosphere which it easily breeds may then inspire feelings of anxiety and fear.

There can be no true joy where distrust, suspicion, envy, and jealousy destroy good relations between men. They bring unrest and doubt into social life and cause men to be suspicious of one another, to be more than cautious and reserved towards each other. This enemy of joy has its worst and most corrupt expression in the system of spies and informers cultivated in totalitarian States. The secret police becomes the principal agent of government and suppression. It is expanded to cover everyone and everything, so that no one is safe from anyone else. The worst of this base practice is that men are compelled by threats and blackmail to spy upon, to testify against, and to incriminate one another.

Generally speaking all forms of selfishness militate against joy,

---

[74] That is, genuine sorrow. Most of the kill-joys mentioned here come under false sorrow.

especially when selfishness dominates in a person's life. The miser as well as the fastidious person, he who thirsts for power or seeks pleasure for its own sake, the lazy person, the narrow-minded man, embitter their own lives and the lives of others. Their joy is either a deceptive joy, or it is achieved through the grief and the troubled conscience of their fellowmen.

True joy is endangered or actually destroyed by excessive and perverted "joys". This happens when pleasures and change are sought merely to pass the time, to divert or to satisfy low desires and lusts. (The motto: "enjoy life" may be very wrong and degrading.) The modern world overwhelms men with unlimited opportunities of diversion, excitement, entertainment – opportunities which are partly good or at least harmless, but partly far from good or harmless.

5. Joy is a very important aim and means of education.

The sources, motives, and great variety of possibilities of true enjoyment ought to be developed in youth. Men should be taught and convinced above all that fidelity to virtue can produce the purest and greatest joy, and that there can be no true joy without it. (Conscientiousness, self-control, zeal in prayer and work.)

Besides positive guidance towards true enjoyment warnings are required against false joy and how to keep away from it. Young people must learn to avoid forbidden "joys", and to observe a reasonable measure in the indulgence of what is permissible. This requires strength of character, self-denial, and a readiness to abstain.

It is a particularly important fact for social life that to do the right thing, active charity, is one of the principal causes of true joy. ("A joy shared is a joy doubled"); and that occasionally it is necessary to be tactful in giving outward expression to one's joy. Outward, and especially noisy, manifestations of joy may become obtrusive and annoying. It may hurt those afflicted with some great sorrow.

From an educational point of view it is highly important to create an environment in which true joy can be developed. In this connection there is very much to be done: for example, providing proper housing and working conditions; private groups fighting publicly against indecent and offensive influences; efforts to overcome social antagonisms; promoting all that is likely to offer true joy to men.

BIBLIOGRAPHY

General Works

Bigongiari, D. (Ed.), *The Political Ideas of St. Thomas Aquinas* (Hafner, New York, 1953).

AFTER an introduction summing up the main ideas, selections are given from the *Summa Theologica* (I–II, Qs. 90–97 and part of Q. 105; and II–II, Qs. 42, 57, 58, 66, 77, 78 and 104) and seven chapters from Book One of the *De Regimine Principum*. The last section of the introduction is rather confusing, and the selection of texts is not as comprehensive as that of Professor d'Entrèves (q. v. *infra*).

Clune, G., *Christian Social Reorganization* (Browne and Nolan, Dublin, 1940).

A GOOD general introduction to the principles of a Christian social order which, while not too profound, covers the ground adequately. The examples are drawn from the Irish situation but this does not diminish the value of the work.

Cronin, J. F., *Catholic Social Action* (Bruce, Milwaukee, 1948).

ALTHOUGH there is little of a speculative nature in this book it is important as a survey of methods of social action being presently employed in the U.S.A. It is comprehensive, covering social action with workers and employers as well as with various types of community groups. The annotated reading lists are an especially valuable feature.

Cronin, J. F., *Catholic Social Principles* (Bruce, Milwaukee, 1950).

THE subtitle of this work, "The Social Teaching of the Catholic Church applied to American Economic Life", indicates that its bias is towards economics rather than politics. Nevertheless the first part, on the Christian Social Order, and in particular the chapter on the social virtues, make it of the first importance. Each chapter is prefaced by extensive quotations from the relevant papal documents and concluded by valuable reading lists.

Cronin, M., *The Science of Ethics* (Gill, Dublin, 1939).

THE second volume of this exhaustive two volume work deals with special ethics and includes a profound treatment of Catholic social ethics as well as a critical discussion of other systems, both ancient and modern.

Davitt, T. E., *The Nature of Law* (Herder, St. Louis, 1951).

A DISCUSSION of the relation between the concept of law and the philosophy of intellect placed in its historical context by an analysis of the relation as expressed or implied in the writings of various Scholastics. A valuable contribution to the concept of law and of obligation.

D'Entrèves, A. P. (Ed.), *Aquinas, Selected Political Writings* (Blackwell, Oxford, 1948).

THIS book contains the whole of the *De Regimine Principum*, the *De Regimine Judaeorum*, extracts from the *Summa Contra Gentiles* and from the *Summa Theologica* (including all the questions from the *Prima Secundae* which deal with law: Qs. 90–7, 100) and passages from minor works. In every case the Latin text is given, faced by a competent and readable translation by J. G. Dawson. Not the least valuable section of this useful compendium is the learned introduction by Professor d'Entrèves.

Haas, F. J., *Man and Society* (Appleton-Century-Crofts, New York, 1952).

A FUNDAMENTAL and standard textbook first published in 1940 and revised by Bishop Haas shortly before his death. It presents a comprehensive Christian sociology with special emphasis on man's economic relations.

Husslein, J., *The Christian Social Manifesto* (Bruce, Milwaukee, 1939).

AN introduction to the main socio-ethical principles of the two great social encyclicals, *Rerum Novarum* and *Quadragesimo Anno*, written at a popular level.

Jarlot, G., *Compendium Ethicae Socialis* (Pont. Univ. Greg., Rome, 1951).
A SCHOLASTIC treatment of the foundations of social ethics – summary in form but containing in its nineteen theses the essential truths of social life.

Kothen, R., *L'enseignement social de l'Eglise* (Warny, Louvain, 1949).
AN anthology of excerpts from papal documents dealing with social principles and practice from Leo XIII to the present day arranged according to topics and joined by explanatory notes. The most complete of its kind, with an excellent analytical index of subjects.

Murray, R. W., *Introductory Sociology* (Crofts, New York, 1946).
A comprehensive textbook, widely used in Catholic colleges.

Messner, J., *Social Ethics* (Herder, St. Louis, 1949).
THIS is an essential work of reference, one of the most profound studies in social philosophy in the English language. The social principles which are elaborately established are applied in detail to economic and political relations, with particular reference to current problems. In general the author inclines to a conservative standpoint while remaining within the broad stream of Catholic social thought.

Osgniach, A. J., *Must it be Communism?* (Wagner, New York, 1950).
THE title is somewhat misleading, for this is a clear exposition of Catholic social ethics, presented as the only complete answer to Communism.

Rutten, G. C., *La doctrine sociale de l'Eglise* (Editions du Cerf, Paris, 1932).
A SHORT concise Thomistic commentary on the two great encyclicals of Leo XIII and Pius XI. Despite its date of publication, the clarity of its statement of principles is still fresh.

Todd, J. M. (Ed.), *The Springs of Morality* (Burns Oates, London, 1956; Macmillan, New York, 1956).
A SYMPOSIUM dealing with morality in all its aspects: its basis in philosophy and theology – moralities outside the Church from that of primitive tribes to modern Communism – its practical application in psychology, medicine, economics and labour relations. The great number of experts and specialists who contribute to this book mark it as an ex-

haustive work of reference on the subject of morality in theory and in practice.

Sheed, F. J., *Society and Sanity* (Sheed & Ward, London & New York, 1953).

A POPULARLY written yet profound treatment of the nature and dignity of man and of his social relations in the family and in political society. Its defect is the minimal reference to the economic order, and it is clear that the author has an exaggerated fear of State interference.

Steven, P., *Eléments de Morale Sociale* (Desclée, Tournai, 1954).

A TEXTBOOK intended primarily for seminarians but deserving of a much wider public. It deals systematically and methodically with the Christian social principles involved in the family, work, civic life and the international order. Naturally most of the examples are drawn from the French scene but this does not detract from the author's clear analysis of basic principles and ideas.

von Nell-Breuning, O., *Reorganization of Social Economy* (Bruce, Milwaukee, 1936). Translated by Bernard W. Dempsey.

A DEVELOPMENT and a word by word explanation of the encyclical *Quadragesimo Anno*. This commentary remains the indispensable accompaniment to a detailed study of the encyclical.

Wu, J. C. H., *Fountain of Justice* (Sheed & Ward, London & New York, 1955).

THIS "study in natural law" includes a detailed historical examination of the natural law as seen in the rise of the common law in England and subsequently in America. It is particularly interesting on American jurisprudence and on the necessary role of the virtue of prudence in the embodiment of natural law principles in common law practice.

Part One

Man in Society

Eschmann, T., "A Thomistic Glossary of the Principle of the Pre-eminence of the Common Good" in *Medieval Studies,* v (Toronto, 1943). From the same author, "Bonum commune melius est quam bonum unius" in *Medieval Studies,* vi (Toronto, 1944). Also "Studies in the Notion of Society in St. Thomas" in *Medieval Studies,* viii, ix (Toronto, 1946, 1947).

THESE long articles by Father Eschmann together make up a scholarly study of the relations of person and society as they are developed in the writings of St. Thomas Aquinas. The primacy of the human person is well brought out, as well as the tie of justice which binds man to the furtherance of the common good.

Gilby, T., *Between Community and Society* (Longmans, London & New York, 1953).

THE author, adverting to the fact that St. Thomas Aquinas has been made to appear the patron of different, and even diverging, social and political causes whereas "his philosophy is too tender, constant and generous for an ideology, still less for a vogue", here presents his thought in its historical existential context. In doing so he shows how the first Western philosopher to chart the independent field of politics wrote his political dialectic under the influence of the different ideas of his period, the Augustinian conception of the Eternal Law, the Roman Law, the feudal medieval culture, the revived Aristotelian philosophy.

Maritain, J., *The Person and the Common Good* (Scribner, New York, 1947; Bles, London, 1948).

HERE M. Maritain develops one of the central themes of his social philosophy: the singularly complex relationship between person and society. Man is a part of a social community and as such inferior to it and bound to serve its ends, but he is also a person with an immortal soul and as such of more importance than anything else in the world.

Ruopp, P., (Ed.), *Approaches to Community Development* (W. Van Hoeve, Hague, 1953).

THIS symposium is a general introduction to the social reality in which welfare projects at the village level must be undertaken, and to the problems and methods of what is now generally called "community development". It places the idea of "community" in perspective, showing its importance in the modern world in mutual aid programmes in underdeveloped areas.

PART TWO

Basic Laws of Social Order

Eberdt, M. L. and Schnepp, G. J., *Industrialism and the Popes* (Kenedy, New York, 1953).

AN exposition of social principles, drawn from papal documents, related to the fundamental idea of subsidiary function with special reference to the "Industry Council Plan". Excellent bibliography and reading lists.

Furfey, P. H., *Three Theories of Society* (Macmillan, New York, 1937).

THE author contrasts positivistic society (based on progress, or the success-ideal) and noetic society (based on deep knowledge, contemplative) with pistic society, a society characterized by its members' dominant common purpose of attaining socially their ultimate supernatural end – a society founded upon supernatural faith.

Maritain, J., *Man and the State* (University of Chicago Press, Chicago, 1951; Hollis and Carter, London, 1955).

THE most comprehensive statement by Maritain of his political philosophy, linking the rationality and freedom of the human person with the spiritual meanings and purpose of the organized political community, and at the same time establishing the principles and aims of Christian democracy.

PART THREE

Justice and Charity

Bezzina, E. E., *De Valore Sociali Caritatis* (D'Auria, Naples, 1952).

A DISSERTATION set out in classical form which is especially good in the chapters on the function of *amor caritatis* in society, on the relations between justice and charity, and on the notion of social peace.

Cantwell, J. E., "A Fourth Species of Justice" in *Social Order*, iv, 6 (St. Louis, 1954).

THE author claims that a fourth species of justice is to be found in the relations between the roughly defined groups of the "haves" and the "have-nots" of the present day. In support of his notion he alleges that it was some such notion that was in the mind of Pope Pius XII in his broadcast on the post-war famine threat, 4 April 1946.

Dempsey, B. W., "The Range of Social Justice" in *Social Order,* vii, 1 (St. Louis, 1957).

A CONSTRUCTIVELY critical review of Drummond's "Social Justice" *(vide infra)* by a Jesuit economist. He interprets Father Drummond's definition to mean that social justice is the radical form of contributive justice, distinct from commutative, distributive and legal justice, which requires that proper goods (material or otherwise but in some sense appraisable at a price) shall serve the common good of all men.

D'Entrèves, A. P., *Natural Law, An Introduction to Legal Philosophy* (Hutchinson, London, 1951).

AN historico-philosophical approach to the notion of natural law with particular attention paid to Grotius whose proposition that natural law would retain its validity even if God did not exist is called by Professor d'Entrèves "a turning point in the history of thought". Most useful for showing the position of natural law in the common law of England and the U.S.A.

Drummond, W. F., *Social Justice* (Bruce, Milwaukee, 1956).

FATHER Drummond maintains that social justice differs from legal justice and has been confused with it because of the verbal identity of aims: the common good. He asserts that this confusion "retards an evolution of doctrine which the encyclical *Quadragesimo Anno* seems to encourage". He defines social justice as "a special species of justice, distinct from commutative, legal and distributive, which requires that material goods, even privately owned, shall serve the common use of all". This is then worked out in a compelling argument.

Faidherbe, A. J., *La Justice Distributive* (Recueil Sirey, Paris, 1934).

THIS thoroughly scientific study treats of the nature and problems of distributive justice. The author finds himself in keen opposition to most modern moral theologians and asserts that according to the teaching of St. Thomas and many of his commentators distributive justice is a form of strict justice, the object of which is a legal debt and so involves the duty of restitution. The study ends with a useful discussion of the application of this virtue to modern circumstances, for example, the question of the family wage as a claim in distributive justice.

Ferree, W., *The Act of Social Justice* (Catholic University of America Press, Washington, 1942).

THIS is an analysis of the Thomistic concept of legal justice with special reference to the doctrine of social justice proposed by Pius XI in *Quadragesimo Anno* and *Divini Redemptoris,* with a view to determining the precise nature of the act of this virtue. While accepting that the formal object of legal and social justice is the same, viz., the direct furtherance of the common good, Dr. Ferree pays special attention to the material object and concludes that the immediate and proper act of the virtue is "the act of social organization". The work concludes with a chapter on the act of social justice viewed in relation to the four causes.

Hering, H. M., *De Justitia Legali* (Paulist Press, Fribourg, 1944).

THOUGH little more than a booklet this was until recently the only work of its kind devoted entirely to legal justice and is the most important philosophical analysis of this virtue. The central point of the analysis is that St. Thomas Aquinas has two distinct conceptions of legal justice: the virtue of the law, and ordaining to the common good. The treatment is technical and the conclusions have been contested (see *Newman*) but cannot be neglected in any thorough discussion of the Thomist conception of justice.

McCoy, C. N. R., "Social Justice in *Quadragesimo Anno*" in *Social Order,* vii 6 (St. Louis, 1957).

THE author takes issue with both Drummond and Dempsey and suggests that the phrase "social justice" as used in the encyclical may not primarily signify justice as a virtue but rather a certain rectitude or order in the disposition of the parts of that whole which is society. He claims that the novelty of the term lies in the relating of the virtue of distributive justice to the governing principle of order, the "justice of the regime". (I–II, 113, 1.)

Maritain, J., *The Rights of Man and the Natural Law* (Scribner, New York, 1943; Bles, London, 1943).

BEGINNING with the vocation of the person, a spiritual and free agent, to the order of absolute values and to a destiny superior to time, J. Maritain deduces the various rights, personal, civic and social, which are significant (perhaps because they are attacked more often than they are upheld) in the world of today.

Newman, J., *Foundations of Justice. A Historico-critical Study in Thomism* (Cork University Press, Cork, 1954).

UNITING and fusing the texts of St. Thomas Aquinas relating to legal justice, the author resuscitates the general intellectual attitude in which the notion of legal justice originally appeared. He traces its use (and abuse) in the intervening centuries, and rescues it from its modern deformations. He holds that social justice is the same as St. Thomas Aquinas' general justice, but suggests that the legal justice of modern times should be renamed civic justice, thus dividing commutative justice into individual justice, between persons, and civic justice, between persons and the State.

Pieper, J., *Justice* (Faber and Faber, London, 1957; Pantheon, New York, 1957).

A SIMPLY written discussion of the traditional threefold relations of justice. The author passes easily from the analysis of abstract ideas to their application in the concrete circumstances of today. Throughout the book he remains very close to the verbal text of St. Thomas Aquinas.

Rommen, H. A., *The Natural Law* (Herder, St. Louis, 1947).

THE sub-title of this work, *A Study in Legal and Social History*, indicates its comprehensive nature. The author traces the history of natural law from Greek and Roman times up to the deviations of the eighteenth century. After the positivism of the nineteenth century the traditional concept of natural law is beginning to make its way again, and the author ends up on an optimistic note. The work is uncommonly well documented and is one of the most comprehensive to be found in English.

Ryan, J. A., *Distributive Justice* (Macmillan, New York, 1942).

THE title is somewhat misleading, as Dr. Ryan is concerned to discuss the application of justice to the distribution of the product of the economic process in its four parts: rent, interest, profit, and wages. When the book originally appeared in 1916, it was a pioneering work of the utmost importance. The work was kept up to date by the author so that the edition of 1942 is still a classical treatment of morals applied to economics. The sub-title, *The Right and Wrong of our Present Distribution of Wealth,* has not lost its relevance.

Vidler, A. R., and Whitehouse, W. A., *Natural Law, a Christian Reconsideration* (S. C. M., London, 1946).

THIS little book is the autcome of discussions between a group of Christians, clerical and lay, Catholic and Protestant, British and Continental. It is particularly good on theological presupposition and on theonomic thinking and the application of the natural law.

INDEX

A

Ability (capability),
and Facility (habit), 220f., 282f.
of man, 208f.
natural capability of doing good,
282f.
social obligation, 172
Abortion, 108, 122, 156, 235,
242, 247
Action,
collective, 78f.
of the community, 78
legal, right of, 295
morally good, 1, 2, 13
motive of: the good, 4, 13, 57,
226f., 240f.
social, 59, 154
true to nature: as social principle,
46f.
Action, human,
all-inclusive, 154f.
and the common good, 107f.
dependent of community, 70
with dispensation, 249
with equity, 253ff.
efficient cause of community,
76ff.
external (and internal), 160,
284f.

external, and human authority,
123ff.
(in itself) good, 129, 155f., 220f.
natural and supernatural, 282
object of justice, 284ff., 312f.
own proper value, 157f.
principles of, 218ff., 225ff.,
240ff.
proper spheres, 282f.
purposeful, 23f., 140, 154ff.
responsibility (independence) of,
56ff., 75ff., 272ff.
true to nature, 140, 209
Action, norm of human, conscience, 56ff., 62ff., 132ff., 288
the good, 4
human law, 124
law, 192
the natural law, 205ff., 229ff.,
247
virtue, 287f.
Activity,
charitable, 348
and essential nature, 209
natural, 209, 212
and perfection, 76
proper to nature of every
creature, 171f.
unique, 151
true to nature, 173f.

369

Man's right (basic rights), 269, 273, 279 f.,
  to freedom of association, 86, 176, 238
  to freedom of conscience, 237, 272 f.
  to legal protection, 238, 273 f.
  to marriage, 235 f.
  to perfection, 236 f., 272 f.
  to personal responsibility, 167 ff., 272 f.
  to procreation (rights of parents), 210, 235, 273 f.
  to property, 235, 273
  to self-preservation, 234, 273 f.
  to social order, 237 f., 273 f.
  to work, 235, 273
  to worship God, 237, 272 f.
Mankind, 70, 312
Marriage, right to, 186 f., 190, 235, 272
Marxism,
  anthropology, 50
  and basic rights, 270
  ethics of, 28, 152 f.
  fundamental errors of, 203 f.
  natural right, 203 f.
Mass, "mass man", 108 ff., 143
Materialism,
  ethics of, 28
  and human liberty, 58 f.
  interpretation of history, 50, 204
  and natural right, 203 f.
Matter and Form, 42
Mean, of virtue,
  twofold: rational and real, 288; in temperance and for-

titude, 288; in justice, see Justice
Means, 156,
  and end, 80
  and immediate goal, 217, 287
  right to, 159
Member, community, 86, 164, 323
  duties of, 323 f.
  must fit into the greater community, 160, 173 f.
  self-administration, 174 f.
  and social justice, 319
  subsidiary function, 171 ff.
Member, of community,
  claim to common good, 291
  and distributive justice, 299 ff.
  duties of, 323 f.; towards members, 167; the whole, 113, 166 f., 323 f.
Mercy, 343 f., 347 f.
  works of, 332, 347 f.
Minority, racial, 239
Misuse, of right, 196 f.
Moderation, of the community, 174
Money, as object of Virtue, 291
Morality, 1,
  and advantage, 9 f., 194 f.
  and denial of God, 213 f.
  and economic life, 10 ff.
  and joy, 356
  and right, 186 f.
  supernatural, 20
Multiplicity, and unity, 144
Murder, see Abortion, Euthanasia, Killing, Suicide

under influence of Holy Spirit,
63
and the "mass", 109 f.
personal, 167 ff., 272 f., *see* Person
right to personal responsibility,
236 f., 272 f.
Restitution,
basis of, 295, 308
in commutative justice, 295
in distributive justice, 306 ff.
obligation of, 296 f., 315
in universal justice, 315
Revelation,
and basic supernatural rights,
276 ff.
and the natural law, 249
source of social ethics, 20
teaching on God, 138
teaching on man, 60 ff.
Reward, 300
Right, 183 ff.
in commutative justice, 292 ff.
conditions of, 186 ff.
confirmation by distributive justice, 303 ff.
creation of, 266
determining judgement in, 304 f.
in distributive justice, 299 f.
due, 183 f.
not end in itself, 186
enforceable, 194
equality, 184, 189 f.
essentially social, 187, 196 f.
exercise of, 251
function of, 186 ff.
inalienable, 196, 269
between individuals, 292

inferred, 265
loss of, 196 f.
and might, 193 ff., 305
and misuse of, 196 f.
and morality, 186
necessity of, 185 f.
norm of law, 191 f.
object of, 188
object of justice, 282 ff.
positive, 251, 253
regulating function, 187 f.
in relation to others, 188 ff.
sense of, 279 f.
sources of, 251 ff.
subject of, 188, 212
and title, 184 f.
and utility, 153, 193
validity of, 197
what it presupposes, 186
Right, division of,
in objective and subjective, 185
in proper and less proper sense,
190 f.
in right in the thing and right
to the thing, 300
Right, of community, *see* Community
to self-management, 174 f.
to self-protection and self-defence, 162
Right, fundamental, 261 ff., 265
characteristics of, 269 ff.
of the community, 275 f.
and conscience, 280
and constitution, 261
declaration of: by natural and
positive law, 266 ff., 271
derivative, 265, 274 f.

Bd. III C

2 vols